Praise for Kiri Blakeley and

CAN'T THINK STRAIGHT

"Kiri Blakeley experienced one of the worst fears that runs through the back of every woman's mind. Not only was her fiancé cheating on her, he was cheating with another man. With humor, insight, and transparency, she takes us on a journey from devastation to renewal, proving that there is no heartbreak that is too painful to overcome."

—**Alisa Bowman,** author *Project: Happily Ever After: Saving Your Marriage When the Fairytale Falters*

"If Erica Jong and Tucker Max had a couple of drinks, a night of hot sex, and then wrote a book, it might end up something like Blakeley's memoir, a frank and wickedly funny account of her life after finding out her fiancé is gay."

—**Judy Dutton,** author of *Secrets from the Sex Lab*

"With wry humor and necessary courage, Kiri Blakeley brings this relationship horror story to life. *Can't Think Straight* is irrefutable proof that the only person you'll ever really know is yourself."

—**Samara O'Shea,** author of *Note to Self: On Keeping a Journal and Other Dangerous Pursuits*

"Brutally honest, self-deprecating, emotionally wrenching, and somehow still laugh-out-loud funny. One can only imagine being faced with such a scenario in her own life. This book is clearly written by a survivor."   —**Kimberly Dawn Neumann,** author of
The Real Reasons Men Commit

"Blakeley's *Can't Think Straight* reads like an edge-of-the-seat psychological thriller as her private hell comes to life on each page. One can't help but laugh, cry, and sympathize as she takes readers to the depths of her ten-year love affair, unraveling lies and deceit along the way. Blakeley's sharp psychological insights are spot-on and her often entertaining style is masterful in this page turner that will make you never look at your significant other quite the same way again."
—**Jonathan Alpert,** columnist for *Metro* newspapers'
No More Drama and *X17* online's *Hollywood Breakdown*

"*Can't Think Straight* is like one of those unforgettable episodes of *Sex and the City*. Meaning, it's the type of book you and your friends will be quoting, pondering, and rehashing, all because Blakeley has captured an unimaginable relationship scenario so vividly, you feel like you are right there with her."
—**Hannah Seligson,** author of *A Little Bit Married*
and *New Girl on the Job*

CAN'T THINK STRAIGHT

A Memoir of Mixed-up Love

Kiri Blakeley

CITADEL PRESS
Kensington Publishing Corp.
www.kensingtonbooks.com

CITADEL PRESS BOOKS are published by

Kensington Publishing Corp.
119 West 40th Street
New York, NY 10018

All Kensington titles, imprints, and distributed lines are available at special quantity discounts for bulk purchases for sales promotions, premiums, fund-raising, educational, or institutional use. Special book excerpts or customized printings can also be created to fit specific needs. For details, write or phone the office of the Kensington special sales manager: Kensington Publishing Corp., 119 West 40th Street, New York, NY 10018, attn: Special Sales Department; phone 1-800-221-2647.

AUTHOR'S NOTE
All names of people (except for the dead) and some identifying factors have been changed. There are no composite characters. With a couple of exceptions, scenes appear in the order in which they occurred.

CITADEL PRESS and the Citadel logo are Reg. U.S. Pat. & TM Off.

First printing: January 2011

10 9 8 7 6 5 4 3 2 1

Printed in the United States of America

Library of Congress Control Number: 2010931891

ISBN-13: 978-0-8065-3330-8
ISBN-10: 0-8065-3330-7

CAN'T
THINK
STRAIGHT

chapter
one

I thought I had escaped it. The family curse: my grandmothers on both sides, my mother. All had grown old alone—victims of divorce and heartless men. I, on the other hand, had been in a relationship for ten years. A good, solid relationship. The kind you want, the kind all your friends want. The kind I never expected someone like me would have.

Yet the lies we tell others pale in comparison to the lies we tell ourselves. And one night my fiancé decides to stop lying to both of us.

"I think I'm confused about my sexuality," Aaron says, as *Sex and the City* drones on the TV in the background.

Just moments before, I'd been in our bedroom, living my normal life. Aaron had summoned me into the living room with a solemn, "We need to talk."

That's the kind of opener that, in movies anyway, usually precedes some bad, or at least important, news. But I'd felt no flutter of fear. Ten years spent in a warm haze of reliably reciprocated love had left me without even a sliver of relationship anxiety.

I was like the family dog coming for its usual belly rub and, instead, getting a bullet in the head.

Not knowing whether to laugh or scream, I do both—a laugh-scream hybrid, a piercing, high-pitched "*Haa!*"

"Why do you say this?" I ask, recovering some degree of decorum.

"Because I'm having fantasies," he says. Then he starts to cry—huge wracking sobs that let me know this is no strange joke he's pulling.

The tsunami of panic in my chest subsides just a bit. Fantasies. *Okaaay.* Aaron, being the most honest and loyal man on earth, not to mention being rather bland in his sexual tastes, perhaps didn't realize that fantasies—even those about the same sex—were normal. He'd probably jerked off to a picture of Orlando Bloom and was having a meltdown about it.

"About men going down on you?" I gently probe.

"And me"—*sob sob*—"going down on them."

Slightly more ominous. Men will fantasize about anything going down on them. But wanting the cock in his own mouth? This just moved from yellow to orange on the sexual-identity alert scale.

"These must be some serious fantasies if you are willing to risk a ten-year relationship by telling me about them," I say.

Aaron's silence confirms the worst. Yes, these are serious.

Panicked, I toss out: "Do you think we should . . . have an open relationship?"

He sort of hiccups and nods.

"Maybe, uhh, I could help you experiment?" I venture.

He looks at me like I'm crazy, then avoids eye contact. "I don't think that will work."

Then it crystallizes. *Haa!* I'm getting it now. He doesn't want spice, playtime, fantasyland within the safety net of our beautiful, if predictable, relationship. He wants to dump me, get out there, and start sucking dicks full time.

"But babe, you don't even like your ass touched. How will you function as a queer?"

No answer.

"Well, babe. You know I can't be your beard."

"Beard?"

"How will you make it as a fag if you don't know the lingo?"

I pause.

"Did you get turned on by the sex scenes in *Brokeback Mountain*?" I ask, as if conducting some sort of psychological evaluation.

A couple of months earlier, at my insistence, we had gone to see the Oscar-winning love story of two homosexual cowboys. During the infamous pup tent scene, when the cowboys first get it on, I'd touched Aaron's arm and giggled, wanting to make sure he wasn't too uncomfortable.

Afterward, he'd hardly said anything about the film. Certainly, it hadn't evoked any "Now *that* was a movie I could relate to!" type reaction.

He shrugs. "Not really. I don't find either one attractive."

Oh, so Jake Gyllenhaal and Heath Ledger weren't good enough for him. This meant he had a "type." We'd moved into the red zone.

"Whom are you attracted to?" I ask.

"Um . . . hairy men."

Hairy men? Hairy fucking men?! I'd spent years mowing this guy's back because he hated the hair on it. Spent a decade shaving between my legs because he preferred smooth pussy. *And he likes hairy men?!*

When the jokes don't make the problem go away, we decide to get drunk. We open beer and a bottle of wine (thank God we have them on hand) and begin smoking like fiends (something we'd never done inside our apartment).

We talked and talked. Went up and down, back and forth, to and fro. I swung wildly from the most psychotically hopeful scenarios ("We can be roommates and live together and have our little affairs on the side!") to the most biting and terrifying visions of my future. ("I have to worry about being a thirty-six-year-old single woman in this city! All you have to worry about is AIDS!")

I didn't see much bleakness in Aaron's future. He was cute and hetero looking and acting. Men would be all over him. His friends were not homophobic and would all support him. His family might be shocked, but they too would come around because Aaron was such a sweet, lovable guy (not to mention he had a gay sister who had not been ostracized). Within a year, he'd be living in Chelsea with his hair-stylist boyfriend, wearing muscle shirts and walking his poodle. Meanwhile, I'd be the head case who scares away men due to my tendency to scream *Areyougayareyougayareyougay?* if they prefer a *Seinfeld* rerun instead of sex.

You hear that cliché: feeling like you're in a waking nightmare. And so it was. I sat in a chair across from Aaron with my bare knees pulled up under my chin, frantically wondering, "When will I wake up from this? None of this can be real."

have no idea how I survived that night. With Aaron still in the living room, I curled myself into the fetal position on the bed and lay in some kind of catatonic state for the next few hours. I think I got maybe two or three minutes of sleep.

I'm not a dumb woman. There had been no signs. I never caught him checking out the waiter. There was never a drunken confession of a high school blowjob from a beer buddy. There were no requests for strap-ons. He'd never come home raving about his new (hot) friend, Brad, from the gym. (In fact, he was always canceling his gym memberships for lack of use.) I'd met guys who told me they'd recently come out, and I'd thought, "Whom exactly were you fooling?" Aaron was *not* one of those guys. His voice had a soft deep timbre; his entire demeanor, from his gel-free hair to his loose cords and scruffy shoes, was relaxed and masculine.

Weren't red flags, pink flags, any kind of fucking flags supposed to precede something like this?

I had accepted that, despite being a Carrie Bradshaw type—thirty-six years old, a writer, and New York City resident—I would never taste *Sex and the City* adventures. In fact, for the past few years, I was never quite certain when I would next experience *real* sex. Although Aaron had never gazed upon my naked form and exclaimed, "Not for me, honey!" things had been going downhill in that area for a long time. But we were working on it. We'd been to therapy. We'd had our Saturday night "sex nights." When was the last time we'd had one?

Anyway, I wasn't about to toss out the best man I'd ever met and take my chances in the dysfunctional dating capital of the world just to find more sex. You only had to read a few of those *Smart Women, Stupid Choices* types of books to know that mind-blowing sex with exciting bad boys was a fast track to heartbreak. Besides, what couple still had hot, or even regular, sex after ten years? I didn't even know whom to ask because no one I knew had stayed together as long as we had.

I thought I'd escaped. I'd picked Aaron, not only because of his appeal to me and our mutual attraction, but because he was so good, reliable, safe. He was nothing like the men in my family. And yet—here it was. I had not escaped.

At some point, I tiptoe out in the dark and find Aaron, where he lies on the couch. I can hear his light snoring. How he can sleep at all is a mystery to me. I kiss his cheek because I think it might be the last time I ever do so.

chapter two

T he second the clock hits 7 A.M., I jump up and call my friend Tyler. I know he wakes up early. Even though we'd never met in person, he's the only one I can think to call.

We'd met in a screenwriters' chat room five years ago and conversed (even flirted a bit) every day by message board and email. Yet it was only a few weeks ago that he'd told me he was gay and that his "wife" was actually a man. About his online misrepresentation, Tyler admitted that he'd enjoyed our harmless flirtatious banter and though we were both loyal in the extreme to our long-term partners, before he knew it, he was caught up in a lie he hadn't quite intended.

He must have some idea what's going on.

Tyler is skeptical. "I've never heard of a guy coming out this late," he says. Aaron, too, was thirty-six. "I think he might just want to be single, travel with his band. He knows you are sympathetic to gay people and thinks this is a better way to get out of the relationship."

Aaron always wanted to be a rock star. Not too many record labels were rushing to sign up near middle-aged men, but his latest self-produced CD had gotten some college radio play, and he booked a future gig in upstate New York. I'd planned to go until he made some noises that "the band" didn't want girlfriends tagging along. He'd also been exchanging a lot of text messages with the new girl in the band, Amber. Some long-dormant jealousy had stirred, and we had a couple of mild arguments about it. But Aaron had said, firmly, "I am not attracted to Amber." And I believed him.

In our ten years together, I had never once suspected Aaron of straying. He never even *looked* at other women. If someone had told me he was cheating on me, I would have held out both my arms and said, "If you can prove this is true, cut them off. That's how much I know you are wrong."

Could this whole gay thing be what Tyler posited? That Aaron didn't have any sexual issues other than wanting to tour with his band, have groupies, and fuck Amber?

Could *anyone* be this diabolical?

I pad into the living room and wake Aaron up. I sit across from him in the same chair I'd been in last night when he'd told me, in the same position, as if there hadn't been a break in the conversation.

"Tyler thinks you just want to be single," I say.

"Well, that's not true." He hesitates. "I've been looking at gay porn. Does that convince you?"

I'm surprised about him looking at *any* kind of porn, let alone gay porn. Sex shops, toys, role-playing, porn. Over the years, I'd suggested all of it. "Sure," Aaron would say, his disinterest obvious. None of it ever happened.

I return to the bedroom to cry some more. I can't be near this complete stranger. I call the magazine I write for, *Forbes*, and leave a rambling message on my supervisor's machine about being sick.

Aaron decides to go into work for a few hours. As soon as he leaves, I run to our computer. Although we shared the Mac, I had never been to his side of it. It had never occurred to me to snoop on him. I'd done a little spying in our first year together, as I was jealous of an ex-girlfriend and kept looking for evidence that he was still in love with her. But after months of finding nothing, I'd lost interest.

And now, bubbling up from the deep recesses of my memory, his password comes to me. He'd mentioned it offhandedly maybe eight years ago. It hadn't entered my mind since. I didn't even know if it was still the same.

The password works. I click into his personal folder. I see JPEGs. I open them. There are pictures of Aaron—of his beard (which he refused to shave off, no matter how much I complained), of his face (he pouts into the camera like Zoolander doing Blue Steel), of his erect cock. That one is labeled "Piece."

I see videos with names like *Big Balls*. I do not open them; the names are quite enough, thank you. I see pictures of muscular policemen in leather, like something out of the Village People. I'm almost more shocked at the bad taste—*how cliché!*—than the homosexuality.

I go to the browser history and pull down the menu.

Over and over, Craigslist ads come up. I click into them: M4M. Oral sex party this Saturday! Man looking to hook up tonight! Want to suck your cock right now!

Worst of all, many of them order: No condoms!

chapter three

O h . . . my . . . God . . ." my friend Julie breathes into the phone.

I've just told her what is happening. Julie has known Aaron for as long as I have. I read her a few Craigslist ads, and, since she's a writer who works from home, tell her I am coming over.

I get on the F train and stumble off at her stop. I stand on the street corner, completely disoriented. I have been to Julie's apartment dozens of times, and yet it's as if I stand in the middle of a strange city I've never been in before. I call her from my cell.

"I don't know how to get there," I say. I can feel the hysteria rising, my breathing getting shallow and rapid.

"Take a left," Julie stresses. "A left."

"Oh God," I wail. "Which way is left?!"

Julie has to come get me.

I call Aaron at work. "You've been cheating on me," I say, taking a chance. I don't really know if he has responded to any of the ads.

Aaron is silent. Then I know it is true.

"How long as this been going on?" I ask in a monotone.

"Two years," he says.

I only go home to get some things so I can stay at Julie's. I warn Aaron not to be there. I try to go straight for what I need and not look at the rest of the apartment: the furniture, the appliances, pictures on the walls, knickknacks. Anything and everything we had bought together. Anything and everything a big fat lie.

There is a long handwritten note on the kitchen island. I can barely look at it. My eyes fall on one sentence:

"I separated sex from love," it says.

I throw the letter in the trash, where I hope Aaron will see it.

At Julie's, she and her boyfriend, Jake, occasionally force me to down a little soup. I have zero appetite, but I think of a male friend who, when he found out his girlfriend had cheated on him, stopped eating and ended up in the hospital with an IV drip in his arm. I want to avoid that fate.

I had hardly been in the office all week. Went in for a few hours here and there, just to try to feel normal. It didn't work. I tell my supervisor, also a friend, what is happening, because I need people to understand why I might appear a red-eyed zombie. "Take whatever time you need," she tells me.

I cry so much that when I suddenly stop, I wonder if it's because my body simply can't produce any more tears. Then I need the stability of familiar surroundings, my cats. I call Aaron and tell him to get out of the apartment. He says he will stay with our friend Ben, who I know is in the process of divorcing his wife.

"Is it him?" I ask. "The timing seems rather coincidental."

"Ben is not gay so far as I know."

I don't know anything anymore. Anything seems possible.

The night I return home, I dig through Aaron's personal belongings. I find a bank statement, call the number on it, and listen to the automated teller run down his checks and balances. I find his passport and Social Security card and hide them. I have no idea what I'm doing other than trying to figure out whom I've been living with for ten years. Maybe I'd discover identification that said he was someone else—someone who'd been on the run for a long time, who had been holing up with me, pretending to be Aaron, pretending to be a straight man who loved me and wanted to marry me.

I sleep on the couch with pillows stuffed up against me for comfort. I can't be alone in our bed; I'm terrified I will smell him on the sheets. I leave the lights and TV on all night, like I'm five years old and scared of ghosts.

In the morning, there's that initial moment when I swim to consciousness and life is familiar and normal for a half a second—then everything rushes back, and I'm trapped in a strange new world I can't shake off.

Occasionally, someone puts forth a theory as to why Aaron has chosen this particular time to come out. One friend suggests that it's all an ego thing—since my career is doing better than his. After all, while Aaron was sputtering along with his homemade CDs and sparsely attended local gigs, I'd been in Los Angeles, making the rounds of Oscar parties for my *Forbes* celebrity beat. At the *Vanity Fair* shindig, I'd accidentally sat on one of the billowy folds of Jennifer Lopez's dress, drawing an icy stare. At the ICM bash, I'd been an arm's length away from Mariah Carey, Elton John and Mick Jagger—all at once. I'd spent a lot of time on television in the past year yapping about Paris Hilton or Gisele

Bundchen. Not exactly the stuff of Pulitzer or Emmy. But it was fun. My family and friends enjoyed seeing me on the tube; liked hearing about celebrities I met or interviewed.

But I knew Aaron didn't have that kind of ego-driven retaliatory nature.

I was more inclined to believe it was our recent decision to end our interminable engagement with a marriage ceremony. Aaron had asked me to marry him about a year into our relationship. The prospect so terrified me that I burst into tears and couldn't put the ring on for months. Over the years, Aaron had been the one pushing for it; I was the "if it ain't broke, don't fix it" hold out. But specter of death—first my paternal grandmother and then my young niece—and the realization that Aaron's elderly mother and my maternal grandmother (who helped raise me) most likely wouldn't be far behind, gave us grim impetus.

Plus, it just started to seem silly and impractical. If I got hit by a wayward cab and lay in a coma, he wouldn't be able to make any kind of decision or arrangement. Once we'd decided, Aaron ran into our local pub hangout, Last Exit, and announced it to his friends, as hyped up and excited as if his soccer team had just scored a goal.

"You know everything about me," I'd told him. "It doesn't get any better, and it doesn't get any worse. I have no surprises."

"Me neither," he'd said.

Me neither!

When I asked Aaron why now, he said, "Because I respect you too much to keep doing this to you."

There was nothing about respecting me enough not to do it in the first place.

13

chapter four

y work voice mail contains a message from Sahana, one of my best friends from Columbia Journalism School:

"It's midnight. I don't know why I'm calling you at the office, as you must be at home, but probably asleep. I don't know if it's the right thing to say, but I love you and am thinking about you, and can't stop thinking about you. . . . By the way, this isn't a gay greeting. I just want to make that clear."

That gives me a good chuckle. A pained chuckle, like you might make if you're told a great joke as you lay dying.

The list of people I have to inform seems endless.

"Aaron and I broke up—"

There's a breath-sucking pause on the other end of the line as the recipient processes this information: the couple who'd survived the longest, the decade-long Aaron'n'kiri phenomenon, has ended. Then I hit 'em with the kicker: "He's GAY!" So much better than "We've grown apart" or even "He wants to be single." But that's not all! Once they get the "*What*?!" out of their system, then I smack 'em upside with the kicker to the kicker: "And he's been cheating on me with men." That's when they drop the phone.

Of everyone, my father is the most maddeningly philosophical. "Sexuality is very fluid," he drones. "My ex-girlfriend lived with a woman after me. And now she lives with a man." Thanks for the paternal outrage, Dr. Kinsey.

On the opposite end, my grandmother wails and blubbers inconsolably and then declares, with a scary finality, "I'm too old for this world!" As if homosexuality had just been invented in the past decade.

Three of my friends (all writers) proclaim: "Think of all the stuff you have to write about now!" They have fun coming up with book titles: *He's Just Not That Into You. . . . Because He's* Gay; *Till Dick Do Us Part*.

Aaron and I fall naturally into an arrangement: he would tell his friends and family; I would tell mine. Aaron was dealing with a more varied array of less-than-ideal responses. His boss: "You're not going to get all bitchy now, are you?" His mother: "Oh, no. Not another one."

Only one person betrayed a streak of homophobia, and it was a young relative of Aaron's known for being conservative in her politics. "All the gays I've known have been so promiscuous!" she hissed, after calling me as soon as she'd heard from Aaron's mother. With Craigslist ads still dancing in my head, I was in no mood to correct her stereotype. Tyler, for example, had been with his partner for 20 years. Instead, I just gratefully gulped down her opprobrium.

Once I knew that he'd informed his lesbian sister, Darlene, I give her a call. I was curious to see if even her gaydar had malfunctioned on this one.

"I had no idea," she says, "but he wouldn't have come out during Dad's lifetime."

It was six years ago that Aaron's father had died. He'd had plenty of opportunity since then. But when would've been a good time? After 9/11, when both of us, not to mention the entire country, were reeling? Or during my niece's illness or in the agonizing months after her death? Aaron had been my rock during that time. He'd been right behind me in the hospital room, crying just as hard as I was, as Ana's hand slowly went cold.

"He says he won't be putting up rainbow stickers and that he hates gay music," Darlene says.

I still can't believe he's saying anything about being gay at all. At the same time, I imagine running into him a year from now: a pride flag draped around his shoulders, Kelly Clarkson on the iPod.

I tell Darlene how Aaron had been cheating on me with men, a fact he keeps conveniently leaving out of his confessions to his family. I need them to know so I can collect the sympathy and so they might share my disapproval. Maybe it's also some kind of little revenge. *I'm going to tell your family how rotten and sneaky you are, so there!*

Everyone wants to know if I'd seen any signs. People are eager to be reassured that something monstrously large can't come along and knock them into another dimension without warning. They want to believe that tragedies can be avoided with the proper precaution, diet, and exercise. It's like when you hear about a random murder. Well, what was he doing on *that* street at *that* time? Doesn't he *know* any better? Unfortunately, there hadn't been a pile of *Playgirl* magazines and Liberace CDs stashed under the bed to clue me in.

I scour the depths of my memory and can really only come up with a few things.

Exhibit number one: the beard.

The hairy intruder had appeared about a year ago. It went through all manner of incarnations: bushy, trim, with mustache, without, with sideburns, without. "You have such an adorable face," I'd tell Aaron. "Stop hiding it."

"I'm experimenting with facial hair," he'd say.

Experimenting with more than that, as it turned out. He'd been sending photos of his woolly mascot to other beard aficionados. Something to do with the subgroup of homosexual men known as "bears," I supposed.

But facial hair doesn't *always* equal gay, right? I cut myself some slack on that one.

There also was his general withholding nature. Aaron, for all his apparent emotional availability, had always been rather reticent and closed off. He had no problem telling me he loved me or saying he wanted to get married, but I could hardly ever figure out what else he was thinking. For all the lip service that Aaron and I, like most modern urban couples, paid to "communication," I often had the uneasy feeling that something was going unsaid. But I never imagined that something would be, "Honey, I like to suck cock."

This brought me to the last and most glaring "clue": our sex life.

If I were honest with myself, I remember our first argument about it happened about four years into the relationship, just after we'd moved from Manhattan to Brooklyn. After two weeks without a peep of erotic interest from Aaron, I'd finally raged at him in the middle of the street as we were antique shopping (he liked antiques—hmm). But over the years, he'd always pushed the issue back onto me: "Well, *you* could initiate. I'm ready whenever *you* are." Eventually, I decided that maybe he had low testosterone levels, which I'd read afflicted some men. Also, I didn't feel particularly alone in this issue. Magazines blared with cover lines like, "The Sexless Marriage," and there was even a popular term to describe it: Double Income, No Sex, or DINS.

There was a din all right—it was so loud, it had rendered me stone deaf.

But the cold hard truth was that there hadn't been much in the way of warning flags. A lackluster sex life here, a beard there, none of it really added up to gay, let alone years of pervasive and masterfully covered up deceit. This was a man who was so honest he would call himself on his own slightly illegal shot in a game of pool, even if no one but him had noticed. And yet he had done this.

I wasn't sure how I was to wade forward in the world with this new-found knowledge: the crippling awareness that you could never know anyone. That, in fact, the person you know best could be the person you know least.

chapter five

Day 3 On Friday, I prepare myself for an evening out—my first since the news. I'm careful to dress to the nines: miniskirt and high heels. I tousle my hair and put on lots of makeup.

I'd always felt that I was an integrated personality, but I suddenly get a crash course in compartmentalization. I split myself right down the middle and push the devastated portion of myself, that portion that would prefer to become nonfunctional, into a bottom drawer. Probably similar to what Aaron had done all these years (only he used a closet). I should have known eventually this discarded side would bang on that drawer, and push and kick until she burst out, and then she'd wreak havoc for having been shut up. But you do what you have to do to get through the next few hours.

I meet up with Julie and her friend at a Brooklyn bar called Loki. As much as I don't want to be the girl who regales everyone with the sitcom-y plot of her boyfriend who turned gay, I can't seem to help spilling it. First of all, it's a good yarn. The writer in me has to appreciate it. Second, it's all I can think about, let alone talk about. Half the time, people respond by telling me about their former boyfriend/girlfriend who also came out. If homosexuals are ten percent of the population, my friends and I seemed to have dated all of them.

"Hello," Julie says, grinning dazedly, like she's just been bonked on the noggin with a wrench. I turn to see a dangerously attractive dark-haired man with a slightly gap-toothed smile next to us on the sidewalk, where we had stepped out for a smoke.

"I locked my keys in my apartment and I'm just wandering around!" he exclaims. His voice had an orgasmic lilt. He could have been a BBC announcer.

"Your voice is beautiful," I purr. Okay, I'm tipsy. "Are you British?"

"Indian."

He doesn't look Indian. Italian maybe. He has deep-set ice blue eyes, like a Siberian Husky.

Julie and I chat with him about the missing keys and then go back inside. He sits somewhere else, but out of the corner of my eye, I catch him staring at us. Audacious. I ignore him and continue telling Julie's friend my gay fiancé story.

Julie's boyfriend, Jake, arrives and we decide to head for another bar. Julie catches up with the Indian guy, whose name turns out to be Rahil, and invites him to come with us. I'm a little miffed. A single guy hanging around with us might attach himself to me. And I want to be free—for the first time in ten years—utterly free. Sure enough, when I break off from the group to go to a deli and buy mints, Rahil trails me. Truth be told, I wasn't even sure if, at this stage of the game, hot men would still follow me around. Apparently, they would. Or this one would. Maybe he could smell my newly devastated, nihilistic state; maybe I was shedding single, horny molecules.

He keeps up a barely intelligible stream of patter. He's in finance but wants to quit his job to become a full-time "djembe" drummer. Not even a rock-and-roll drummer—some kind of Caribbean music drummer. It doesn't sound like the kind of thing that will offer steady employment.

Back in the bar, Rahil and Jake get into a fight about India. I can make out only snippets of it.

"There's one billion poor people in India and what are *you* going to do about it?" Jake demands.

The evening moves on and everyone gets drunker. I usually limit myself to two or three drinks, but tonight I'm going to get blitzed. Numb myself but good.

For March, it's unseasonably warm. We sit outside at some tables. I tell Rahil that I'd just broken up with my boyfriend of a decade because he is gay and had been hooking up with men behind my back for years. Aaron had said "two years," but I figured that was like a woman revealing the amount of men she'd slept with—you could safely double it.

"My friend in India keeps telling me she thinks I'm gay," Rahil responds, cheerily. "I looked around the room and *tried* to find a man I was attracted to, but I couldn't!"

This seems like the kind of red flag I wish Aaron had waved.

"But you're straight?"

"Straight, straight, straight!"

"Prove it."

"How?"

"Whom do you fantasize about?"

"Angelina Jolie?"

"That's who my boyfriend always used to say."

"Cameron Diaz!" he backtracks. "Cameron Diaz!"

Jake gets jealous that Julie is talking to some guy for too long and they get into a fight. Rahil and I decide to give them some space. We go upstairs, order drinks, and raucously sing to the U2 song blaring from the jukebox. I'm not a U2 fan, but singing along somehow becomes a lifeline to the living. Just to be able to stand and open my mouth and not have it spew out something about Aaron. I feel like someone should congratulate me.

At some point during all of this, I notice that Rahil is looking better and better. Alcohol and sexual deprivation will do that to you.

Rahil and I go out for a smoke. As he speaks, I feel my eyes zeroing in on his lips. For how many years had I gotten the drunken urge to kiss a strange man in a bar and not done it? How many nights had I gone home feeling guilty and unworthy because I'd even *contemplated* letting another man's lips near mine?

As I watch Rahil's lips, I realize there is nothing stopping me for the first time in ten years. Nothing. Invisible steel bars had been raised. So I lean in and kiss him.

I don't know what his reaction is, because I'm too drunk to see it. But he doesn't pull away. He puts his tongue in my mouth. I'm pleased he doesn't try to take out my tonsils, drool on my lips or do any of those other nasty things I remembered happening when I was last single, back in my early twenties. I'd always thought Aaron was the best kisser I'd ever had. But Rahil's technique is more formed. His tongue has a plan. It doesn't just come in and feel around in the dark.

Nevertheless, I'm too drunk or too emotionally sandblasted, or both, to enjoy it. Well, I enjoy it the way you might when you throw a stick for a dog: a pleasant enough way to pass the time, but not exactly a turnon.

I look back through the bar window. Julie is giving me the thumbs-up sign with her eyes.

Rahil wants to give me his number, but I refuse to take it or give him mine.

"I'm sorry. I'm in no place for that right now."

"That's fine, I totally understand," he trills, and heads off into the darkness.

The next day, I force a little polar ice cap over my heart and haul Aaron's most cherished possessions—his guitar and some music equipment, even our shared computer, since it contains his Pro Tools software and original song compositions—over to Julie's. I tell the super to change the locks, and then I inform Aaron he will get his things back after he pays a lawyer to transfer his shares in the co-op to me. I was going to lose plenty of sane brain cells, but I refused to lose one dime because my boyfriend couldn't admit he was gay.

chapter six

Day 5 Julie and I sit in Loki, drinking already. I'm the new but by now familiar Kiri: depressed, wallowing, overtalky—and drunk.

My eyes shift to the left and, suddenly, there he is. Sitting right near us in the almost empty bar, that presumptuous grin plastered on his face: Rahil. The only guy, besides Aaron, who I'd kissed in ten years.

The three of us are mutually stunned—pleasantly so, on my part. He looks better than I remembered him looking, maybe because I'm microscopically less emotionally dead. Maybe because he's an Adonis compared to the other early afternoon guzzlers sprinkled around the bar, their eyes glued to the basketball game on TV. But this time, less obvious is his annoying, slightly hyperactive personality; more noticeable is his toned build, wavy dark hair, and blue-green bedroom eyes.

Over the previous few days, I'd decided I was going to take a year to play the field and explore my sexuality. I wouldn't, couldn't get emotionally involved with anyone. The idea of even going on a date with a man, having the kind of conversation where we exchanged hopes and dreams, made me weak with nausea. But sex with Aaron, when it actually happened, had always been so predictable: touch here, lick there, orgasm. Like playing connect the dots. This could be a good opportunity. You could get down and dirty with a guy you didn't really know—didn't really *want* to know.

Like Aaron, I was going to separate sex from love.

I ask Rahil to a game of pool. He's good, but I hold my own. I'm hyperaware that the knocking around of pool balls is just killing time until we kiss.

At the end of the second game, I notice Julie's disappeared. I make my move, pushing Rahil against the pool table. We kiss and rub against each other. He's hard. I feel my juices flowing—it isn't anything I'd felt since the early days with Aaron—and nothing I'd felt Friday night, when kissing him had felt akin to kissing a lamppost.

He asks if I want to head to the couches in the back of the bar, where no one is. "It's not a back alley," he offers. True.

We get to a couch and make out like two teenagers in a hormone frenzy. He pushes up my shirt. When his hands get to my bra, I'm a bit embarrassed at the padding and small boobs. Aaron had always said he liked, "No more than a handful"—which turned out to be truer than I ever imagined. Maybe hetero guys only wanted big knockers.

"I've lost some weight recently," I say, hoping that will explain the A cup. Rahil doesn't seem to care—or even hear me.

It's nice to be with someone who is enthusiastic and passionate. He kisses my neck and holds my face and calls me "beautiful." All stuff Aaron hadn't done in a long time, if ever.

"You know what the worst thing about making out is?" I ask. "It makes you want to do more. But I can't."

"I understand," he says, "but that doesn't mean we have to stop kissing."

If anything, this guy is totally unflappable. I could imagine seeing him in a month and thinking, "I made out with *that* guy?" But right now that's part of the appeal. He's everything Aaron isn't, and I realize this is why I chose him. He's verbose, flighty, flaky, and sexual. Very sexual.

He insists I put his number in my cell phone. He has somewhere to go and that's fine by me: I'd done enough grappling on a dirty bar couch. He wants to walk me to the subway, but I wave him off. That would be too much like a date.

"So, uh, please don't be offended if I don't call you. I'm in such a weird place right now," I stammer.

"Kiri," he says, his voice smooth as an island vacation commercial, "call if you want to call. If you don't want to call, don't. If you want to kiss, we'll kiss. If you don't, we won't."

I didn't think there'd be a shortage of men attracted to an emotional wreck of a woman who just wanted a little physical interaction. In fact, I was fairly certain I'd never again find myself so attractive to the opposite sex. Wearing an "I'm not looking for a relationship" sign would be as magnetic as having double Ds.

end up staying at work late. Not *working* late—I hadn't done any real work since the breakup—but hanging around. I'm in the office of an editor, Paul, draped over his couch, completely exhausted. We chat intermittently about my "situation." I mention how my sex life had been lacking for such a long time, that, who knows, if Aaron hadn't confessed,

I might have ended up cheating eventually. Then I'd be the one with the guilty conscience.

"I can't believe he left the Ferrari idling in the garage like that," Paul observes.

"He turned out to be the Ferrari," I grouse.

One of the million things I'm pissed about is that while I'd been frustrated to the point of daily masturbation, Aaron had been out there getting his rocks off for real.

"Now you are free to do what you want!" Paul, married for twenty years, says. I think I detect some envy in his proclamation.

I groan and bury myself farther into his couch. I have a permanent cigarette-and-alcohol-induced hangover. Paul asks if, what with feeling so exhausted all the time, I might be pregnant: "Wouldn't that be ironic?"

"Look," I say, "he isn't gay for nothing. If I'm pregnant, let's alert the Vatican."

Still, Aaron and I had sex since he'd started his little Craigslist romps. This meant I had to get an AIDS test, despite him swearing he'd never had anal. I didn't know if one could get AIDS from a blowjob. Was this a question I could call 311 about?

Without any immediate plans—except the depressing unfamiliarity of an apartment without Aaron—I get a little restless and decide to check Aaron's email. Sure enough, he hasn't changed the password. Dummy. The inbox is empty; he'd gotten rid of the evidence there.

But there are a few things in the trash. I check it. As soon as I see an email from "John Doe" with the subject line "Thanks" my heart leaps into a galloping frenzy—cold saliva fills my mouth. My entrails feel like they're about to slide out my ass.

From Aaron: "John: Thanks for last night. Thanks for being there to listen and allowing me to vent and thanks for letting me stay over."

Stay over! My heart does a sickening flip-flop in my chest.

"As you can imagine, I'm going through a huge upheaval in my life right now but I would definitely like to continue seeing you in 'real life' (versus fantasy). We still have a lot of getting to know one another to do but I look forward to that. I know fuck-all about how to go about this kind of thing but I guess it's just one baby step at a time, right?"

I become freezing cold. My entire body is quivering with fear, with anger, with a betrayal so absolute that I'm almost literally blinded by it. I'd never had an asthma attack before, but I'm breathing so fast I think I could faint.

John Doe replies that he is glad Aaron is comfortable with him and that he looks forward to getting to know him better. He signs it: "Xxxxxooooo ☺ Peace."

Okay, first off, a grown man making *xoxo*'s and a smiley face? A grown man signing off with "Peace"? This guy needed to be taken out of the gene pool. Being gay, I guess he had taken himself out of the gene pool. But maybe not. Maybe he had a wife and kids and was fucking around just like Aaron. Didn't they realize that their little "fantasy" lives destroyed real lives?

This email said these hookups weren't just anonymous M4M encounters. I didn't know if Aaron was in love with this man, but he clearly had some kind of friendship or emotional connection with him. The emotional betrayal kicks me in the gut even more than the physical ones.

A tornado of devastation flashes into my mind: going home, taking Aaron's CDs, albums, clothes, financial information, mail, anything I can find, and smashing it, stomping it, burning it into oblivion. The vision is so white hot, so imminent, that I know I'm a mere subway ride from its realization.

I see the morass open up: the deep, black, bitter hole into which I was about to plummet. If I did this, Aaron would shut down. Communication would cease. Maybe he would even have me arrested for destroying his personal effects. He still had legal rights to the apartment: maybe he would get a locksmith to break in or begin wrangling for market share on the co-op.

I make a Herculean effort to slow my breathing. I look at the precipice to which I have come. I peer over the edge.

I back away from it.

Aaron was gone. He was—or was in the process of—moving on. I needed, for my own sanity, to do the same. Revenge is just another form of clinging to the old life.

But Aaron is the only one who can help me. He's the only one who can explain to me what had happened, how far this had gone, how long this had been going on, what had gone wrong.

chapter seven

Day 8 "I feel like I'm supposed to kiss you," I say. Old habits.

Aaron looks kind of scared.

"Come on, let's kiss then," I insist, and peck him on the lips. He relaxes ever so slightly.

I sit at the bar and order, my hands still shaking. Aaron had agreed to meet me at Boat, a Brooklyn watering hole. I hadn't told him what I wanted to discuss, just that we needed to talk. To Aaron's credit, he had yet to shut me down and took all my phone calls, no matter how unpleasant he must have known the exchange would be.

On the subway ride over, I resolved to be calm in my dealings. If I came in screaming at him, he'd clam up or even leave.

I'd also noticed complete strangers on the train giving me a look—a look that said, "Welcome." They recognized me now as one of their own. I had passed over into an eerie twilight world populated by those whom life had kicked in the teeth. They offered me a kind of solidarity.

I wait until I've had a couple of sips of vodka and say it.

"You're having an affair with some guy who calls himself John."

He shakes his head and starts to argue. I hold up my hand.

"Please! Just let me finish." I take a deep breath. "You're having an affair with some guy named John and you spent the night at his place."

"Can I explain?"

"No."

I begin to weep and shake. "I know you haven't been honest with me, or even yourself, in years. But I need you to be completely honest for one night. I think I deserve that."

He nods. "Now can I explain?"

I let him. John, he says, is one of his online hookups. They'd kept in touch—I didn't ask how much—but John had once been married and Aaron hoped to get some insight from him. If you can believe it, his actual name is John, from which he got his Internet handle, "John Doe." I guess Aaron didn't choose him for his cleverness with words.

Last night, they'd met at Vegas, a bar I'd been on my way to at the same time, but had very fortunately (especially for Aaron) opted for another dive a block away. Aaron had talked and vented until he was too drunk to make it home. Then he spent the night at John's.

"Nothing happened."

I don't know why at this stage of the game I still expected him to be faithful. But I decide not to press the issue. We weren't living together anymore, and he could do what he wanted. I just didn't want to hear about it.

I tell Aaron that the anger that surged through me when I read John's email—so overwhelming, so horrifyingly large—made me worry I would do something I could never take back. Some of the poison filling me up to the neck needed to be drained or I would drown. Only the plain, ugly truth could do it.

I keep my voice as steady and clinical sounding as I can. "Did you have anal sex or give it during the time we were together?"

"No."

"Did you use condoms when you gave or got blowjobs?"

"No."

No condoms! said the ads.

I puff out my lips and take quick breaths, as if I'm in Lamaze class.

"How many times have you done this?"

"A handful? A dozen?"

Jesus Christ. Aaron and I had *lived* together. I knew where he was at all times. He never came home at 3 A.M., reeking of Axe body spray. But a couple of times a year, I went to Los Angeles to interview celebrities. And then there was the past year. I'd been away quite a lot. Last April, every weekend for five weekends, I'd taken the train to Washington, D.C., where my grandmother was dying of cancer. A few months later, I'd taken another train to a Boston hospital several times, to watch as my only niece, seven years old, died of complications from a cancerous brain tumor.

"When did you do all this? When my grandmother was dying? When Ana was dying?"

"Whenever. After work."

Aaron worked about twenty-five minutes from our apartment. He usually got home about forty minutes after work ended. So these things were fifteen-minute encounters? How were you ever supposed to catch or even suspect a man of cheating if he only took fifteen minutes doing it? If your man walked in the door every night, perfectly normal, saying "Hi, baby," and kissing you and then cooking dinner, how would you suspect? Shouldn't he come home with a shamed face, retreat to the bedroom, and curl up in the corner, wracked with guilt?

That's what I would have done.

"When did you start having these feelings? Be honest."

He blabs on about not knowing, not being able to pinpoint it. But then he hits upon something, almost as if the memory comes as a surprise.

"Remember the 'Have good day' guy?"

He means the elderly Italian tailor in our former Brooklyn neighborhood—the one we lived in before we bought our own place. The tailor had probably been in the country for decades and still left the *a* out of his usual "Have good day!" goodbye.

I nod.

"Well, he was taking up my pants one time and, uh, he had his head down there and was running his hand up my pant leg and, uh, I got aroused."

Aroused by the "Have good day!" guy? He must have been eighty.

"And you don't remember anything like this happening before?"

"No."

So that was it. You send your fiancé to the dry cleaners one day and he comes back gay.

"I've always had this vision of my life—what I wanted, what it would be—and none of that ever included a man," he says.

Mine never included a homosexual fiancé, either, but there you go.

I again press him as to whether the viewing of *Brokeback Mountain* had affected him at all.

"Want the truth?"

"No, I'd like you to keep lying to me."

"Okay. The truth is, I ran into John in the lobby. I saw him as soon as we came in and I spent the rest of the time being nervous about it."

Unbelievable. I hadn't sensed one goddamn thing amiss. There I was, sitting in the darkened theater, having a good chuckle at the small town naïveté and pitiable cluelessness of Heath Ledger's on-screen wife, and I was unknowingly in her same position. I doubted that John had just happened to come to the same screening—one or both men had probably planned it. Maybe they got off on watching the movie at the same time. Having their little secret.

Sitting there gazing at me with so much tenderness, Aaron looked so innocent. At a time like this—when I could hear him, see him, chat with him—I could forget all this crap. Forget that he was blowing guys while I was at work or home feeding the cats or watching a loved one die in another city. For this moment, he was the person I liked being with more than anyone in the world.

"I don't know if this will happen, but it would be nice if, maybe, somewhere down the line . . . we could be friends," I say.

"Like *Will and Grace*," he laughs. When the joke falls like lead, his eyes well up and he nods. "It's so brave and healthy of you to be here saying this to me."

"Or stupid."

We share a subway ride like we had thousands of times before. We hold hands like we used to. We call it the "Bizarro World": something so familiar, and yet so starkly strange.

When my stop comes, I turn and kiss him goodbye.

By the morning, I've stopped feeling so magnanimous.

I wake up around 6 A.M., as I have every day since the breakup, my mind racing. I leave Aaron a message on his cell, which I know he'll have turned off. It's become a habit, an easy way of spewing to him without it turning into a dialogue.

"I just want to say that you would come home with some guy's sperm on your breath and kiss me. I never even saw you brush your teeth. That's just gross. And, you know, at the end of the day, when the orgasm is over and the spark begins to fade, you're left with a human being whom you have to figure out if you can live with, trust, believe in, respect, have stuff in common with, talk to, listen to, and love being with. We had all that. You know how hard that is to find? Look at all our friends in their thirties who are single and have been for years. Everyone wants what we had. I just hope when we're old and alone, we don't look back and say this was a fucking huge mistake."

Well, I hoped I wouldn't look back and say it was a fucking huge mistake. I didn't wish the same for him.

chapter eight

Day 9 Paul, the married editor, and I go out for a drink. There's the familiar electric current between us, but I'm too depressed to play with it. He looks slightly wary. Maybe he thinks I'm going to hit on him. Maybe he's worried he'll hit on me. Maybe it's none of the above and I can't read people for shit anymore, if I ever could.

He tells me how he and his wife have an "understanding," that sometimes "shit happens" and if it's a "one-off," it's not a big deal. The shock of what an illusory moral world I'd been living in—apparently alone—hit me again.

After two drinks, he decides to make a beeline for the train. "My wife wouldn't want me hanging out with you for too long."

I look at him quickly. "What do you mean?"

He backtracks. "I mean she wouldn't want me to hang out too long. I like to get home and cook dinner."

He leaves and I contemplate my new status as The Woman Who Wives Will Not Want Their Husbands Hanging Out with for Too Long.

Here I am: tipsy, pathetic, and alone. I guess I'd have to get used to it—but not tonight. I make some drunk-dials to friends, but none of them pick up. I call Aaron. He answers and I sound like a fool, telling him I'm drunk and lonely. Why shouldn't I tell him? He's the one who made me this way.

"I'd say let's go out, but I have rehearsal with Amber."

Amber. The girl I'd been jealous of just a few weeks ago.

It doesn't matter. Two nights in a row with Aaron would be too weird. I hang up and decide to call Rahil. It's purely to hear another human being's voice.

He picks up and I babble that I'm drunk and pathetic and apologize for calling.

"Why are you apologizing?" he trills. "I thought we had discussed this. We are just having fun!"

There's something comforting about a guy with his head in the clouds when the earth under your feet has buckled and caved in. The connection drops and I can't reach him again. I feel so desperate calling guys. I'm the opposite of desperate: I don't give a fuck about anyone or anything. But they don't know that.

On the walk home, the reality of my new life begins to settle on me. I hadn't been lonely for ten years. I'd forgotten how it felt, how deep it cut, what one did to alleviate it. I let my mind slip into those darkest of dark thoughts. *I don't want to feel this way forever. But I will feel this way forever. I need to stop how I feel.*

But how could I kill myself? I had no idea how to get a gun. I had some pain pills left over from a recent tooth extraction, but only enough to barely warrant a stomach pump.

It takes me two phone calls to crawl back up the side of the dark, slimy well. A friend I've known since college talks me down with her therapist-speak: "Just one day at a time, Kiri. Just get through this night."

As for my mother, because she is so devastated, I spend most of the conversation trying to convince her how this is actually a good thing. Subsequently, I almost convince myself.

My mother is certain that Aaron will see the error of his ways. "He's going to regret this. I know he will."

"Mom, what does it matter? Am I going to wait around to find out if he regrets it one day?"

I neglect to add that I could never again live with a guy who might not only pick up some groceries on the way home from work, but a blowjob from a dude on Craigslist.

Rahil calls and apologizes for the dropped signal. Damned technology. I'd refused him my number, but because I'd called him, his phone trapped it. Things were a lot different from a decade ago, when I was last single. You could actually call a guy and hang up without him knowing it was you.

We chat for a little bit and then I come around to the point, my first attempt ever to set up some kind of booty call.

"We could, uh, meet at Loki. Maybe. And, ah, play some pool."

"Sure, sounds great."

"Well, um, I could, um, call you Sunday afternoon and maybe you're free or maybe not and we could meet up or not meet up, it really doesn't matter." Smooth.

Again, he's unflappable. "Kiri, let's just make plans to meet up. People do make plans you know."

"But plans are so . . . adult." I want nothing to do with the real world.

"Okay, then let's not. Maybe I'll see you sometime."

"Wait, are we meeting Sunday or not?"

He laughs. "You just said you didn't want to make plans."

I'm going to say a lot of things. A lot of fucked up things that make no sense. We agree to call each other Sunday. What I don't tell him is that I can't handle any rejection right now. Not even from a booty call.

"I'm sorry I'm being so crazy," I say.

"You're not crazy. You're just having a tough time. If I thought you were crazy, I'd run five miles."

In the morning, I fantasize about heavy petting with him. That scares me. I'd been with one man, one body, for so long. I wasn't up for any strange surprises.

chapter nine

Aaron comes over to pick up some of his stuff. I'd thought the sight of him packing up his things and taking them out of our life together would send me over the edge—but when the day comes, I'm too hung over to get weepy about it.

He brings cat food and litter and coffee, as requested. He was always thoughtful and reliable like that—except for those times he was sucking off strange men, of course.

I lay on the couch nursing my massive hangover while he rustles around in our bedroom gathering his belongings. I rouse myself enough to get in a couple of digs at him.

"I met an A&R guy last night," I say. "Ordinarily, I would have told him about your band. But I told him about a different one instead."

Aaron swallows this in silence.

I pick up the International Baptist Church flyer the Bible thumpers had left under the door that morning.

"Babe, you might want this," I say, brandishing the flyer with its "God Loves You" message printed on the front. "You could use God in your life."

No reaction. Aaron is nothing if not good at shutting down.

Once his stuff is ready, he stands by the door, looking at me with his tender brown eyes. I'm not sure if they reflect love or pity. I'm sad and steely at the same time. He moves in to kiss me goodbye and I feel his lips for what might be the last time ever, who knows.

After he leaves, I walk in tight circles around the apartment, trying to catch my breath.

That night, I go out with Jocelyn, a friend from college, to Cafe Improv to see a comedienne friend of hers perform. I thought I handily won the award for most juicy life at the moment, but Jocelyn doesn't ask many questions about my situation. She's too focused on her own boyfriend issues: he makes no money; she pays for everything; he's leaving for the summer to work in a little theater in Rhode Island. How any of this was remotely as interesting as my gay boyfriend I didn't know, but I was tired of talking about myself anyway.

We meet up with her comedienne friend at McGee's, a nearby pub. But after a while, I'm restless. I'd had ten years of conversation with my friends, and I'd have ten more. What I hadn't had in ten years was male attention I was free to reciprocate, and it was all I craved right now. These girls weren't interested in flirting.

I step outside and call Julie. "Why are you home?" I ask. "Isn't Jake out of town and you should be out getting into trouble?" Then I apologize. It's the kind of thing Jake probably fears I'm saying to Julie when he's out of town.

"Don't be ridiculous. I was planning on going out anyway. I'm meeting some friends at Loki first, then Gate."

Loki—where I keep running into Rahil. The evening is looking up.

Julie tells me she'll already be at Gate by the time I get back into Brooklyn, but I direct the cab to Loki anyway. Fuck it. I'm looking for him. I admit it.

Inside the dim bar, a man passes me and we lock eyes, recognition taking a moment to sink in. We laugh. It's Rahil. I stammer something about looking for Julie, but maybe, now that I think twice about it, she's somewhere else.

He tells me he's headed into the city to see his friend, who is visiting from London, but he doesn't seem in a rush to leave.

At Gate, Julie is surprised to see Rahil trailing me, and we chuckle over the "coincidence" of it. I don't volunteer that it was self-determined.

Julie moves to a back table.

"I think she's giving us some alone time," Rahil says.

"Alone for what?" I ask, moving my hand to his waist.

Within moments, he's on his BlackBerry, telling his friend to meet him in Brooklyn instead.

We make out at the bar. We move to the back table and make out there. Rahil's friend from London arrives and we ignore him and make out. People come and go and still we make out. I go to the bathroom and return and we make out even more intensely because I'd been away for two minutes. We joke about my bothering to put on lipstick, because he's going to eat it off anyway. If he turns for a moment to speak to someone, I suck on his earlobe. If I talk to someone, his hand travels to the inside of my thigh or up the back of my shirt. It's that kind of thing, the thing that when you're in a good, solid, long-term relationship, makes you want to cheat. It's better than sex—it's the anticipation of sex.

Luckily, Julie's with me that night. Any of my other friends would have lost their stomach for it and left by now.

Someone brings up the idea of relationships, what men and women want from each other.

"Women want safety," says Julie, who writes about sex for magazines and has lots of theories on the topic.

"I just want heterosexuality," I volunteer. "It's my one requirement right now."

"Don't you think what you want out of a person changes depending on where you are in your life?" Rahil asks, reasonably enough.

"No!" Julie snaps. "Women want safety."

"I agree with Rahil," I announce, thumbing his palm. I'd agree with whatever the fucker had to say right now. There was WMD in Iraq? You said it, buddy. Nuclear war has its advantages? Sure enough, pal.

At four in the morning, Rahil and I are alone on the couches downstairs in the dark recesses of a different bar. Everyone else had gradually drifted away. Rahil's hand is up my shirt and under my bra.

I decide I'm going to tell this person whatever I'm thinking at any moment in time. Games are for long-term relationships. I don't have to play games with this one.

"You're goddamn sexy," I say. "I love your eyes."

"I think we should still meet up tomorrow," he says, referring to our plan to "play pool" on Sunday.

"You might be sick of kissing me by then."

"Kiri, I am only going to say this once, so you better listen. I am dead attracted to you. I wouldn't be here if I wasn't. And I am not going to get sick of kissing you. So if you want to meet up, let's meet up. And stop thinking so much."

I push him off me, sit up, and meet his gaze. "I want to be totally honest with you about something," I say. "I am not ready for any kind of relationship and it sounds like you aren't either."

Somewhere during our nights together it had come out that Rahil's ex-girlfriend was in the process of moving out of his apartment. "She likes to do her thing and I like to do mine," was the only explanation he'd offered. I didn't want or need to know more.

I continue: "I just want that out there, because I know how guys are. They think all women are dying to marry them and start spitting out their babies. And that's not the case here. You are free to do what you want and so am I. So don't freak out if I call you, and I won't freak out if you call me."

"You won't fall in love with me, and I won't fall in love with you. I get it."

I cover his eyes while I kiss him. "Have you ever been blindfolded?"

He laughs, as if I'd asked if he'd ever watched television. "Of course I have!"

When the bar shuts down, we get kicked out. I hadn't been out this late in God knows when. I'd forgotten what the color of light looks like this early in the morning: glassy gray.

"Can I at least show you the outside of my apartment?" Rahil asks.

"I am *not* going up to your apartment."

"I know. I just want to show it to you."

We walk a block and he points to it. "See? The one with the fire escape."

When the sight of his fire escape doesn't get me any closer to coming upstairs, he hails me a cab.

chapter
ten

I call Rahil late in the afternoon to beg off meeting him. One, I have another nauseating hangover. Two, I'm worried we're going to overdose on each other. I want to keep up the excitement and mystery. But he's the most persuasive man in the world. Or maybe it's easy to be persuaded. Either way, I find myself at Loki, tired and hung over and still somehow horny as hell.

We play a little pool, but I'm too wiped out to enjoy it. I can really only think about when we're going to start kissing. We do soon enough, but then we spot a big group of middle-aged locals setting up a table behind us for some guy's fiftieth birthday party.

"We should make out in front of them the whole time. They might like that," I suggest.

"I have an idea. There's this apartment. It's near here."

"I'm not going to your apartment."

"I won't lock the doors. You can run out at any time."

"I'm not going to your apartment."

I knew damn well I was going to end up in that apartment.

"Look," he says, his eyes drilling holes into mine, "here's the ground rules: no one takes off any clothes. If you take off your clothes, I'm kicking you out. And any time you want me to stop anything, you say so, and we stop."

I had the feeling he'd gotten a lot of girls into bed with that little speech.

His apartment is your typical Brooklyn walk-up: hardwood floors, small rooms, a rundown kitchen and shabby bathroom. But nice views.

"You can see the penis building from here," I remark, pointing out the old Williamsburgh Savings Bank building on Flatbush Avenue, the top of which is shaped like a phallus. It's always auspicious to mention a penis as soon as you enter a man's apartment.

"Where are your sex toys?" I ask. At the bar, Rahil had regaled me with his knowledge of sex toys. The man had moved to New York City only a few months ago, yet he'd already decided that the best sex shop in town was Tic Tac Toe on Sixth Avenue. I'd bought my first vibrator the week after Aaron left. I'd always been worried I might get "addicted" to one and not be able to climax without it. That turns out to be a fallacy.

Rahil leads me to his dresser and opens the top drawer. Inside is a whip, some kind of strange plastic stick with large beads on it (for the ass? the pussy?) and a vibrator.

"You're not using any of that stuff on me, you know." I meant the toys in the drawer, not toys in general.

"I wouldn't exchange sex toys! That's quite unhygienic. I always send them back to my ex-girlfriends."

Quite thoughtful of him.

He shows me his box of specialty condoms, the "best condoms in the world," he calls them. At least he uses condoms. And I appreciate that he isn't hiding his dirty side from me as Aaron had done for so long.

We start off kissing on the couch, but soon that becomes too small. "Let's move to the bed," I suggest, knowing he won't suggest it himself. Unlike a lot of men, he has self-control, and knows that a little patience will get him what he wants faster in the end.

We roll around on the bed and he puts his hands inside my panties, his fingers in my vagina. "That feels like a wet pussy to me," he observes.

Here it is, the moment of truth. I put my hands down his pants and feel his cock. It's a bit of a disappointment. I'd hoped it might be the "piece" that hung on Aaron. But I had to face it, the odds of finding that again might not be so good. At least it wasn't tiny. It was doable. And besides, Rahil had a way with his fingers, a way of savoring foreplay, of making it the main meal, which made cock size somewhat irrelevant.

This man has ideas. He turns me around and fingers my pussy and ass from behind while kissing my neck. Three things at once! Impressive.

He's so unabashedly sensual about everything. If I kiss his neck, it's "I love having my neck kissed." I could never get a reaction out of Aaron when I kissed his neck, so I would stop after one or two halfhearted pecks. When I bit and sucked on Rahil's nipples, it was, "I love what you're doing. It feels so incredible." Aaron's nipples had been off-limits for the entire time I'd known him. I wondered if Aaron had managed to tap into his sensuality with men—if he allowed them to turn him on where I couldn't.

On the verge of coming for the first time (yes, there would be a second), I tell him a fantasy: that we are doing this in front of a bunch of strangers. I think he says, "I'd like to try that," but I can't be sure. My mind is elsewhere. After my second orgasm (he insisted on the encore), I begin to get a little nervous that my hand manipulations haven't done much for him. After all, he still hadn't come. But I needn't have been concerned. When he decided it was his turn, he had no trouble. Good thing. In my state of mind, if there were any last-minute sagging of the penis, I would've taken it as a bright neon sign of latent homosexuality.

We smoke a cigarette on his couch. "It's amazing that we managed to do all that and not take our clothes off," I say.

"I knew we *wouldn't* have done all that if we'd taken our clothes off."

Neat trick, that.

I glance at my watch and say I have to go. It's still early, but I don't want to hang out and make postcoital chat. Plus, I tell him, I really need to eat something.

"Then we'll go get something to eat," he says.

"I said *I* needed to eat something, not *we*."

"You meant to say 'we.' "

"No, I didn't."

Rahil walks me to 4th Avenue to find a cab. It's biting cold and I lean into him. He puts his arm around me and doesn't ask when we will see each other again.

chapter eleven

I fly to Palm Beach to visit my grandfather, Bernardo.

Born into a noble Portuguese family, former diplomat, man about Georgetown, multilingual author whose first book was published at age twenty-four, and once so handsome he was under contract with a Hollywood studio because he resembled a more masculine Tyrone Power, Bernardo's now ninety years old and preoccupied with his coming death. This, according to him, is set to happen any day now, despite his being in perfectly fine health, his mind as sharp as twenty-five-year-old's, able to dredge up incidents, places, and people from decades ago with finely pointed fidelity.

Here's a guy who'd always gone his own way: he'd had three wives (all gorgeous enough that they'd modeled professionally) and couldn't stay faithful to any of them. His first wife, my paternal grandmother, had been the recipient of one of his most audacious displays of womanizing:

three days into their Catskills honeymoon, he'd snuck off to cheat on her with another newlywed.

Of course, he's an old man now, his Don Juan days behind him. He's lonely, tottering around his tiny Palm Beach apartment. It would have been nice if he'd had a wife to keep him company. But they probably would have driven each other nuts. Besides, we all die alone.

My grandfather had heard about the breakup but not the reason for it. When I get to the "He's GAY!" part, he does the standard-issue "What?!" Then, unlike anyone else I'd told, he starts laughing. "I thought it would be something more dramatic."

"More dramatic than that? You set the bar pretty high."

"Why would he want to be with a big hairy man when he could have you?"

"Actually, it's big hairy men he prefers. How'd you know?"

At dinner, I ask my grandfather if any of his marriages had been "open."

"With Roxie," he says, naming his third wife. "She liked women. She'd bring them home for a threesome. She loved to go down on me while the woman went down on her."

Yep, this from my ninety-year-old paterfamilias. We'd never limited our conversations to grandfather-approved topics like heartburn and baseball.

"Did you ever get insecure because she liked women so much?"

"To a certain extent."

But despite having a wife who brought women home for him, the marriage still fell apart. I never quite knew what had happened, except that Roxie once mentioned how she'd filed for divorce after Bernardo disappeared for four days over Christmas. I guess even if you give a man total sexual freedom, you still expect a modicum of reliability.

My grandfather and I are walking back from dinner when Aaron calls. He's been staying at the apartment to watch the cats and updates me on them, then tells me he cleaned the bathroom. "You didn't have to do that," I say.

"It was disgusting."

I tell him how my grandfather doesn't get him at all. "He's revolted by men," I say. "He doesn't understand how anyone could prefer a man over a woman."

Aaron chuckles, hesitantly. I'm twisting the knife a little, making him feel like less of a man.

"Well, baby, so far we've broken up so you could spend more time drinking at Last Exit. Are you doing any real work on yourself?"

"I've been to a couple of gay bars."

Ask a stupid question.

"In Chelsea?" I gulp.

"There are gay bars in Brooklyn."

Ask another stupid question.

"How's that going for you?"

"Not too good. I can just about say hello."

I can picture it: Aaron, paralyzed with shyness. He was never good at the pickup.

Over dinner, my grandfather had told me that a great passion requires great suffering on both sides. He'd only felt it twice in his life, on neither occasion with his wives. The first time was when he was twenty-two, with an older woman whom he'd followed to America (I have her to thank for being American). Then there was a woman named Christina. He considered her the great love of his life. The relationship was fraught with jealousy, raging dramas, blistering arguments, and phenomenal sex. One night at a party, after seeing Bernardo dance a little too amorously with another woman, Christina had extinguished her cigarette on his hand (he still had the faint scar) and then tried to burn down his apartment.

Yet even this supposed great passion couldn't stop him from straying. Christina had once walked in on him having sex with her best friend. I'd asked him why he couldn't keep it in his pants—not even for his soul mate.

"Because," he said, "I always wondered if I was a good husband, a good father, whether I would get a good job. One thing I knew I could do well was to get women into bed."

We all have our strengths, I suppose.

chapter twelve

Day 18 "What's the longest passion can last?" I ask no one in particular.

"I've read lots of studies on this," Julie declares. "It's three years."

"Three years!" everyone exclaims. I'm not sure if we all think three years is too short or too long.

"Wait," Julie says, "maybe it's three months. I can't remember."

A group of us are on 14th Street at Ipanema, a rundown, glaringly lit little joint. I wish we could go somewhere else, somewhere darker, more intimate, with lighting that won't reveal every flaw—but my halfhearted attempts to corral everyone are resisted. I have a reason for wanting to look good—Rahil is on his way.

When he does arrive, he's like a jolt of caffeine to the evening, jubilantly introducing himself ("Rahil here!") to all and sundry, before turning to me and growling, "You look fantastic." He doesn't look so bad himself, with his light green T-shirt a bit too tight. It's not long before we're full on in the PDA department and people are beginning to move away from us like we're contagious.

Rahil begins working one constant theme: going back to his apartment.

"No."

"All we'll do is what we're doing right now."

"No."

I hadn't been out of the game so long that I didn't know that a girl was still expected to kick up a fuss as a prelude to sex—that is, if she wanted to make it more interesting (for the guy, at least).

"If you'd called earlier in the week, we'd be there now, because that's what I was going to suggest we do," I say. "But you didn't call me until an hour ago. Look. I'm a low-maintenance girl. I'm not asking for dinner or any courting. But I do ask for a plan so at least I know whether to take other offers or not."

"But . . . but . . . you said you didn't like to make plans!" he sputters.

"For all you know about women, here's a very rudimentary thing you seem not to know. A woman can change her mind at any time."

"My mistake. It won't happen again."

Julie, Jake, Rahil, and I catch a cab back to Brooklyn. Jake gets in the front seat and keeps looking back with what I imagine is a look of disapproval. Is it directed toward me and the fact that I'm acting so slutty so soon? Or toward Rahil as a kind of warning to tread carefully with me? Or toward Julie, who every once in awhile gives Rahil a drunken, overly friendly embrace?

After dropping them off, Rahil and I head to Loki for one last drink. But we don't drink. We make a beeline for the back couches, which are deserted, and sit kissing and fondling. I make sure to flash him my pink lace panties, the ones I'd just bought from Victoria's Secret. Not the kind of thing you bother with in a ten-year relationship.

The apartment refrain is never far from his lips. "We'll just kiss, nothing more, you can leave at any time. I want you to feel safe. . . ."

Of course we end up back at his apartment.

We're all over each other on the couch until he picks me up and carries me to the bedroom. I'm acutely aware that this is a calculated move, certainly one he's practiced many times, but it's still one of the hottest things anyone has ever done for me. I love the way he comes, noisily and lustily, holding nothing back.

"I'm going to leave early in the morning," I say. "Don't be upset if I don't leave you a note."

"You don't have to leave."

"But I'm going to."

About 6 A.M. while Rahil sleeps, I'm crawling around on the floor, trying to locate my clothes. My grasping hand touches upon a bunched-up wad that turns out to be a frilly white shirt and a thong—neither of which are mine. Could be the ex-girlfriend's things, but if so, it seems strange stuff to leave behind. At any rate, I'm amused by it. It's further evidence that I'd picked the right person to have a purely sexual fling with.

Walking back from his apartment toward 4th Avenue to find a cab, I think of the term "walk of shame." With my mussed hair and cakey makeup and still wearing last night's dress-up clothes, it is indeed a walk of shame—giddy shame—as if my bruised sexuality is hanging out there for the world to see, point at, judge, and secretly envy.

I can't believe this is my life.

* * *

Late that afternoon, I manage to drag myself into the cat shelter, where I've volunteered for seven years, cleaning cages and feeding homeless felines. The animals are so simple. Some are scared and need a little coddling. Others are stretched out and happy. I'm just glad to have something to concentrate on besides my own drama and lust. At 6 P.M., Rahil leaves me a message. I'm beyond surprised to hear from him so soon.

"Bottom line, I want to see you," he says.

At midnight he arrives at People Lounge on the Lower East Side, at my friend Lily's thirtieth birthday party. I'd been drinking a lot before he got there, hoping that the more I drank, the more I'd find other people interesting. But it doesn't work. My mind is fixed on Rahil's arrival and that's a little scary. I couldn't begin to rely on one person to make my evening.

I'm excited for him and Sahana to meet. Both are talkative, opinionated, a little crazy, and Indian. After the two of them gab to the point where even I can't get a word in edgewise, Sahana takes me aside.

"He's unlovable, but funable," she says.

"What the hell does that mean?"

"It means you're safe. He's fun. But you're never going to fall in love with him. He's unlovable. Don't tell him I told you that."

Back at his apartment, Rahil carries me to the bed again. I love to look at his expression when I kiss him, the way he leans into me and purses his lips slightly, sometimes licking them, waiting for the next kiss, full of desire. It's only after getting kisses like this that you realize that something had been missing from your other kisses.

When we're done, we wrap our legs around each other, and he tucks his head into the crook of my neck, gives two heaving snores, and falls asleep. The desire for sexless affection is so strong in humans, even in those where the relationship is based purely on sex. Aaron had always been such a delicious snuggler, though in the past couple of years, it had been pretty much one sided, up to me to snuggle. But about a week before I left for Los Angeles in March, to attend the Oscar parties, I'd felt him curling around me from behind. "You spooned me last night, baby," I'd said the next day, pleasantly surprised. "I did," he'd smiled. Maybe he'd known then it would be the last time.

In the morning, Rahil makes me Indian tea. He never seems in a hurry for me to leave, though we both know it's going to happen. It's difficult to keep the conversation at the superficial level. At some point you run out of light banter and things creep toward the "get to know you" talk. It creeps very slowly, but still it creeps.

I fight it. The less I know, the more I can cloak him in my own fantasy. If I find out he voted for Bush, or hates cats, or once spent time in prison for child molestation, the less likely I'm going to want his fingers up my vagina.

I lie with my head on his naked lap, and at some point I realize he's rubbing his penis while talking to me.

"Good lord, what are you doing?" I laugh.

"What?" he asks, innocently.

"You don't do that on the subway, do you?"

"Certainly not. I'm only perverted when someone wants me to be."

I had gone from Aaron, someone so repressed he hardly liked anything touched, to a guy so sensual he couldn't keep his hands off me *or* himself. I wondered why I couldn't find someone in the middle, but maybe this was what I needed now, as maybe Aaron was what I needed then.

I still have dreams about Aaron: short, nonsensical, gut-wrenchingly sad dreams about my best friend leaving me. After one, I awake with a jolt and realize I need to see him more. Cutting him out of my existence is not working. I don't know how people who lose their life partner after fifty years, who are older and may not have the big city distractions I do, survive. I guess they slowly die of a broken heart.

That night, Rahil calls to make plans for Friday. The "plan" is to go to his apartment . . . period. Something about the call makes me feel so generous that when I speak to Aaron, I tell him that when he comes over to get the rest of his things, he can bring boxes. I'll give him some bowls, plates, glasses, towels.

"But I keep all the good stuff," I say.

That night in my dream, Aaron is animated and emotionally expressive like I'd never seen him—and it's because he's free to be himself. I feel so horrible about that, as if he'd been forced to be someone else for ten years.

Then we get into an argument. "Well, *you* like men," he says, explaining his own attraction.

"Yes, Aaron," I hiss. "But I'm a girl!"

Good God, I'm becoming a red stater in my dreams.

I remembered the night Aaron and I had met at Boat. I'd asked him to help me understand how I might spot this kind of thing in future relationships.

"When the sex goes bad . . ." he'd sighed, trailing off.

How that had galled me! I'd spent years trying to convince Aaron the sex wasn't quite right, and he'd always played it off like it was fine. Eventually, I'd come to accept that it was better to have a lukewarm sex life and a great relationship than the reverse.

It's not that you don't see the warning signs, or ignore them. It's that after ten years you learn not to freak out about them. You've gone through so much crap together and are still together that a gradual widening of interests or dwindling of a physical connection doesn't set off the alarm bells that they might only six months into it. After a man comforts you through the World Trade Center collapsing before your eyes, through the deaths of relatives, and through hundreds of more minor crises in between, you don't expect him to suddenly take a U-turn out of the relationship—and into the arms of a big hairy man.

The next afternoon, I go to my hair salon to pick up a diffuser that my stylist, Katie, had ordered for me. Aaron uses the same place, the hairdressers all know him. They are dumbfounded by my news.

"Are you going to get therapy?" Katie asks, wide eyed.

"Everyone keeps asking me that. I'm not much of a therapy person."

"I'm just saying, you might want to consider it," she warns. She tells me about a male friend of hers who was with a woman for ten years, got married, and a year into the marriage found out his wife was having an affair with a woman.

"Please don't tell me the past eleven years have been a lie," Katie's friend had begged his wife.

"I can't tell you that," she'd answered, less than diplomatically.

Subsequently, Katie continues, the man got into a car accident. "And he died!"

"Because he didn't get therapy?"

"Because his head wasn't in the right place. He wasn't concentrating."

"Well," I say, "I don't drive."

chapter thirteen

That night, I go out with Lily, Sahana, and Julie. We hit Union Bar and sit near a group of men ranging in age from the twenties to the sixties: three young guys, their father, and their uncle, out celebrating the uncle's birthday.

One of the young men is like a game show host. He sits in front of us and barks, "Where are you from?" and points at us one by one for an answer. Then he makes us each guess what he does for a living. I wonder when we get our year's supply of car wax. After Aaron, who spoke every word with deliberate sincerity, I find myself drawn to the guys who take the conversation off my shoulders.

This game show host and I begin dancing. He's actually quite good, twirling me around as I flop to and fro, always catching me firmly.

He sticks his tongue in my mouth. It's stationary and bulbous, like a plug. He tells me, "You're as good a kisser as you are a dancer." The line is laughable considering how little I'd reciprocated. But having all of my emotional nerve endings suddenly sliced off is freeing in a way: I'm much less irritated by people I would've normally dismissed, more willing to dance, to mingle, to throw myself into the carnival of life and kiss its barker.

Monday night, as I make far too much tuna pasta salad because I'm accustomed to making it for two, and I futilely try to find something on TV, the Aaronless apartment gapes at me, cruel in its aberrant emptiness. I'm introduced to that heart-palpitating restlessness that attacks newly single people, the kind that makes you want to claw your skin off.

I've completely forgotten how to be alone.

The night before, Rahil had texted me, asking if I was "recovered" yet from the weekend. We'd emailed back and forth a couple of times that day. On the subway ride home, I angsted over how utterly disastrous it would be if I developed emotions for him—if I hadn't already. I wondered whether women were even wired to have purely sexual relationships, and how lucky men were that they were capable of it—hadn't Aaron said his hookups were just sex while I was love?

I thought about ending it with Rahil. Before I got attached. Before he hurt me.

chapter
fourteen

Day 28 Rahil is to come over to my apartment tonight. My idea. He'd originally suggested going to see a movie, but I'd found that a little off the mark. Going to a movie, buying popcorn, sitting together, and holding hands? What, what, what was the point? So he would come over.

As I'm waiting, the phone rings.

"It's me." *Aaron.* I can't believe he's calling. "What are you doing?"

"What am I doing?" I squeak.

"Yes."

He'd said he would leave the calling up to me because he didn't want to press a relationship I might not want. He sounds down. Is he going to tell me he misses me, this is all a mistake, he isn't gay anymore? No, I'm not that stupid.

"I'm waiting for a guy to come over," I say. I get a little thrill out of it.

"Oh."

"Is something wrong?" I ask.

"No. I've just gotten used to our Wednesday nights."

"Our" Wednesday nights consisted of two Wednesdays in a row, both tearful and fairly torturous. Why on earth would he be hankering for another? My guess is this was the first night Aaron didn't have plans with his bar buddies, or soccer practice, or band rehearsal, or some other thing to distract him from the fact that he was no longer part of a couple. Craigslist, I supposed, was good for the cock, but not necessarily for the soul.

"You're lonely, huh?"

"Maybe."

"Yeah, I know, Aaron. I've had plenty of nights where I sat here in shock that you wouldn't be walking in the door any minute."

"I'm sorry if I ruined your night."

Rahil's cabbie gets lost so it's half an hour before he makes it to the apartment. He bounds up the stairs, kisses me, hyper as ever. I show him the gift I'd gotten for him the day before. It's a copy of a photo from my decade-ago nude modeling days: hair obscuring my face, one tiny boob popping out of a little black dress. Rahil is as excited as a kid at Christmas.

"This changes the whole tenor of the evening!"

I show him the whole nudie portfolio. He oohs and aahs over each shot of my nipples. It's the kind of caveman behavior that Aaron always lacked. "We have to kiss some now," he insists.

Making out soon leads to petting on the couch. At my request, he gets a little "rough" with me, pinning my arms above my head and yanking my pants down to my knees. Unfortunately, he keeps up a frenzied whipping motion with his fingers, when I tend to like a slower, more deliberate caress, and rather than tell him to slow down, I just fake an orgasm. I don't know why. Maybe it's because he's trying so hard. Maybe it's because I'd told him I preferred it slow on a previous night, and he obviously didn't remember, and I didn't feel like repeating myself.

We finish off in the bedroom and by that time I'm ready to smoke a cigarette and order in something to eat. The whole thing had been a little pedestrian. The kissing had lost some of its spark. About five years into my relationship with Aaron, I'd felt as if I were kissing my brother. This is creeping in with Rahil after only four weeks.

Also, by now, the fantasy is dissolving. I knew Rahil had grown up in a small manufacturing town outside of Bombay. I knew he had a brother and a slew of cousins. I knew he'd thought about becoming an actor, a writer, anything creative, but that just wasn't done in his town or family, and so he went into finance. I knew too much.

"People get mad when I say this," he says, "but my goal is to have a full relationship with five different women at the same time."

"A full relationship? Not just fuck buddies?"

"A full, real relationship."

"You better move to Utah."

"People always say that," he sighs. "Or Saudi Arabia."

I challenge him on whether he'll have enough time for this kind of thing. He admits that maybe three women would be more time manageable.

"Well, good luck with that."

Now I definitely knew too much.

"This booty call thing is kind of weird," I say. "I don't know the ground rules."

"Do whatever you want to do. Just make sure to keep your feelings in check."

I'm unexpectedly stung.

"Rahil, there's a reason you got this job. You seem like a great guy. You are a great guy. But I couldn't fall in love with you."

Yet I'm dully aware that I'm only half believing what I'm saying. It's clear that my wiring is kerflooey—mouth, brain, heart, and pussy all working different sides of the room.

A friend of mine tells me she's tested positive for HPV (human papillomavirus), a strain of venereal disease that puts her at high risk for cervical cancer. She feels horrible, like a slut, even though she's only had sex with five men in her entire life and used a condom with each one, every time. Her doctor tells her she could've gotten the virus just from petting or from the base of the penis, which the condom doesn't cover. Because the virus could've lain dormant, undetectable for many years, until now, she doesn't even know which guy to blame it on.

This news sends me into a slight state of panic. Here I am having sex—"protected" sex, but that hadn't helped her—with a guy I hardly knew anything about. One who'd surely had many, many sexual partners. And then there was Aaron, who'd taken it upon himself to blow and fondle strange men, who were no doubt blowing and fondling other strange men, and women too, who knows.

In the morning, I call Aaron at work and tell him about my friend. I demand that he get me the results of his AIDS test in writing. He'd already told me he'd tested negative. I'd already tested negative. But I needed to see it. He emails it to me later in the day. Negative.

My friend's diagnosis is a kick in the head. I realize that no matter how careful you are, you still take a risk every time you have sex. Whether it's with one person or twenty. My unformed idea of taking one year to "explore" my sexuality, to have sexual relationships with more than one man, maybe several men, quickly begins to lose its appeal. But I'm not ready for a boyfriend either.

So what to do? Wrap myself in Saran wrap? Demand a detailed doctor's note from every sexual prospect? Stay celibate, so that the first guy I wanted to fuck, I did invent some emotional attachment where none existed so I could justify making him my boyfriend?

No guarantees. You could use a condom every time you had sex, and still get a sexually transmitted disease. You could be seven years old and die of a cancerous brain tumor. You could pick the guy all the relationship books tell you to pick—good, stable, loving, committed, one who makes you feel safe and cherished. And he could turn out to be gay.

Earlier in the evening, before my friend called, I'd stopped off at Last Exit, the bar Aaron and I had always hung out at. I knew Aaron wouldn't be there because he was at band rehearsal. I'd touched on the situation with a few of the regulars there. They were basically Aaron's friends, all of them. Only one had bothered to email me after the break to ask how I was doing. I wasn't even sure why I was there, except for the lack of other plans, and maybe the enjoyment the shock value of my appearance would cause.

"He's not evil," a regular informs me. "He's not burning babies."

I'd been in one of my Zen-like moods where I thought everything had happened for the best, something I'd been forcing on myself so I wasn't constantly consumed by a fireball of anger. So I'd agreed with her. Yes, that was true, Aaron wasn't *evil*.

But after my friend's news, I had a somewhat different view. Wasn't it evil to take a person's trust and mutilate it so completely? To put the health of the person who loves and believes in you at risk? I remembered now, about two years ago, Aaron had seen what he thought were fleas crawling around in his pubic hair—but he had pubic lice, commonly known as "crabs." I'd trusted him so implicitly that I'd teased: "Knock it off with the Thai hookers, babe." Of course it must be from a public toilet seat. *Of course it must.*

Maybe what Aaron had done wasn't *evil*, it wasn't *burning babies*, but I thought it was pretty shitty nonetheless.

If Aaron had had a string of anonymous women on the side, I suspected I would have received a bit more sympathy from his friends. But they were too busy going to great pains to prove they weren't homophobic to offer any round condemnation. Even my own friends would ask, in concerned, hushed tones, "How is Aaron doing?"

In February, we'd celebrated Valentine's Day. The card he gave me was of the excruciatingly sappy variety, but I loved it anyway. I was never jaded when it came to Aaron.

At the bottom of the card, in his own writing, he'd added, "I usually don't like these pre-printed cards, but I thought this one was perfect. I LOVE YOU!!!"

I had cried because I couldn't believe I deserved this kind of love, couldn't believe I had somehow pulled it off.

Three weeks later, he was gay.

chapter fifteen

Day 32 My friend Pam is in town, visiting from Los Angeles. At Union Square Bar, we chat with a married couple from New Jersey, Angelo and Missy, who are getting drunker and louder as the night wears on. I smoke a cigarette with Missy outside, and tell her about Aaron coming out after ten years.

"Do you want me to have him killed?" she asks, deadpan. "I'm half Italian. I know people."

Back inside, she loudly informs Angelo of my situation. Angelo, a red-blooded heterosexual male of the meat-eating, beer-drinking, Florida-vacationing variety, can't get over this news.

"You are so hot, you would turn a gay man straight!" he crows.

He wants to meet Aaron, to "beat some sense" into him. He's genuinely baffled and, I think, slightly insulted by the whole thing. Where

Angelo came from, a man didn't suddenly turn gay on a cute blonde girl who's willing to sleep with him on a regular basis.

Sahana arrives and the three of us head to Underbar. There's a group outside competing to get in, and not even my plea that I'm a journalist who writes about bars (um, yeah) gets us ahead of the pack. So we split there and move upstairs to Olives, in the W Hotel bar. Boredom begins to settle in. I find myself repeatedly checking my phone for any sign of life from Rahil. He'd called earlier and told me he'd be out with two married friends. But there was another reason he'd called.

"Did you talk to Sahana today?" he'd asked.

"Sure. Twice." I thought it was odd he was asking about Sahana, whom he hardly knew.

"She didn't say anything about running into me last night?"

"Nope."

Rahil recounted how he'd been at a performance space to see his ex-girlfriend, Hayden, do some kind of circus act, or flying trapeze act, or whatever the hell it was she did. And whom did he happen to see there but Sahana and her fiancé, Pradeep, who were coming out of their yoga class.

"Weird she didn't mention it," I'd said.

"It was so surreal. I never thought I'd be introducing your friends to my ex-girlfriend."

"When do I get to meet her?"

He'd stammered and flailed around. "Well. . . . uh. . . . sometime, I guess, it might be awkward, I don't know, but we're all adults, so. . . ."

After I'd hung up, I'd called Sahana.

"You're keeping some gossip from me."

"I wanted to tell you in person."

"He already told me. So what happened? What's the ex like?"

"I have to tell the whole thing in person, with facial expressions, hand gestures, and voices."

"Uh, okay."

At Union Bar, Sahana launches into the story.

"Let's get the vanity thing out of the way first. You are a hundred times better looking than she is."

I hadn't asked, but that was good news, I guess. It would have been a little daunting to hear his ex was a supermodel.

"Is she brunette, blonde? White, dark?"

"She's very tall, like four inches taller than he is, so they look really strange together. She's white with red hair, and it's really curly, like an Afro. She doesn't seem feisty. She's not rat-a-tat-tat. She seems rather sweet and naive."

The sweet and naive part threw me. I'd seen her drawer full of sex toys.

Sahana drops her voice and adds: "She's *really* young." Then: "He seemed nervous that we would rat him out."

Well, I'd figured he was still sleeping with the ex. I'd seen her panties on the floor and the expensive salon conditioner in the shower, the kind no guy would bother with. For the purpose of not spreading SDTs, I did wish we were being monogamous. Hell, I wished he were a virgin. But that wasn't what I was dealing with, and I took the risk on my own terms. I, too, had no intention of being monogamous, if opportunities arose.

Though I wondered if I was even capable of juggling more than one sexual partner. It suddenly occurred to me I had tried that once before—in my mid-20s. I had just moved to the city, and was still having the occasional cross-ocean get-together with a British guy, Nigel, whom I'd met when I'd lived in England for a year at age nineteen and on the student exchange program in college. At twenty-four, I'd finally lost my virginity to him. Yes, I said twenty-four.

Two years later, Nigel had helped me move to New York and then came to visit me over New Year's. But I'd met Aaron a couple of months before and, although we weren't that serious yet, was sleeping with him. I figured I could do the whole casual sex thing with both of them. But I couldn't bring myself to even touch Nigel. It was a huge disappointment for him. Who could blame him? Flying three thousand miles only to get the cold shoulder in bed. We'd ended on bad terms. But was it prudishness on my part or was it because I'd developed real feelings for Aaron? Or was it because I was incapable of having sex with more than one man at a time? *Crap*.

"Anyway," Sahana continues, "I think Rahil's fun. He might actually be a good guy."

Boy, did he have her fooled!

At 3:30 A.M., just as I get into a cab, Rahil texts and tries wheedling me into coming to his apartment. Once I get dropped off in front of my building, I call him.

"Four A.M.? I have my standards, you know. They may be rather low right now, but I have them. Anyway, you should come out with us tomorrow. I don't know what happened last night, but you've really won over Sahana. She wants my other friend to meet you."

"I thought she'd go back and report that I was with some girl and hate me!"

"She thinks you're crazy, but fun."

"She thinks I'm crazy?"

"You *are* crazy."

"What does that say about you that you're sleeping with a crazy guy?"

"It says I'm crazy too, but hopefully it's a temporary state of mind."

"I think it means you've always been crazy, but you're just now getting a chance to indulge it."

The next day, I do a Google search for Hayden, Rahil's ex-girlfriend. The combination of her unusual forename and the name of her flying acrobatic troupe instantly brings up her page on a social networking site. She's all of twenty-two, hippyish, into yoga and all things India. She has a bright red mop of curly hair, a somewhat doughy body, and a face that, no matter how long you stare at it, refuses to clarify itself as either plain or beautiful.

Then I thumb through old photos of Aaron and me, something I hadn't had the stomach to do until now. There we are in Costa Rica, in November (five months until gay). Here we are at my last birthday party, at the restaurant Rosa, in September (seven months until gay). And then at his birthday party—the surprise one I'd thrown at Last Exit, his favorite bar. I'd gathered all his friends together, managed to single-handedly corral a cake and a batch of balloons onto the premises before his arrival (all on an extremely windy, rainy day), and had everyone yell "Surprise!" as he came in. He'd told me it was the best birthday anyone had ever given him.

Now I can't look at his grinning face without it taking on an element of the macabre: He had already started blowing strange men. He already knew we were doomed. Yet he looked in the camera and smiled.

I text Rahil: "When can you next service me?"

Then I call Aaron.

"Hi," he answers, his voice soft, tired.

"What are you doing?"

"I came straight home from work for the first time in weeks."

"You sound exhausted."

"I am."

Trolling Craigslist must take its toll.

I tell him about my looking at old pictures, and how they made me sad, empty, nostalgic.

"I know," he says.

That's his answer for everything.

Rahil calls on the other phone and I hang up with Aaron.

"You mentioned servicing?" he chirps.

"Yeah." I try to cover my embarrassment with a laugh.

"Well, Thursday I'm going out with Hayden. Friday might be okay, but it depends on my brother's arm. Did I tell you he broke his arm? I might have to go to Boston."

I hesitate. I know I shouldn't say it, but the words fly out of my lips.

"I'm not sure why you and Hayden broke up if you're going to choose to spend time with her rather than your booty call."

"You need to get more booty calls going so you don't have this problem," he says, helpfully.

I feel my ire rising.

"Look, I told you from the beginning that there were no strings attached," I say, a bit too strenuously. "But you did say 'ex-girlfriend.' Some people might take that to mean a girl you're no longer fucking. You just might want to change that description in the future, that's all."

I had walked into this trap with eyes wide open, and there shouldn't be any whining when the door slammed shut behind me. But whine I would.

"I just want you to know you don't have to hide things or lie about things," I harp. "If you tell me you're going to the library and you're really going to a whorehouse, you don't have to tell me you're going to a whorehouse. Just don't tell me you're going to a library."

"Have I done any of that? I could have told you I had 'other plans' on Thursday. But I said it was Hayden."

This is true.

We hang up and I feel like crying. It's the idea of being second best that makes the lump in my throat swell. Incongruous as it sounds, Aaron may have been climbing the stairs up into strange, maybe dangerous, apartments and blowing anonymous, maybe dangerous, men, but he'd always been there for me. No matter what my mood—sad, angry, bored, stressed, neurotic—he was my rock. He was the kind of guy who would not only hold your hair back while you puked but would also clean out the toilet afterward. And now I was running around in the real world, with guys like Rahil, who had no allegiance to anyone except themselves, and who didn't even bother to hide it.

But what was my real problem here? If I was going to be brutally truthful, it was that I expected to trump anyone else: a brother with a broken arm. An ex-girlfriend. Especially one I considered not as pretty as myself.

But there was an emotional history between Rahil and his ex that I couldn't compete with, and I shouldn't expect to. He and I had not known each other long enough to have an emotional connection, but even if we had, I'd steadfastly denied us one. No movies, no dinner plans, as little conversation as possible. Yet I somehow expected to take top priority. These thoughts swirl manically in my brain to the point where I have to let them out.

I grab my cell and text Rahil: "Forgive me for being a selfish bitch. If I'd had plans, I wouldn't have cancelled them, yet I expected you to. I have a lot to learn from you and Hayden. You have such a healthy relationship."

I had a different view of "healthy" now. I used to think Aaron and I had the healthiest relationship imaginable—no drama, no insecurity, few arguments. In reality, the cancerous parts had just been suppressed, hidden. I felt like I was seeing the light for the first time. The idea of romantic love, that you find one person who suits you in all aspects of your sexual, emotional, and spiritual life, was a crock. We all knew "that" couple—whether they were friends, acquaintances, our parents, or grandparents—who seemingly were all and everything to each other, forever, always. For me, it was my great-grandparents. Married for sixty-eight years, good years, years still filled with love and affection. (Until my great-grandmother got Alzheimer's and became convinced her husband had been exchanged with a replica.)

But, now that I really thought about it, my great-grandparents hadn't slept in the same bed for as long as I could remember. Of course, they were old, and their inability to navigate the stairs to the top-floor bedroom had necessitated a move to the living room couches. This couldn't have meant much action, if any. Had that perfect relationship, the one that had seared itself into my young impressionable mind and haunted my adulthood, not been perfect after all? Who even said that "action" had to be part of a good relationship anyway? Certainly I'd come to that conclusion myself with Aaron.

Was that ideal relationship we caught glimpses of in others even worth striving for, because you'd never find it, because, like a white unicorn bounding somewhere in our peripheral vision, it was merely a fantastical chimera? Or could it be that if two well-suited people somehow ended up being torn apart only by death was it, more than anything, just an extreme stroke of good fortune—or maybe even the consequence of laziness?

chapter
sixteen

That night, I dream about Christmas. I shudder awake with fresh ripples of panic.

I'd spent the past ten Christmases with Aaron. Last year, we'd carried a tree home and set it up in the corner of our newly purchased apartment, and decorated it together. Aaron was closer to his family than I was, so he'd no doubt go home for the holiday. I guess I'd have to go home now as well. Home to the bare bones of a family: a very ill grandmother, a mother who still drove me crazy, a sister who probably wouldn't be around. No niece anymore. No children from me. No man now either.

The thought of an Aaronless Christmas wasn't the only thing causing predawn anxiety: I had started to think about Rahil almost constantly. I fret about the last email I'd sent him. Not because it'd said anything emotionally revealing, but because it was long. Funny how it's fine for two newly involved people to talk for three hours while laying naked in each other's arms, but to send a three-paragraph email in the cold light of day might be considered too intimate. I hadn't had the nascent relationship jitters in over a decade. I'd forgotten how anxiety producing they could be, how they could hijack your thoughts to the exclusion of almost everything else.

The next night, Rahil calls. Two minutes into the conversation, his normally live-wire tones take on a dull cadence. "Hayden and I are officially and truly exes now," he says. "She met some guy and wants to explore that relationship and be exclusive to him."

Good for her. I guess she's not that stupid after all.

Not what I say.

"I'm sorry. Are you all right?"

He's all right, but sounds like what he is: a man who was happily having his cake and eating it too—and just had it taken away from him. I offer to meet him for a drink, to "be there" for him.

I'm not sure why I do this, except that a little over a month ago, I was a quivering mass of confusion huddled in a bar. Rahil, a complete stranger, barreled onto the scene, distracted me, made me happy, or at least sexually fulfilled, and this in turn made my transition with Aaron slightly less devastating. Did he do it all on purpose or out of some noble character? No, he saw a pretty girl in a bar and wanted to get laid. But who cares what his motive was. The end result was the same: this guy helped me through the most difficult period of my life. I felt I owed him.

I cab it to Loki. When Rahil arrives, I try to keep the talk away from his troubles, toward something light and amusing. I tell him how my grandfather had had an open relationship with his ex-wife. I tell him about my plans to go to India in November for Sahana's wedding. All the while, he sits so close to me I'm practically inhaling his exhaled breaths. He punctuates his sentences by firmly touching my leg, and stares at me intently with his deep-set blue-green eyes. When I speak, there's a slight tremor in my voice, because the sexual desire he inspires in me is so palpable it's embarrassing.

We get drunker and the night gets longer. We do a lot of kissing and grappling on the back couches. At one point, he is either going on about Hayden, or going on about how he can easily separate sex from emotion, and I begin crying. It's mostly because of the alcohol, but maybe it's a little of all the breakup talk too, and maybe also it's his persistent refrain that I should go back to his apartment and have sex with him even though he's torn up about Hayden, because after all, there's no emotion here, and he can dehumanize me like a blow-up doll. Well, he doesn't exactly *say* that, but it's pretty darn close. So I cry.

"What's happening?" he asks, nervously.

"This just all reminds me of everything," I blubber.

The scenario flips and suddenly Rahil is the one comforting me.

"I can't believe I brought you out here to talk about my ex-girlfriend after what you've been through. What an idiot I am."

Again he tries a hundred different ways to talk me up to his apartment. One of them must have worked because ten minutes later, that's where I am.

We enter the apartment and hit the ground running, feverishly yanking off each other's clothes. In two seconds, we're on the bed and he's inside me. I don't even know how a man gets a condom out of the drawer, opens it, and manages to put it on in the time it takes to blink, but it has to be more than practice. It has to be some innate ability. Immediately after he comes he gasps, "I'm so glad you came over! *So* glad!"

"You knew I would," I say, quietly.

"No, I didn't."

Afterward, we move to the couch. He stares off pensively. One side of my brain is inflamed with how rude he's being, sitting there unabashedly mourning his ex-girlfriend minutes after fucking me, the other side knows exactly what he's feeling down to the tippy toes.

"I'm sure she loved you and does love you," I say, rubbing his back. He nods.

"Do you want to get into bed?" I ask. He nods again.

We get under the covers and he curls as close to me as he can, tucking his head under my chin, and wrapping his entire body around me. I kiss him on the forehead like a little boy.

"Your heart is beating so fast," he says.

"Is it? Interesting."

To paraphrase Rhett Butler, God help the woman who ever really loved Rahil. He was like the sun. When he shone on you, you felt warm and happy and alive. But you couldn't and shouldn't expect him to shine on you alone.

I wait until he falls asleep and then slip out from his embrace.

chapter
seventeen

Day 44 I meet Aaron at a local pub so he can give me a copy of our mail key as I've lost mine. He looks the same: Aaron, my Aaron. His face is as familiar as my own. Maybe more so, as I'm sure I've spent more time looking at him than at myself.

After a drink, I broach the subject of his "gay life."

"So . . . these gay bars, where exactly are they?"

"Are you sure you want to know?"

"I wouldn't have asked if I didn't expect an answer."

He tells me about one in Park Slope, where there is bad "gay music" that he can't stand, and then one in the East Village that has a better jukebox. I giggle nervously and stare at him with wide eyes, as if this is all some protracted prank and he's about to guffaw and tell me how gullible I've been.

"I never expected we'd be having this conversation," he says. "Maybe it's too soon."

"It's okay," I say, half convincingly. "However, I admit I'm glad you're not with anyone."—I couldn't bring myself to say "a boyfriend."— "Maybe that's selfish of me."

After we've both got a good buzz going, Aaron suggests we make our "triumphant return" to Last Exit. I come up with a few excuses, but finally agree to it. It will be amusing to "shock and awe" the regulars. It's unnatural and awkward for us to walk together without touching, so we instinctually reach for each other's hands and clasp them together.

To our disappointment, there's only two regulars at the bar, and one of them is a guy we call "anti-social, social Tim," for he loves to come to the bar and sit in the middle of the group, only to say absolutely nothing. Later on, a few others show up, so our demonstration doesn't go entirely unappreciated.

We do what we've always done: chat, put our hands on each other's legs, and peck each other on the lips before making bathroom trips. Nothing seems to have changed.

But then Aaron launches into a story, broadcasting it to the regulars hunched around the bar. His doctor's receptionist had called him at work and said, ominously, "The doctor would like to discuss something with you."

Aaron, thinking this means his HIV test is positive, almost has a heart attack.

"Tell me now," he'd demanded. "Tell me what it is."

"It's your cholesterol level," the receptionist responded. "It's quite high."

Bah-dum-dum! The crowd bursts into laughter.

I'm mortified. We're actually in a bar, laughing about how Aaron had cheated on me with strange men, putting us both at risk for AIDS.

I wait until we're outside smoking before I burst into tears. Aaron apologizes profusely. But the truth is, none of it matters. It's all funny. A joke. Ten years of my life: a drunken punch line.

At the same time, my brain synapses, which apparently hadn't gotten the memo about Aaron being a diabolical liar, perversely go about traveling their well-worn routes, and I fret about his cholesterol level. Was one of his blowjob buddies going to take over my job of nagging him to stop eating so much pizza, so many French fries?

Back inside, "I'm Coming Out," by Diana Ross plays loudly over the bar's speakers. Who knows why the disc jockey, not knowing Aaron or me and unable to hear our conversation, chose that song at that particular moment. But you couldn't make this shit up, could you?

Well, I guess you could. But I didn't.

chapter eighteen

Day 45 Rahil and I are downstairs at the QT Hotel in Times Square, where you can swim in the indoor pool right up to the bar. He's still in shock over Hayden choosing to explore a monogamous relationship with some other guy rather than continue her third-rate status with him. I can see him beginning to do what so many men do—romanticize the one they can't have. Women tend to romanticize the one they've got.

Nevertheless, we have a great time—splashing about in the pool, making out by the bar and in the sauna. But then he asks if it's okay if he goes home alone to sleep, pleading exhaustion from swimming and drinking.

"Of course," I say. It's the first time he's shown a disinterest in sex, but I decide not to read into it. I have an early flight in the morning to Los Angeles, where I'm to interview the "supermodel turned mogul" Tyra Banks.

* * *

The singer Fiona Apple is on the plane with me. Tiny, pretty, and as glum looking as you might expect someone who makes her type of lovelorn music to look. I'd listened to her latest album, *Extraordinary Machine*, every day since the breakup. The lyrics to "Oh Well" I sang into the hallway mirror.

> *My peace and quiet*
> *was stolen from me . . .*
> *What wasted unconditional love*
> *On somebody*
> *Who doesn't believe in the stuff*
> *Oh well.*

I can't bring myself to say anything to her. What is there to say after all? Hey, my boyfriend turned gay and your album really helped me through it?

At the LAX baggage claim, Fiona hauls bags as large as herself off the carousel, without help. I bet she's a girl who never gets romanticized either.

On the set of *America's Next Top Model,* I meet with Tyra Banks for my profile. She's no-nonsense. She doesn't giggle or bat her lashes. No way does Tyra get romanticized. She probably loses out to a lot of 22-year-old models with nothing to say. Just as I was certain I would lose out to Hayden, the 22-year-old flying trapeze artist.

When I'd first met Aaron, he was still hung up on some single mother who worked in a beauty salon. He finally got over the beauty shop broad, but not until it almost destroyed our budding relationship. Once we got back on track and had been together for a while, I'd come to the realization of how supremely lucky I was to find a man who could love an ambitious, opinionated girl like me. The realization that I might never find another left a cold pit of fear in my heart. Maybe only a gay man could love a strong woman.

After my interview with Tyra, I drive back to Santa Monica and call my friend Andrew, who happens to be in town from New York. He's staying with a couple named Jude and Jennifer. They've been together for seven years and seem an ideal match. But over the course of the evening, and a few too many Johnny Walkers, Jennifer starts complaining how Jude still hasn't asked her to marry him. Her sweet personality begins to morph. She becomes a hellcat, drunk and belligerent. Jude is clearly annoyed with her and they bicker loudly, screeching at each other down the empty streets. I'm beginning to see why Jude hadn't gone ring shopping yet. Barring the first few months, Aaron and I never had these issues. We'd hardly ever argued. But the next morning, Jude and Jennifer are as lovey-dovey as newlyweds. They would probably go on to get married and be together forever, whereas Aaron and I were finished.

Was getting along too well a bad sign?

chapter nineteen

Back in Brooklyn, I arrive at Rahil's apartment just as he's getting out of the shower. He immediately swoops in and begins kissing me, pushing me over to the couch.

"Can I take this off?" I ask, indicating my coat.

"No. You get to do what I tell you."

I have to laugh at the "get" part.

"You can't speak more than five hundred words tonight," he orders.

I defiantly say something and count the words on my fingers. Five.

"I've been waiting for this all week," he says.

"Me too." Seven.

Within an hour, we'd done pretty much everything two people can do to each other, and I'd learned a few new tricks.

We order in Thai food and then go to a bar, where I call Julie, leaving her a message to join us.

"How are you feeling about this situation?" I ask Rahil, once we've ensconced ourselves at a back table. "Do you feel like we're spending too much time together?"

"Not at all," he says, breezily. "It's working out great. If I get one ounce of romantic feeling for you, I'll let you know."

"Thanks," pushes out of my lips. "That's reassuring."

We go to another bar. He checks his cell, sees Hayden left a message, and sits listening to it, head cocked intently.

"You can leave to go see her if you want," I say, not really meaning it.

"I wouldn't leave you to go see her."

"I'm just saying you can if you want. I'm your booty call and she's your true love."

He shrugs and hangs up. "She's asleep by now anyway."

I tell myself that he probably isn't *trying* to make me feel like shit. He's just uncannily doing a great job of it anyway.

A little later, Julie joins us.

"Guess who I ran into outside?" she asks, breathless. "You have to guess."

"Aaron?" I venture.

"Yes!" she cries. "He was alone."

Aaron didn't know anyone in Park Slope. "He must be out trolling the gay bars," I say, and grow quiet.

Rahil excuses himself, as if to let me feel whatever I'm feeling in private. Julie and I step outside for a smoke.

"Did I weird you out?"

"No. I mean it's weird to hear he's out at gay bars, but it's not like I didn't know this."

"I invited him to come here with us and he was going to, but then he asked me if you were with anyone. When I said yes, he changed his mind."

"That's probably for the best."

A couple hours later, Rahil and I are walking back to his apartment. We pass a bar and he points out that it's full of men, *just* men.

"It must be a gay bar!" I exclaim, and lurch inside. The bar is extremely dark. I walk up and down, scanning the shadowy faces, but I don't see him. I don't even know why I went in, or if I'd found him, what I was supposed to say. When I come back out, I cry a little. Rahil puts his arms around me and comforts me.

"Love sucks," I mumble.

"Love sex?" he asks, mishearing. "Me too!"

Later, as we lay in his bed and I feel him beginning to fall asleep, I slip out from his arms. He grabs me back.

"Where are you going? Stay, stay."

"I'm just getting water," I respond, gratified that he wants me to stay, although, by now, I knew him well enough to know that didn't mean much.

In the morning, we lounge naked on the couch, drinking Indian tea. He'd told me the night before that he had a brunch meeting with Hayden, so I ask him what time he has to leave.

"Something came up and she had to postpone until this afternoon."

I tell him that my email buddy, Tyler, is coming into town that night, and how he and I had been emailing for four years but had never met in person.

"He's coming into town to meet you?" Rahil grins. "Sounds like someone's going to get laid tonight!"

"Before you go any further with this fantasy, Tyler is gay." I relay how Tyler had told me for years that he had a "wife" and that he'd only confessed his homosexuality a few weeks before Aaron did. "I'm the girl who turns men gay," I conclude.

Hayden calls. Her plans have been canceled, and she can meet up with Rahil earlier. He hangs up and looks at me.

"Do you mind if I go?"

It wasn't so much a question that begged an answer. I could tell by his energy that he was already halfway out the door.

"Of course not." I keep my voice steady, but begin to dress at a furious pace.

"Slow down. You don't have to leave this minute. Want to hang out here? You can sleep or whatever."

"That would be weird," I mutter. "I should go home anyway."

"Let me take a quick shower and we'll walk out together."

He heads to the bathroom and I stand in front of his dressing mirror, brushing my hair. I look down and see a packet of photos. I leaf through them: pictures of Hayden and her friends. I'm struck by the plain moon face, the big-boned body. In one photo, she's wearing some kind of dominatrix outfit. Perhaps that's the attraction: a meeting of kinky minds.

Before we leave, I take one last look around. "Did I forget anything?"

"If you did, it doesn't matter," he says. "You'll be back."

Rahil is fairly glowing with contentment. He must figure he's bagged two of his five-woman dream harem.

Later, on the phone with Sahana, I tell her the tale in all of its gory detail: how Rahil, as I lay there naked, having just blown him, had jetted out the door to meet his ex-girlfriend. I announce that I'm going to break it off with him. To my surprise, she tries to talk me out of it.

"It sounds like you have a great booty call—he's fun, you like him, he likes you, and he's reliable," she says. "Your ego took a bruising, but

I think you'd be crazy to let this thing go when it's so good for you right now. Anyone else you get involved with is going to have issues too."

"Great."

"He's smart. He doesn't want to ruin a good thing. I'm sure if you tell him to modify his behavior, he will."

"Look," I counter, "the next time I want to be with a guy who runs out to meet another girl before the sperm on my lips is even dry, I'll make some money at it."

I meet up with Tyler that evening. He's a blond-haired man in his early forties with a soft, wise expression.

We have dinner and then walk around the East Village, gossiping and laughing. He rechristens Rahil "Ra-heel." Since Tyler doesn't drink, we stay away from the bars and eventually end up at a psychic's. The psychic cups my palm.

"You made a career change about two weeks ago," she pronounces.

"Um, no."

"Two years ago, you made a major change in your life."

"That's when my boyfriend started sleeping with men, does that count?"

"That's *his* change," Tyler corrects, "not yours."

chapter twenty

Day 53 I delete Rahil's information from my cell phone. But I know it won't do much good, since he'll call me. And at 6 P.M., he does.

The first five minutes are nothing but laughs. I tell him how I'm in the process of walking to a bar to meet Julie, who has left a message that she's in the neighborhood, but that I'm becoming more and more convinced the message is actually two days old.

"Just remember that anything I promise you isn't good two days later," he jokes.

"Anything you promise me isn't good two minutes later," I respond, my laugh only slightly forced.

I take a seat on a nearby bench and prep myself.

"But actually, I wanted to talk to you. What I would really love is, well, if you and I take a break, maybe a month, and then maybe reconnect. Because, with the whole Hayden thing, you're in such a bizarre head space right now."

"I don't think it's bizarre," he parries. "I think it's normal."

"Okay, wrong word. But I would love to reconnect when and if it becomes more clear."

"Do you mean when I'm over her?"

"Yes."

"I don't know if I will ever be over her."

"I understand," I say, keeping my voice calm, "but I'm not your consolation prize."

"I wish you had said something before it came to a head like this. What did I say that was so objectionable?"

There were so many things I couldn't even decide which one to dredge up to throw at him first. There was the time he'd told me he would choose Hayden over Angelina Jolie. The time he told me he wouldn't be even a "tiny bit" sad if he never heard from me again. And, of course, the time he ran out of the apartment, off to meet his ex, without even offering breakfast to the girl (me) who'd just blown him. It seems Rahil had devoted a significant amount of time to getting to know a woman's anatomy, but none at deciphering her feelings.

"You're smart guy, I don't need to go into that," I state, simply.

He starts getting flustered. "I thought we had clearly delineated lines in the relationship."

"They are clearly delineated. I just didn't realize that they were going to make me feel like dog shit."

"I'm sorry you're reading it that way."

Sorry indeed. I begin the final kiss-off: "I'll never forget how you helped me through this difficult period. And I think you and I can be friends. Just not now."

"Okay. I respect your wishes."

"Take care of yourself." I hear my voice echoing down the suddenly distant cell connection.

"You too."

For about three hours, I feel really good about the conversation. Happy. Triumphant. I had ended it, not him. But after a couple of drinks at a nearby bar, I just feel depressed and lonely. And I hate Aaron for putting me out here again to get my feelings trampled, when I'd thought I was done with all of that.

chapter twenty-one

That night, Aaron comes over for dinner. He'd been to see his mother in New Jersey that weekend. She'd either come around about having a gay son or at least had learned not to grouse too loudly about it, and had given him some leftover crab au gratin to take home. The mere fact that he was in possession of crab au gratin, which had always been our favorite, made it natural, almost obligatory, that he offer to share it with me. Obviously, we were flailing around when it came to accepting our new roles as separate entities, one of whom had perpetrated a decade-long semifraud on the other.

I cook broccoli and corn and make a salad. Aaron slices and dices vegetables on the kitchen island, just as he used to. The carrots he chops down to tiny little particles.

"I don't remember you cutting the carrots that small when we were together."

"Are you saying it's a gay thing?"

"You said it, I didn't," I laugh.

We eat while watching *American Idol*. I put Bacitracin on a boo-boo he'd gotten while playing soccer. Aaron had always been half lover, half child to me.

When he begins putting his shoes back on at the end of the evening, I have the urge to ask him where he's going. *Where, Aaron, where are you going? You live here.*

We sit on the couch and cuddle. I cry silent tears because I miss him, because I'm scared of my future as well as his, because I don't know if I'll ever find anyone who loves me as reliably as he had, and seemingly still did. And because we'd gotten to this place—this place of friendship and familiarity. Yes, there are a few happy tears too.

The next day, I receive an email from Rahil. He apologizes for his "less than gentlemanly behavior" the weekend before and admits that he was "less respectful" than he should have been but that his "emotional state" had gotten the better of him. Who knew he had an emotional state?

"We'll pick up the pieces in due time," he promises. Or is that a threat?

That night, I go to Last Exit. A couple named Sam and Sarah are in town visiting from San Francisco, where they'd moved in September, and the gang has gathered there to welcome them back.

When I arrive, Aaron is already there. He orders me a drink and we chat. When Sam and Sarah arrive, Sam locks eyes with me, surprised at my presence. "The last I'd heard, it was acrimonious between you two," he says later.

"I guess I had two choices," I say. "Cut him out of my life or be friends. I chose to be friends."

All night, people keep coming up to me, almost paying tribute, proclaiming how amazing it is that Aaron and I are still talking, and how brave I am. But all it takes is a millimeter scratch beneath the surface to reveal how things aren't so amazing and brave.

"So do you still see John?" I ask Aaron, as we sit outside smoking a cigarette.

"Yes," he says.

I'm stunned. Since Aaron had been out cruising the gay bars, I'd assumed that he and John were finished.

"Well, I don't like him," I pronounce, turning abrupt.

Turns out that Aaron was having the type of casual sex arrangement with John that I'd attempted with Rahil. Men were much better at that type of thing. It was in their molecular makeup. Since women could get pregnant, their DNA was wired to fall in love. Otherwise, why bother? Why risk a painful birth, and possibly even death, and raising a child, all for a no-strings-attached screw?

Aaron is taken aback. "He's a nice guy," he stammers.

"Nice? He was messing around with you even though he knew you had a fiancée. That is not nice. It's sleazy. I don't ever want to meet him. He's lucky I didn't get in touch with him and say a few things. Next time you see him, tell him Kiri says to fuck off."

Back in the bar, I can't shake my simmering anger. Aaron takes the hint and leaves. One of the crew, Dave, notices my change of mood and asks me how I'm doing. I tell him what happened.

"Shouldn't you be mad at Aaron rather than this guy you don't know?" he asks.

"Of course I should!" I say. "But I can't, not if we're going to be friends. It's be mad at him, or be mad at John. Because I have to be mad at someone."

I ask Dave, Aaron's drinking and soccer buddy, whether he'd ever seen any signs. Maybe I'd just been too close to the situation to be a reliable observer.

"Not really," Dave says. Then something dawns on him. "Well, there was one thing. You know, when guys get together, we talk about what women we think are hot. Like there's this bartender at The Brazen Head. We'd go there after games, and all go on about her: 'Look at that ass,' that kind of thing. Aaron never joined in." He pauses. "I thought it was because he was so devoted to you."

Ha! So that's how you could tell if your man might be secretly gay? He's not ogling other women behind your back?

After another drink, Dave edges closer and asks me what I want out of life.

"Just fun," I shrug. "In whatever form that takes. And not having expectations, just taking each day as it comes. Maybe that means hanging out with friends. Maybe it means having a booty call. Maybe it means I meet the love of my life. And as long as no one gets hurt, I'd like not to expect commitment or monogamy."

If you want to see a guy's eyes light up, give him the above speech.

"What do *you* want?" I ask Dave.

"The same thing."

"What a coincidence," I laugh.

I get home at 3 A.M. and leave Aaron a drunken, rambling message. The kind I hadn't left since early in the breakup.

"How dare you tell me John's a nice guy? I know you think what you did was nothing, but as far as I was concerned, I was in a relationship.

And that means what you did with John was cheating. And that makes him a slimeball."

I begin to realize that the friendship between Aaron and myself had been based on a form of denial I'll call "separate but same." We didn't live together anymore, my reasoning went, but other than that, everything was the same. The only problem with this philosophy is that it wasn't remotely true. Aaron was gay. But anything that reminded me of that reality triggered an emotional meltdown. If our friendship was to survive, I'd eventually have to base it in the (sur)real world—the gay world.

I didn't know when, or if, I could.

My mood wasn't helped by the fact that over the past couple of days I'd missed Rahil so much my bones ached. I didn't miss him as a person, God knows. I just missed our intense physical connection. It was a nasty joke life played giving you those kinds of sexual sparks with someone for no real reason.

chapter twenty-two

Day 62 My friend Lily invites me to something called "French Tuesdays" at Bed, a club in the Meatpacking District. Bed is called Bed for the obvious reason: beds were cast around the room in lieu of couches. French Tuesdays turns out to be a bi-weekly roving party consisting largely of very attractive dark-haired Europeans, mostly French, mostly clad in black tailored suits, the dress of choice for financial types. You actually had to submit a photo before you were granted membership into French Tuesdays, so it's no surprise that, for the most part, everyone was damn gorgeous (though guests, like me, were not subjected to the face control).

My heart sang as I took in the crowd and realized I'd stumbled across one of New York's best-kept secrets: Unlike most of the city, the men here easily outnumbered the women, and they all appeared to be well groomed, gainfully employed and, at least on the surface, straight.

Lily, her friend Lisa, and I make the rounds, stopping to talk for about fifteen minutes to whichever group of men catches our fancy before we move on to the next.

By 11 P.M., I'd been there for four hours and had had enough. I was drunk, and although I'd had a great time, I hadn't managed to exchange numbers with anyone. That was fine. It was enough to know I could come back and pillage this treasure trove in the future.

I decide to make one last trek to the bathroom before departing. The bathroom attendant is a large black woman who barks out orders and wields a little alarm that she sets off near the stall doors when she determines that someone is taking too long.

A man standing in front of me turns and makes a joke about the "bathroom Nazi." I laugh and begin teasing him that he better get out of the loo in time. When I return from my own trip, I vaguely wonder if he'll be waiting for me. He is.

"Did she set off her alarm on you?" he asks.

"She set it off before I even sat on the toilet."

"Can I buy you a drink?"

"Oh no. Just because you got stuck in front of me on line doesn't mean you owe me a drink."

I wasn't trying to get rid of him. Drinks here were so expensive, I felt guilty about it. I wasn't used to hanging around guys who had money.

"Don't be ridiculous," he says.

"Champagne. It's twelve dollars." I hand him a ten-dollar bill. "You can pick up the extra two bucks. How's that?"

I ask him if he came with anyone. Maybe I wouldn't be leaving just yet, after all.

"My two friends. But they left because they said it was too straight here. They're gay."

"Are you?"

"Am I what?"

"Gay."

"No."

"Are you sure?"

He laughs. "Yes, I'm sure."

I lead him through the throng, to the bed where I last saw Lily and Lisa. Lisa is dancing with some bald, sallow-complexioned man whom James (my bathroom find) christens "the undertaker." James, a 31-year-old banker, is as cute as a button. He has an angelic face, and a sweet, somewhat naive manner about him. He isn't one of the swarthy bad boy Frenchies I'd been looking to connect with, but he'd do.

Suddenly, I notice that his fingertips flash with reflected light. "Are you wearing nail polish?"

"Uh, yeah. Some girl put it on."

"Um. And you're not gay?"

"No!" he laughs, again.

Well, Aaron never wore nail polish. Or had gay friends. Maybe this was what straight guys did.

Soon, I recline on the bed like a pasha and pat the space next to me. James lies down with me and I begin to kiss him. On a kissing scale of 1 to 10, with Rahil being a 10, he's about a 7. I hit him with my fun slut routine and ask him whether he's ever been blindfolded. He pauses shyly and says, "No. But I'd like to be." He rubs the small of my back in awkward circular motions, like you might rub a cat the wrong way.

The next day, on the phone, I recount all of this to Sahana. I'm missing Rahil's expert kisses and caresses.

"American men grow up with sex," she says. "It's easy to get. Rahil had to try so hard to get a girl in India. Girls there don't lie on beds in bars and kiss men. So he had to develop all this technique, and really devote himself to it. Here, a guy has a penis and thinks that's all a girl needs. Americans have always been my worst lovers."

"Please don't tell me any more."

"There's plenty of Indian and European men you can find," she reassures me.

"Sure. But once I get serious about a guy, I don't want to worry about him getting kicked out of the country."

At Bed, before I knew Americans were unskilled lovers and why, James (Canadian) asks me if I want to get together the next night, or over the weekend. I tell him I can't, as I'm headed to Connecticut because my grandmother is having an operation. He takes his chances and politely inquires if I'd like to accompany him back to his apartment. I think I actually babble something about being fine with going back to a man's apartment the second or third time I meet him, but not the first. I was certainly setting myself up for an interesting sophomore encounter, if there ever was one.

He walks me to the taxi stand outside.

"Are you going to give me your number?" he asks before I hop in the cab.

I flip him my business card.

In the morning, I'm surprised to find an email from him in my inbox already. He tells me how glad he was to meet me and that he hopes I want to get together soon.

What a sweet, courtly young man. Something would turn out to be horribly wrong with him, I was certain.

chapter twenty-three

I get to the Russian Vodka Room, a dark little place with a piano man, and sit at the bar, waiting for James. I order a Ketel One and soda and try to gulp myself into a fast buzz, as I'm anxious that when James gets there I might not be attracted to him. After all, when I'd seen him last, I'd been six drinks into the evening.

When he arrives, I still think he's cute, maybe not as much as I remembered, but definitely cute. We chat about how he used to live in Paris, where he grew up in Canada, first-date-type talk.

I tell him I'm thirty-five. It's a small lie that, I thought, bought me a lot of time. Everyone knows that at thirty-six, one suddenly has more in common with a fifty-year-old than a thirty-five-year-old. At least, so says every marketing survey in the world. None of that had mattered until I found myself suddenly single at thirty-six. But let's just make that thirty-five, shall we?

By the time I'm well and truly buzzed, I feel a sexual frisson every time James holds my gaze with his pretty hazel eyes, and it's all I can do not to kiss him. Finally, we move in to lock lips, possibly at the same time. He has a wet kissing technique, heavy on the tongue, and I have to keep pulling away to dab at my lips with a napkin.

We move to another bar and sit there kissing and kissing. When I leave to go to the bathroom, I realize my panties are sopping wet. So much for his kissing technique not being up to par, parts of me must have liked it quite a bit. For a shy man, he sure knows how to work the apartment angle. He must mention his place fifty times, in fifty different ways. Eventually, the repetitiveness of it sort of brainwashes me or hypnotizes me, or something, because I say yes, let's go.

We walk there and he stops me twice in the street, pulling me into him for a kissing session. "You just look so good," he says. There's something about the combination of his shyness and his sexual attraction to me that's an incredible turnon. Whereas Rahil's sexual desire had always come off as calculated and practiced, with him remaining in complete control, James seems a little goofily bewildered by the whole thing.

We get to his apartment, a beautiful studio with a stunning view of the Hudson River, and he's kissing me before I even get my coat off. We fall into his bed and off come the clothes.

"But no sex," I command.

His cock is huge. It's a pleasant surprise. A bit of a shock, actually.

"Do you have any lube?" I ask, expecting him to have all the accoutrements of sluthood, just as Rahil did. He says he doesn't.

"What do you masturbate with?" I'm being the no-nonsense dirty girl. This isn't about romance, ya know.

"I don't really," he says.

Does that mean he doesn't use lube, or doesn't masturbate? I didn't think rubbing a dry penis would work, so I engage in some high-risk behavior and give him a blowjob. When he comes, it's the light sigh of a kitten.

"You're the quietest comer I've ever had!"

He uses his hands to give me an orgasm but I have to direct him where to go. I don't know if this means he's inexperienced, or if his girlfriends just hadn't taught him quite properly. Rahil would have insisted on going down on me, but James makes no move in that direction.

"Do you like going down on girls?" I ask.

"Yes. But I thought I'd keep on doing what I was doing."

"I'm pristine down there, I swear."

"I'll remember that next time."

He walks me to the subway, and before I disappear through the turnstile, he kisses me again. "Can we see each other again soon?" he asks. I like the way he puts "soon" at the end of the question. I say we can.

That Friday, James and I meet at Fat Baby, on the Lower East Side, where Andrew is playing an acoustic set. James is late (he'd first gone to the wrong venue). When he finally gets there, he sits down next to me and grins shyly. He's about the cutest thing I've ever seen.

We talk a little about music. I tell him that John Mellencamp is an old favorite of mine, and he says that he thinks "Jackie Brown" is his best song, and I can't believe it, because I totally agree. I think this might indicate some kind of cosmic connection, but then I remembered how Rahil had played Fiona Apple the first night I'd spent at his apartment, the exact song I'd been listening to before I left for his place. No cosmic connection there.

But mostly, James and I kiss and kiss. When we leave the bar, I ask where we should go next.

"I know a private club on ——rd Street."

"Really? A private club?"

"Yes. You get a key and everything."

It's not until we're in a cab and several blocks away that I realize the "private club" is his apartment. I think he's truly more diabolical than Rahil when it comes to getting a girl in the sack.

We have sex once, and yes, he goes downtown. He's not bad, not bad at all, but I can't concentrate. Maybe it's the dirge from Argentina wailing from the DVD player, music more appropriate for a funeral than a night of hot sex. The fact that he doesn't like either his ass or nipples played with, and his lack of emotiveness during foreplay, all reminds me of Aaron. Reminds me too much. When James makes no move to have another session, as Rahil would have, I lay there in a puddle of disappointment.

"Maybe we're not sexually compatible," I offer. I'm sure it's what every guy wants to hear postcoital.

He seems confused. "But everything we just did—"

"I know. Maybe I'm used to the guy I was just with. He would want sex five times a night."

Perfect. Before the sheets are even dry, I'm comparing him unfavorably to my last sexual partner.

"Is he still in the picture?"

"Not really. I told him we should take a break. I don't know what the future holds there."

"He wanted a relationship?"

"Nooo. It was purely sexual, to be honest. What about you? Are you seeing anyone?"

"I was, a few weeks ago. But I felt it headed down that relationship path. That's what she wanted. So we had to have a talk."

I didn't ask if he didn't want a relationship with her or if he just didn't want one, period.

"You know," he says, "you have such a physical presence when you enter a room. Men really notice you. It must be difficult for a boyfriend."

Aaron had never seemed to mind. For obvious reasons, I now realized. James's comment stayed with me. It was one of the nicest things anyone had ever told me. Though I imagined I wasn't the first woman he'd said it to.

I get dressed and he walks with me to his building's back exit. In the empty hallway, he grabs me, pushes me up against the wall, and kisses me passionately. We don't stop until we hear the door behind us click, as someone is opening it.

We quickly run out the other door, laughing.

chapter twenty-four

Before I head into the animal shelter on Sunday afternoon, I call James and leave him a voice mail:

"Hi. I feel like I dumped a lot of crap on you last night and that I owe you an apology. Obviously, I'm dealing with some issues right now. We're all dealing with our own issues, but I shouldn't try to make my issues into yours. If you decide to run screaming from me, I wouldn't blame you for a minute; if you don't, great. And you are fine in bed, great in fact. I hope I didn't give you a complex."

I thought that sounded psychotic, yet reasonable—or reasonably psychotic. I imagine that he might immediately call back and tell me how, oh no, of course you don't need to apologize, of course everything is fine, of course I want to see you again. But he doesn't. That's probably a good thing. If James stayed away from me, it was proof of his own good mental health.

I realize I'd been self-medicating, not only with booze and cigarettes, but with sex. Rahil had been the perfect prescription—someone who saw me as a sexual being and made no demands on me emotionally. For the first time, I understood how people had sex addictions. The serotonin rush doped you up as much as any drug. Rahil had also managed to prop up my shaky sexual confidence by reassuring me every step of the way that he found me desirable, not only by wanting to have sex almost constantly, but by articulating his desire. All the "I want you so much" and "you feel so incredible" and "what you're doing feels so good" stuff. When I got James, a guy who was much less verbal, and for whom one good romp did the trick, and who didn't suck on my body like a crack pipe and bury himself in my vagina like a drowning man clinging to a life raft, I not only hit smack up against the wall of my own sexual and emotional insecurity, but began to suspect he had sexual problems. And to make it worse, I'd verbalized my discomfort to him.

When I'd left James's apartment, my first thought was to get in touch with Rahil again. He was the stronger drug. He medicated better. James, with his sweetness and restrained, almost repressed, sexuality gave me Aaron flashbacks. I had always attributed Aaron's lack of overt sexuality to sincerity (why pay lip service to how much you want someone if you actually do?) and shyness. But it had turned out to be gayness. So now I distrusted shyness, distrusted sincerity, because I distrusted my judgment of those qualities. With someone like Rahil, I could always say, "Whatever faults he has, and there are plenty, at least he's straight."

A few hours later, James calls and asks what I'm doing that night. So much for his mental health.

I toss out a few words of pop psychology: "I'm probably just staying in and spending some time with myself, I haven't done enough of that. I need to learn to be alone."

"But does that mean we can keep seeing each other?"

"I'd like that. But maybe instead of rushing into bed, we can grab something to eat. We've established that we're sexually attracted to each other. Maybe we should figure out if we even like each other."

"I've already figured that out. I like you."

I guessed there would be plenty of time to relearn how to be alone. At any rate, how can you resist a cute guy who tells you he likes you? I couldn't. Not yet anyway.

chapter twenty-five

Over the next couple of weeks, James would email frustratingly vague offers to get together like, "How is your week looking?" and "I don't have any plans yet this weekend [accompanied by a smiley face]" and, the worst, "I'd like to see you again sometime soon!"

I suppose I could have just made things easy on myself by saying, "Great. How's eight P.M. Friday night?" But he'd had no trouble asking directly for a date the first couple of times. So I didn't know what all the beating around the bush was about, unless the fact that he'd already beaten the bush made him downshift into neutral.

I would get irritated and email back that "sometime soon" meant nothing to me and that I'd already made plans for the weekend, which was true. I figured if you're not asking a guy for dinners, for movies, for a diamond ring, the least you can expect is a bit of advance notice.

I'd forgotten how pulsing with angst not being part of a couple could be. The last time I'd been single, it was 1995. I didn't have anything but a regular old landline phone. These days, you didn't just wait for a man to call, but you actually counted the minutes between when you emailed him and when he responded.

This new dating world consisted not only of waiting for the phone to ring, but of checking email, cell phone, BlackBerry, dating and social networking sites, IM boxes, message boards, and God only knows what else yet to be invented.

I'd so cherished the fact that Aaron and I had gotten beyond all this. When we first dove in, we'd hit some rough waves, gotten slapped in the face a few times, but we kept paddling and reached beyond the break, to smooth water. Now here I was again, paddling, paddling, and getting a mouth full of brine.

I began to have the sinking realization that "casual" relationships could be just as complicated as the real thing. Only you got none of the benefits of the long term—no one was there to take care of you when you were sick, or to fix something in the apartment—and only the hair-pulling frustrations. Oh, and the sex was hotter. Or maybe it just seemed hotter because it was fraught with uncertainty.

I was torn between wanting to continue on the way I had been— using men for fun, for sex—and maybe wanting to inject some romance into the proceedings. Maybe a little dinner, a little walk in the park. But I was probably still too much of an emotional cyclone for that. If I stressed out when a booty call like James sent me emails so vague they would take a CIA operative to decode them, what would it be like when a guy I'd really gotten to like disappeared after a month or two?

* * *

113

Aaron and I meet up at the only bar in our immediate neighborhood, Shenanigans, a blue-collar dive, for a drink. Nursing a slight vodka buzz, I ask him about his attraction to men. I do so haltingly, with my hand almost up near my face, as if his answers are physical things that will fly at me.

"Is this a trick question?" he asks, cautiously.

"I make no guarantees on my responses." Yet I prod him more.

He tells me how Amber, his wingwoman at gay bars, will point out men who are checking him out, but he is never interested. They, apparently, are too effeminate for him. "I want men to be men," he says.

Men who are men like women! The bitter thought races through my brain before I can PC it.

"As soon as I hear a lisp . . ." he shudders.

"I'm sort of in a place where I'm open, because I'm not looking for the perfect man," I tell him. "When Rahil sat down next to me and babbled away like an imbecile, I ordinarily would have brushed him off. But I was open to it, and while it didn't end well, it was six weeks of fun I wouldn't trade in. You might be missing someone really great because he's more on the Jack side than the Will side."

He nods. I can't believe I'm giving him advice on dating, perhaps getting him closer to finding a man he can love. I'm not sure if I'm doing it because I want him to be happy or because I want him to be impressed with my openness. Maybe it's a bit of both. If I don't get comfortable talking to him about this stuff, if I just buried my head, I was bound to get the shock of my life sometime soon.

I ask him if this is a phase that he's working through, or if he thinks he will ever go back to women.

"I don't know," he says. "But my attraction to men is strong enough that I have to have relationships with them on some level."

Good God.

On the street corner, before Aaron turns to head back to his new apartment, I hug him and catch a whiff of the familiar sweet scent of his neck, the smell I'd spent a decade inhaling. It's like my guts spill out of me onto the pavement.

chapter twenty-six

Day 82 Early in the evening, I go to a birthday party for one of the Last Exit regulars. Aaron is there, and we spend our time huddled together chatting, as if we're still a couple. I think we simply don't know how to be in a room together and *not* huddle together like we're still a couple. But within a couple of hours, I leave to meet James at Vegas, a nearby bar.

He's already there when I arrive, looking absolutely as adorable as a human being has ever looked. But within minutes, I can tell something is off. Ordinarily, he would've been all over me, and he would've been talking up going to my apartment, but instead, I catch him looking elsewhere while we kiss, and he doesn't once mention the apartment.

"Are you okay?" I ask him.

"I'm just tired," he says. "Been in the sun all day."

"Didn't you take a nap?"

"Yes."

Hmm. A healthy, strapping thirty-one-year-old man takes a nap, comes all the way to Brooklyn to meet a booty call, and shows up tired. We play some pool with a couple of guys, and James goes up and down on his energy level. Sometimes, it's the old James—hand between my legs. Sometimes it's the new "tired" James. Again, he asks about my "date" on Friday. I hadn't really had a date. It was something I'd told him to teach him a lesson about sending me vague last-minute emails.

"Is that what's bothering you?" I ask.

"No," he says, "sometimes my energy level is low."

I'd just spent ten years with a man whose energy level—*sexual* energy level to be precise—could best be described as comatose. My patience level for men with a low energy level is not at a very high level.

"Maybe you should go home and I'll go back to this party I was at," I say.

"If that's what you want."

"Did you meet someone this weekend?" I suddenly sputter. "Do you really not want to be here?" I can't figure him out. We'd spoken on the phone in the afternoon and he'd seemed so excited about coming to see me.

"No, nothing like that. I'm just tired."

We go outside. Maybe I'm giving him mixed signals: the supposed date, my saying I wanted to return to the party. Maybe he's the one who feels I don't want to be there, and he's reacting accordingly. I decide to lay it on the line because I need to know what he's thinking, and he's not volunteering anything.

"James, I don't want to go to the party. I want to stay with you. I really like you. We can go to my place and just talk—or relax. Whatever. But I need to know what you want. If you want to go home, don't feel guilty about it."

"I'll have to go home eventually anyway."

Okay. There it was.

I take a deep breath. "Let me walk you to the subway."

We walk a block. At the stop, I hug him. "It was really great knowing you. We had a couple of great nights."

He seems taken aback. "Are you saying we can't see each other again? This is it?"

"Well, *yeah*. You don't seem that into me. The one thing I ask for right now is for a guy to at least be into me when he's with me. And you don't seem into me."

If someone I liked said this to me, I would have argued. Fiercely. But he doesn't. Maybe he doesn't like me. Maybe he doesn't understand why he has to say he likes me, when it's already been established.

"That's the necklace you were wearing on the night we met," he says, fingering it.

He remembers the necklace I had on three weeks ago. Does this make him enamored of me or is it warning sign of potential gayness?

We hug each other. The smell of his cologne clings to me all night.

I walk back to the party, shell shocked. When I get there, Aaron is gone. Probably left to meet some guy.

Dave, the host, asks me why I've returned. I tell him. He spends an hour lecturing me how I shouldn't be hooking up, that it's unhealthy, that I should be by myself. Considering that Dave regularly took young females home from the surrounding watering holes, I find this a bit offensive.

"Dave, you're having your fun. I don't know why that's okay for you, but not for me. I'm at my sexual peak and I've been sexually deprived for the past few years."

"You're at your sexual peak?"

"A woman in her thirties? Sure."

I can practically see his brain shift into a higher gear.

The party begins to wind down. Around 3 A.M., I find myself lying on Dave's bed, with him next to me. We mostly chat about sex. He likes to tout his skills.

"How do you know you're so great?"

"No one has ever complained. Everyone leaves here happy."

"Uhh, have you seen *When Harry Met Sally*?"

"It's not just what you see and hear, but what you feel."

I think he's referring to spasms. "You can fake those too."

"I mean temperature. You can't fake temperature."

"Temperature?"

"Sure. A woman's temperature rises when she has an orgasm."

"And how do you feel this?"

He indicates his "thermometer"—the one he was born with.

I shriek with laughter.

The party is down to the skeletal remains—just me, Dave, and a few other girls. The girls are out on the terrace, leaving Dave and me alone in his studio.

"You know, Kiri," he drawls, "I'm just going to say this, maybe because I'm hammered."

Uh-oh. I freeze. Aaron and I had once played a game: if he and I ever broke up, which one of his friends would be the first to hit on me? I suspected I was about to get my answer.

"I really feel like kissing you right now," he says.

"That's probably a bad idea."

"*Probably* a bad idea?"

"It *is* a bad idea. I'm going to try and stay out of that Last Exit pool, if you know what I mean."

But ten minutes later, my curiosity (and the booze) gets the better of me. I decide to kiss him. He has a tongue that works very hard—snaking here and there, licking the roof of your mouth, your teeth, practically doing somersaults.

"You should stick around after everyone leaves," he says.

The man had lectured me extensively about how I shouldn't be indulging in booty calls, and now he's trying to become one himself.

I wouldn't have stayed no matter what, but I might've been more tempted if the kissing had worked for me. But it didn't.

"I don't think so, Dave. I'm going to see you all the time."

I phone a car service and make my goodbyes.

"You and I are going to have words about this!" he calls as I scoot out the door.

In the morning, I wake up feeling terrible about how I'd treated James. The poor guy had done nothing but show up tired. He'd been sweet to me all night. We'd had a nice conversation about Proust. (He'd carried *Remembrance of Things Past* with him to read on the subway. I think it was at that moment that it crystallized for me that James was not a secret player.) But I hadn't been able to shake the feeling that something was off, missing. I'd ignored my instincts for so long with Aaron that I was determined not to ignore them anymore. But were my instincts all haywire? James's "Aaronness" made me panic. I needed too much sexual reassurance right now. If you were non-communicative, you could be hiding something. If you were tired, you could be gay.

And most of all, I felt that if I was working this hard on the third date, there must be something wrong.

So, of course, I call him and leave a message.

Then, like a crack addict reaching for the pipe, I email Rahil, tell him I've broken with my latest "booty call," and ask what he's up to.

James returns my call. I'm totally shocked to hear from him. I was certain I'd scared him off. This guy might be as mentally unbalanced as myself. I apologize for being a basket case.

"I like basket cases," he says.

I suggest that we meet up sometime "as friends," but that I couldn't and shouldn't keep torturing him. He claims to be fine with that.

I hang up and notice that I've missed a call from Rahil or at least someone with his prefix. I dial it.

"Ohhh my gaaaaawd. Is it really the famous Kiri Blakeley?"

My goodness—to hear that hyperactive Indian lilt again.

"I wasn't sure it was you," I say. "I deleted your name from my cell, so only a number showed up."

"How childish is that?!" he cries.

We jabber half incoherently at each other for about half an hour. He diligently refrains from mentioning Hayden, though he does say he's taking aerial acrobatic classes, which she does as well. The very idea of him twirling around midair, wearing tights, makes me giggle.

"So you were wanting me to come over to your apartment, right?" he asks.

"No. I have to write an article."

"I was joking!"

"Oh, too bad. Because I was going to tell you to come over."

"I know how this works. I'll say yes, and then you'll laugh at me."

"Yep."

"Don't you miss me in your bed at all?"

"Of course. But I'm being serviced."

He informs me that, no, he hasn't been cutting a swath through the vaginas of Brooklyn, that he's been working on his hobbies, his acrobatics, his yoga, his "djembe" drumming. I'm sure it wasn't for lack of trying.

"Well, it was good talking to you."

"You too."

We say nothing about the possibility of seeing each other again.

chapter twenty-seven

Day 84 I've had my profile up on the dating site Match.com for two days and there's a bewildering array of "winks" from men in my inbox. Many of them look as if they've just gotten out of prison, or hoped to get out eventually. A few aren't half bad. One looks like a model, but his profile made it clear he just wants sex. Naturally, I email with him for a few days. The whole thing is a huge and addictive time waster.

At night, I simultaneously write a story about Tyra Banks's "media empire" and chat with Match men. One of them, a good-looking 43-year-old with whom I have a running gag about him being a convict, turns out to be something almost as bad—an actor. I think of my friend Jocelyn, whose actor boyfriend sleeps all day while she picks up the bills.

On Friday, I have my first session with my former therapist. A few years ago, Aaron and I had gone to couples counseling with her for our sexual problems, which consisted solely of a lack of sex. It seemed to help for a few months, but then her invoices almost depleted my flex spending account, so we stopped going. Couldn't she at least have picked up on the fact that Aaron was gay since she'd cost me so much money? Though her professional judgment was cast in doubt, I still felt as if I needed an emergency session.

Since the city is suffering through some kind of mini-monsoon, making subway service spotty, we speak over the phone. She agrees with me that after my sexual starvation with Aaron, I deserve a little *la dolce vita*, and that, in fact, exploring my sexuality is important. But she's concerned about whatever emotional pain might accrue from my exploration.

The next night, when I receive an email from Rahil saying that he doesn't think I'm as "detached" from our relationship as he is, I know what the therapist means. I shoot back an email telling him to get over himself, but his choosing to describe himself as "detached" is another bullet to my ego.

I wouldn't have been emailing Rahil at all except that once again James disappointed me on the sexual front. Friday, James and I had met up at QT Hotel, along with Julie and Jake. "He's very cute," Julie tells me later about James. "But a little hard to talk to."

"Do you see the Aaronness?" I'd asked.

"Oh, yah."

But I'd gotten to the place where I could appreciate and even enjoy James's quiet low-key nature, his intellectuality. And when we had sex that night, it was definitely interesting. He'd pushed my face into the mattress and grabbed my hair. I liked it—except when he got a little Robert Chambers on me and bent my neck too far. But once again he didn't perform oral sex, or use his hands, or make any attempt to make sure that I had an orgasm.

I guess men were like New York apartments: you were never going to find one that had everything you wanted.

Rahil calls in the late afternoon. He wants to talk about my last email, why it had seemed so "hostile." I tell him it's because the language he sometimes chooses to use is rude and hurtful.

"How?" he asks. "Let's talk about this instead of emailing."

"You really want to talk about this?"

"Yes."

"Well, don't argue with me about what I perceive as rude."

"Fine."

I run down the litany of slights, while admitting that I'm hypersensitive to rejection at this point in my life and that he probably doesn't even realize the effect he's having. He has an explanation for each thing he'd said while we were seeing each other, sometimes throwing back rude things I'd said to him ("I could never fall in love with a guy like you" was one—I was surprised he even remembered that), and once or twice he even coughed up an apology.

After about forty-five minutes of this, he makes some kind of impassioned plea to keep exploring the relationship: "Let's figure out ways for you and me to have fun. When we're together, let's talk about us. I promise to keep the rest of my life completely separate."

It's more emotion than I'd ever expected to hear out of him, which shows you how low my standards of emotiveness had become.

"Do you have a girlfriend?" I ask. "I deserve to know that."

"No, I don't have a girlfriend."

"Are you working behind the scenes to get back into a relationship with Hayden? If I'm going to hear in two weeks that you're in a monogamous relationship and can't see me anymore, I don't want to waste my time."

"No, I'm not." But he makes it clear that he doesn't know what the future will hold; and I agree that I don't know what it holds for me either. Maybe we'd both meet someone we'd want to get serious with. Whenever we talked about the future holding a serious relationship with some phantom person, we were never referring to each other. I couldn't figure out why that was.

"I don't want to be the girl you're just biding your time with while you're hoping to get with someone else," I say.

"You're not."

"Okay."

"Do you want to meet for a drink?"

"I can't guarantee anything will happen."

"Let's just meet for a drink then."

So we do.

"Why are you still wearing this?" Rahil asks, indicating my diamond engagement ring. We sit close together at the bar in Loki. The feral sexuality in his deep-set eyes makes me nervous. I don't understand why every girl in Brooklyn isn't throwing herself at him. It's like he's a giant magnet and I'm a paper clip.

"Because it's pretty," I say. "I like it. And it's never stopped anyone from hitting on me. It didn't stop you."

There are two reminders of my life with Aaron I couldn't bring myself to give up yet: one was my engagement ring; the other was the recording of me saying, "This is Aaron and Kiri" on our home answering machine. If I erased it, and replaced it with "This is Kiri," then it was real.

On my second vodka soda, my nerves begin to settle and soon Rahil and I are chatting easily, like old pals—well, old pals who take every opportunity to fuck each other senseless.

We move to another bar and sit on the same wooden bench where he'd once told me he hadn't developed "one ounce" of romantic feeling toward me.

"This music is killing the atmosphere," I say, referring to the heavy metal screaming from the jukebox.

He swoops in. "How's the atmosphere now?" he asks between lip locks.

"Dangerous."

"How so?"

"I've decided I'm not going to sleep with you. Like pot leads to cocaine leads to heroin, kissing is the gateway drug."

Within a couple of hours, I call a car service; we wave goodbye to each other as the car pulls away. Rahil was never happier than when confronted with the challenge of trying to seduce a girl. I thought it best to keep him happy for now.

chapter twenty-eight

The worst happened. I'd spent every day since I'd seen Rahil wondering when I'd see him again—and if I should.

"If you enjoy being with him so much, why are you denying yourself his company?" Tyler asks.

I knew exactly why. I figured there was a big pot of pain at the end of this particular rainbow. I imagined his speech: "Kiri, you know we've always had this sexual connection. And I really like you as a friend. But I don't have that kind of attachment to you. I don't have one ounce of romantic feeling towards you . . ."

I knew I didn't want to close any doors for myself, but I also knew that whatever I felt for Rahil was so overwhelming that other men just kind of paled in comparison. I'd be setting myself up.

In that 6 A.M. sleepless netherworld, the one that becomes my constant companion after the break, I have an intense flashback: Early in my relationship with Aaron, he was sleeping soundly in our bed when I'd whispered, "I love you, I love you . . ." over and over into his ear. I'd hoped the words would work their way into his subconscious, burn themselves there.

I remembered how quickly he'd told me he loved me: our first or second time after sleeping together, about two months into the relationship. I remembered how frightened I'd been that I'd lose him, that he'd stop feeling that way, and for how long I would have dreams that he was leaving me, and would wake up weak with relief that he was still warm in my bed, still loving me, that he hadn't changed his mind. If I could fall into that pit of insecurity with Aaron, what would it be like with a guy like Rahil?

During our phone session, my therapist had reassured me I would find the sexual connection I had with Rahil with someone who could also give me an emotional connection like I had with Aaron: that I could have both. Really? Was there someone out there who could give me both? Where was he? And what secret would he have, keeping stored away until the moment I let my guard down, completely trusted him, and wrapped my life around him? What tentacled creature would reach out from the tiny unnoticed subspace of our relationship and fling me back out into the world, this time when I was older and even less able to bounce back?

On Thursday, I email Rahil and ask how his weekend is shaping up and whether he'd like to get together. I actually come out and use the words, "I'd like to see you." I figure he's been making all the moves, why not?

But by Friday afternoon, I'd gotten no answer. Was he sitting there staring at the email and not answering because he hadn't enjoyed our time together? Because he thought I wasn't as pretty as he remembered? I didn't kiss as well as he remembered? I was too mean to him? I didn't sleep with him? He'd changed his mind? Or maybe it had all just been a trick—get me hooked again and then be the one to leave.

Did men sit around and stress about this shit?

By late afternoon the next day, he calls and asks if I want to go out that night. After all that stressing, I plead that I'm too tired. It'd been a crushing week getting out the *Forbes* celebrity issue.

"Wouldn't you like a nice massage?" he purrs.

"I'd love that. But I'd fall right asleep."

Let the record show that I was too tired to see a booty call. I vowed to cut a guy some slack the next time one claimed exhaustion.

The next day, he begins texting and asks what I'm up to.

"Thinking about what I'd like to do to you," I reply.

He tells me to get my ass to his place.

"I have female trouble," I text back.

Female trouble be damned, he says, insisting we meet up.

Aaron comes over, bringing cat litter, per my request. He sits on the couch and we smoke a cigarette. I'd been going through a period in which more of my anger about the situation was bubbling to the surface. I just kept thinking about how old I was—almost 37. Sure, maybe I looked younger (I still got carded), and maybe I was at my sexual peak, and I didn't expect to get to the point where men didn't hit on me any time soon, but I knew very well I was just biding my time with guys like Rahil and James. As I'd noticed on various men's Match.com profiles, even guys in their forties were hoping to date girls in their twenties. Instead of aging a few months since the breakup, I felt like I'd suddenly time traveled forward two decades—I was supposed to be dating men my father's age.

I didn't reveal my anger to Aaron. I did, however, let him know that I had someone coming over later—and maybe that was a sneaky form of showing my anger.

"For dinner?" he asks.

I refrain from saying, "Hopefully there will be some eating involved," and opt for the slightly less crass, "I don't think there will be much food involved."

"Oh. Another guy?"

"The first one. He called last weekend and made a case for himself. We'll see how it goes."

"That's all you can do."

When Rahil arrives, I'm waiting for him in my robe, freshly showered, and I practically devour him the second he walks in. I'd never been with a man who was so vociferous in his enjoyment of sex. He lets me know every step of the way that he's appreciating whatever it is I'm doing. If I even fingered his belly button, it was, "Oh my God, I love that. You have no idea." A girl could get used to this kind of positive reinforcement.

Later, we order in Thai food and sit on the couch eating. My cell bleeps and I check it. A text from James, who is out of town at a conference: "I'm bored. You should come meet me tomorrow. There's a big bed in my room." I giggle and put the phone back down. Rahil, sitting a foot from me, says nothing. It's my true pimp moment: one naked guy sitting next to me, another (possibly naked) guy texting me. So this is what it felt like to be a man!

Now that the specter of Hayden is out of the way—or at least Rahil finally realized mentioning her wouldn't do him any good—conversation isn't like tripping through a landmine-strewn field anymore. We're able to babble smoothly about anything: music, my cats, his family. I launch into a comic routine about what I think he'll be like at fifty years old: A paunchy old man with few teeth and several illegitimate children, pathetically hitting on college girls in bars. He'll be living in some hovel in the Bronx, with a shared bathroom, and every once in a while I'll feel sorry for him and stop by with some leftovers.

"Will you fuck me?" he asks.

"No."

"Come on!"

"Well . . . maybe a pity fuck."

I tell him he does a lousy job with time management. "You couldn't even juggle two girls. How are you going to juggle five?"

"How do you know how many I'm juggling right now?"

"If you're juggling more than me, you're doing a better job of it."

"I learned my lesson."

"Time management," I stress.

He pulls me to him. "I love kissing you," I say, as I do so. It's the first time I'd ever used the word "love" in any context with him, and I wonder if it makes him nervous because he doesn't return the compliment. Our faces are so close together I can see every strand of gray entwined throughout his black hair.

Later, he walks me to a nearby gas station to buy cigarettes, and then I call him a car. We sit on my building's steps and kiss until it arrives.

I get back to the apartment and text James, telling him I can't join him at his conference, "but we'll have fun when you get back, I promise."

That evening I pour some heavy-duty sold-in-hardware-stores-only type drain cleaner down the bathroom sink and then make the brilliant decision to try and clear the drain of gunk with a Q-tip and my fingers. Seconds later, my fingertips start to burn. I hurry to the kitchen sink and shove my fingers under the cold tap, letting the water rush over them until the burning subsides. Then I start to panic. What if something worse had happened? Ordinarily, Aaron would have been there to help me, to give me advice, or to drive me to the hospital if needed.

Now I'm one of those single people at the mercy of freak accidents—one who could die alone in her apartment after cracking her head on the tub, or choking on a piece of bread, or getting pinned under a falling bookcase, and who isn't discovered until someone, maybe the superintendent, maybe a friend, maybe the police, pries open the door, and there's the body, decomposed, or half eaten by starving pets.

chapter twenty-nine

I meet Aaron at Last Exit for a drink.

"I've been a little depressed lately," he says, as we sit outside in the warm June weather.

"Why?"

"Confusion over what to do next."

"You mean with your music?"

Aaron never brought up his other confusion unless I asked about it, and I hadn't. But nope! He means his other confusion.

"My orientation."

"You think you might not be gay?"

"It's just a question of what percentage."

Greeeeeaaaaat. So he broke up a ten-year relationship because he's gay, and now he's not sure if, mathematically speaking, he's gay enough.

"I'll be pissed if you end up with a girl," I tell him. You could always count on me to offer words of empathy.

"I don't think that will happen."

The conversation brings me even lower than I'd been lately.

"I'm not going to lie, Aaron. I've been depressed too. Thinking about my future, being out here single. Why couldn't you have done this when I was twenty-nine?"

Aaron groans and buries his face in his hands.

When he decides to leave, I consider walking him to the subway and riding back with him, as I'd done hundreds of times in the past, but it would be too much tonight.

"I think I'd like to leave alone," I say.

"Really?" He seems sad.

"Really." I kiss him goodbye.

Around the corner, I stop and drunk-dial Rahil. I remembered how he'd called me when he was in a tizzy about Hayden, and I thought he owed me one. But there was another reason I was calling: Three days earlier, we'd been as intimate as two people can be. That feeling of intimacy lingered with me, despite the fact that in "casual" relationships you are completely entwined physically and emotionally one day, and the next you wondered if it would be too pushy to email a polite hello.

Rahil picks up and I begin blubbering how Aaron told me he wasn't even sure he was gay.

"Calm down, calm down. Are you upset because you feel like the reasons he ended the relationship aren't what he originally told you?"

"Ye-es."

"I'd say come over here, but I'm on my way to meet a friend. If you don't want to be alone, call me, and come meet us."

"Thank you. I'll be all right."

I walk to a nearby bar. The taverns of Carroll Gardens had lately become my refuge from a cold, cruel, sexually confused world. There I run into Sebastian, a very handsome bartender who used to work at Last Exit. Somehow I'd never noticed how handsome he was while I was with Aaron. We chat for a while and then Rahil calls.

"I just wanted to see how you are. Come out with us if you like."

"I'm fine, don't worry about me," I say. "Thank you for giving a crap."

Before I leave, Sebastian gives me his phone number. He is cute, but he had a certain reputation. I figure I'll break him open in case of emergency.

At home, Rahil calls again.

"You okay?" he asks.

"I don't have my head in the oven."

"Not in the microwave either?"

"No. That would be messy. My head would explode."

"I'm sorry I couldn't have just invited you over."

"Of course not. It's not your job to worry about me."

"We're friends," he says.

The lyrics from a Fiona Apple song pop into my head:

What a cunning way
to condescend
Once my lover . . .
Now my friend

Later, my other "friend," James, sends me a series of sexually explicit emails detailing the rather kinky things he'd like to do to me. Sometimes friends like this are all you have.

chapter thirty

Day 101 My father picks me up and we drive to Bethlehem, Pennsylvania, a quaint former steel mill town where my paternal grandmother, Marie, had grown up. We were burying her ashes; she'd died of cancer the year before. My uncle also came, as did his wife, their two kids, and two of my father's other three kids (my half siblings).

At the cemetery, we all stand around the urn and the beautiful plaque and give our little speeches and reminiscences about Marie. It's the first important family occasion where Aaron isn't present.

Marie and my grandfather, Bernardo, were married for about ten years, every one of them filled with strife. My grandfather, as he would go on to prove with two other wives, wasn't quite cut out for the institution of marriage—at least, not if that institution required any degree of sexual fidelity. My grandmother, an otherwise intelligent, highly practical, and commonsensical woman, had a weak spot for my grandfather that no one, least of all their two children, could fathom. Time after time, she took him back after he'd stray or even move out of their apartment for long stretches. My father called his parents' kind of love "bad love."

Eventually, they divorced. My grandmother, possibly exhausted, never dated another man.

The term "bad love" could have been applied to the kind shared by my mother and father as well. After a few years of determining that they were absolutely unsuited for each other, the situation culminated with my mother discovering, three months into their official and final separation, that she was carrying me. Whoops! They were then pressured into a marriage neither one particularly wanted, and separated within weeks. While they managed to retain some degree of civility, I never saw my father much while growing up. Until I entered adulthood and began to understand, or at least sympathize with, some of the complexities of human relations, I'd held my father's "abandonment" against him.

My mother went on to marry a violent and abusive man, and they had my sister. There followed several years of watching my mother get the crap beaten out of her by a drunken lout.

It was this long, tortured family history of male-female dynamics that I had been trying not to repeat when I bonded with a man like Aaron, a man without a mean bone in his body—a man who would never lie to me or leave me.

Whoops!

When I get back to the city on Sunday evening, I call James because I'd said I would, but I leave him a message that I'm too tired to go out. I tell him to call back if he feels like chatting, but he doesn't. Why call a booty call to chat?

He knew I'd been in Pennsylvania to bury my grandmother's ashes, but what was that to him? Aaron had texted me to see how I was, but Aaron didn't want to have sex with me. Without anyone to dump my emotional baggage onto, I decide to call him.

"I'm a little depressed," I tell Aaron. "Burying Marie's ashes and then coming home with no one to talk to."

"I know," he says. "I thought about that."

Aaron tells me he is still depressed too—he still doesn't know if he wants to be with men or women.

"What triggered this?" I ask. "Are you seeing girls you're attracted to or something?"

"I look at them on the street."

"I look at girls on the street too. Doesn't mean I want to sleep with them."

"Well, that's what I have to figure out."

"Are you seeing anyone?"

"No."

"You would say that, though, wouldn't you?"

"I'm not. I'm in no place for dating."

I didn't know what I wanted either. On the one hand, I wanted to explore a range of possibilities and not commit myself to any of them—I admit I was enjoying the sexual excitement of uncertainty.

On the other hand, I wanted someone who would comfort me at the cemetery when I scattered a loved one's ashes and who would then bring me back to the hotel to make committed, overly-familiar and slightly boring love to me.

The upside was that I was in a better place than Aaron. At least I knew which sex I wanted to pursue.

chapter thirty-one

I attend French Tuesdays, which had accepted me as a member. This time, it was held at China Club. James had told me he would be there. I run into him and his friend around 9 P.M. just as the place is getting packed to the gills with drop-dead gorgeous guys.

After four or five drinks, the temptation gets to be too much. As James stands ordering another round, I begin making eyes with a cute guy on the dance floor. When he beckons me to join him, I shake my head, point at James's turned back, and toss the guy my business card.

I catch James's friend staring directly at me. *Busted*. Rather than wait to get tattled on, I pull James aside and tattle on myself.

"I hope you don't mind if I gave a guy my number," I say. "I consider us both single. I didn't know if it would be awkward with both of us coming to these things, but you're free to flirt if you want."

"Why don't you go work the room?" he suggests.

"I did before you got here," I grin.

"I'm fine with it." And he genuinely seems so.

But about an hour later, as we sit on the couches, I notice a dark mood descending over him. I try to pry out of him what's wrong, but it's like pulling a tooth out of its socket with my bare fingers.

And then suddenly, those words every man, woman, and child dreads to hear . . .

"I just want to make sure that we can remain friends," he says.

The "let's be friends" speech again? I was surely making a lot of friends these days.

"I mean, you are seeing other people and stuff," he continues.

"Does that bother you?"

"No."

"We can talk about it if it does."

"Not at all. It doesn't."

Okaaaay.

"Are you going home?" he asks.

"Where else would I go? We're just friends, right?"

He says nothing. *Right.*

"Would you walk me to the subway?" I ask.

We leave the club. As we cross the street, James grabs my arm and begins rushing me forcefully in another direction.

"Where are we going?"

He doesn't answer, just keeps rushing me forward, as if we're trying to outrun an avalanche.

"Are we going to your apartment?" I ask, breathlessly.

"Yes."

"Why James? Didn't you just dump me?"

As James hurries me through the lobby of his building, I wave at the doorman. "I want him to see me in case you plan on killing me," I tell him.

We get to his studio, and begin forcefully tugging, pushing, and pulling at each other, practically fighting, tearing off our clothes as we do so.

After *bang bang bang* sex, I try to move his hand between my legs. He grins and resists.

"Are you going to sleep?"

He smiles and nods.

"But what about me?"

He just grins some more.

"You don't care if I come or not?"

No answer.

"You know this is the last time we're going to see each other, right?" I whisper.

"Is it?"

"Yes."

I get up and begin dressing. Then the peculiarity of the evening overtakes me, and I plop onto his couch. He sits next to me.

"What is it?" I ask, rubbing his hand. "I can't figure what's up with you."

"I just . . . feel like . . . we don't have chemistry," he stammers.

Hmm. Call me crazy, but you generally don't drag a woman across town to your apartment when you don't have chemistry with her. Or do you?

"Why? Because I asked for an orgasm?"

He makes a face. "That's just so mechanical."

"It's not mechanical when *you* come, which you do every time. Don't I deserve the same?"

His expression remains stubbornly blank. I sigh and get up to leave. He tries to walk me out, but I stop him.

The trains are slow and it takes me a good hour to get home.

The next day, I email him some kind of apology. He emails back apologizing as well, and then he tells me I'm a "fun and interesting person" and that he "enjoys our discussions" and he hopes we can remain friends, but that we should stop seeing each other.

His email is so uncannily similar to one I had sent Rahil after our break, right down to the "fun and interesting person" line, that I wonder if there isn't some "let's be friends" template fire branded onto the collective unconscious.

I write back that being friends is a good idea, and then expect not to hear from him for days, if not weeks. But within an hour, he's emailing flirty sexual banter. He then asks, "So who are these guys you're seeing?"

My heart does a little leap. He is jealous after all? Does he want me to stop seeing other men? If so, what would I say? It would be nice, surely flattering, to have someone want to be with me exclusively.

But there's Rahil. . . . and there's the guy from French Tuesdays to whom I'd tossed my card—he'd emailed that day and we'd arranged to meet for drinks . . . and there were so many other men . . . and, frankly, as adorable as James was, we didn't work on many levels. . . .

I email him promising never again to mention other men, but he responds: "I was just curious. I like open conversation. You don't have to hide anything."

Craaazy. James is a flat-out loon.

That night, I swallow my pride and call Rahil. Since the Sunday afternoon we'd spent together a week and a half ago, he hadn't made contact once. I'd sent him the *Forbes* celebrity issue at his request and gotten no response. I'd initiated a couple of casual bantering emails. No response. Liquored up after a party one night, I finally dial him.

"Let up on the new girl and give the old girl some time," I say into his voice mail. "There must be a new girl since I haven't heard from you in so long. Give you a good shag, that's a way to get rid of you. Anyway, I'll be in Park Slope tomorrow night, if you want to meet up. Just for a drink, it doesn't have to go further. I hope I didn't do anything horrible that you didn't answer my emails."

He never calls back. Wow. How pathetic can a girl get?

Why, why, why had he bothered to pursue me with such hotness only to run in the other direction?

chapter thirty-two

James emails me some stultifying details of his evening before ("took a walk, fell asleep with a book and a glass of wine"). It was clear—at least to *my* mind, I didn't know about his—that he continued to fancy me despite his "we have no chemistry" and "let's be friends" speeches. You don't get rid of a girl by continuing to email to her every hour or so.

I go to a goodbye party for Paul, who is leaving for an editorial position at another major magazine. He not only was my office crush, but also was the only editor who gave a hoot about my career. So the parting is extremely sad on my end—possibly on his as well, as when he hugs me goodbye, he says, "I'll miss you the most." Assuming he'd said that to everyone, I mention it to a coworker whom I knew he was fond of. "He didn't say that to *me*," she smirks.

In a moment of weakness, I text James, asking if he'd like to join me at the party, and then immediately regret it. Not only am I too exhausted to deal with the vicissitudes of James's moods and our relationship in general, but I'm with all my coworkers, and it isn't the "get drunk and make out" kind of evening that he and I are accustomed to. But he texts back asking where I am.

"How do I email a polite rejection to a booty call?" I survey my colleagues. Taking their advice, I tell James that the scene is dying down and I intend to go home.

It hadn't escaped my notice that Rahil still hadn't called, so I make a last gasp of an effort to reach out to him. "Wow, I never expected you to ignore a call of mine. If you don't want to hang out, that's fine, but I hope you're okay," I say into his voice mail, trying not to sound like the blubbering idiot I obviously sounded like.

As I come out of the subway at midnight, I see that he's left a message. I listen to him tell me that he isn't ignoring me, but that work is crazy, that so-and-so is in town, that his brother is coming to town, and blah blah blah. . . .

Once I've established that he isn't lying in a hospital somewhere, that I'm merely getting the "I'm busy" blowoff, I hyperventilate for about three minutes.

Since my conflicted feelings about James are so fresh, I can imagine exactly what Rahil might be feeling: A whole bundle of lust tied up with general feelings of friendliness and a heaping handful of ambivalence accentuated by a strong desire not to lead anyone on.

The next day, I email Rahil, pretend not to remember calling him ("I need to lay off the booze") and tell him to have fun with his guests. It's the only way I can think of to acknowledge his call while still keeping the ball in his court. I never get a response.

James emails asking what I'm doing over the weekend. Two weeks ago, I would have been exhilarated over his interest. This time, I ignore the query. One more scene of sexual frustration followed by a long subway ride home was going to cement our estrangement, and I didn't want that to happen yet. I'm not sure if I'm holding on to him out of selfishness or genuine fondness. Maybe it's a little of both.

I receive an email from William, the guy I threw my card to at French Tuesdays. We had already exchanged a few messages discussing where we'd meet for drinks; where he orginally came from (Montreal), and where I worked. William mentions that it's supposed to rain all weekend, which might prevent him from a) attending a Yankees game or b) playing golf.

Yankees? Golf? I think I might have finally hooked a confirmed heterosexual! And suddenly I realized why I'd been with a gay man for ten years.

But the rain, William continued, would allow him to spend more time with his dog. Opening up the attachment, I find a photo of said slobbering canine.

Don't get me wrong. Every year, I give unwise amounts of my meager salary to animal groups. I've volunteered at an animal shelter for seven years. But there's something that creeps me out about getting a picture of a guy's dog even before the first date. (A few days later, I receive an email from a Match.com prospect in which he says that he shares his life with his Jack Russell terrier and that he's very happy to keep it that way. In that case, I wondered why he had a profile on Match.com which, so far as I could tell, was a website for human beings to find other noncanines with whom they'd like to share their lives.)

That night, I meet Aaron at Last Exit. I give him a book I'd bought for him titled *The Way Out: The Gay Man's Guide to Freedom, No Matter if You're in Denial, Closeted, Half In, Half Out, Just Out or Just Been Around the Block.*

Glancing at the title, one of his friends sniffs, "Well, been around the block maybe."

chapter thirty-three

While I'm at the shelter, James leaves a message. On the subway ride home, I debate whether to call him back and conclude that it's my duty to call, that I can't leave him hanging as Rahil was able to do to me. He isn't anything other than a sweet, somewhat depressive, somewhat confused young man whom I'd made like me.

I also decide I'll avoid any deep conversations, such as the nature of this so-called "friendship," or the fact that he finds discussing our sex life to be "mechanical," or, most of all, where the clitoris is and why it's important.

On the phone with James, I hear a dirge playing in the background; he tells me it's an old Soviet song from the 1950s.

"It's very interesting," he assures me.

But it isn't enough for James to be listening to one foreign language at a time; he's also watching a nature documentary on the French channel. Meanwhile, I sit drinking in the inanity of *My Fair Brady* on VH1. The scene doesn't bode well for our long-term compatibility. Hell, our short-term compatibility was in major doubt.

I call my grandfather to talk about Portugal, his birth country, advancing into the semifinals of the World Cup.

"I'm sort of semicasually seeing a guy who speaks four languages and reads Proust," I tell him.

"Ah!" he exclaims. "A civilized man. I'll have to meet him."

During the ten years I'd been with Aaron, my grandfather had consented to meeting him only twice and, that, only after some intervention from my father. I could be dating an ax murderer, but if he reads Proust, he gets my grandfather's stamp of approval.

Late that night, anger and humiliation about Rahil's casual dismissal gushes over me like a thick, hot paste. I lie there plotting little revenge scenarios. I imagine going to his apartment, throwing something (I'm not sure what) at his window, and screaming up at him that he has a "needle dick!" I imagine telling him that his ex-girlfriend looks like a drag queen (she kind of docs). Then I get up and replay his messages. Was leaving double messages on both my cell and landline a sign of someone in avoidance mode? Or could he just be genuinely busy and I was asking too much of someone to whom I'd given my own slew of blind-traffic-cop-on-crack signals?

Or had he just been out for revenge—out to prove that he could get me back in the sack after I called a "break" and, once he did, it was his turn to leave?

Theories aside, I found it wearily ironic that the man who'd given me the impassioned "let's continue to explore our relationship" speech had disappeared, while James, with the "let's be friends" and "we have no chemistry" speeches, was in daily contact.

I recognize William right away by his very short, almost bowl cut hair. Our date is at the Hotel Gansevoort in the Meatpacking District. We sit at a little table opposite each other, and I avert my eyes from his laser-like scrutiny. It's still light out, that shade of pale greenish, unflattering light that hits just as the sun sets in summer, and my skin hasn't been doing too well lately, and, of course, I'm a bit older than he is. His eyes twinkle when he sees me, but since he doesn't say anything, I'm not sure if it's a twinkle of approval or amusement.

He has gorgeous teal blue eyes, but something about the combination of his broad, slightly crooked nose, wide lips, and big ears gives him a more geeky appearance than I'd noticed through my vodka goggles and the dark lighting of China Club. He also has a couple of yellow teeth, but at least they are far on the sides. I wonder which flaws of mine he's ruminating on. There's something to be said for meeting in low lighting, at least until you get to know each other.

We chat pretty easily. He's from Canada and works as a "project co-ordinator" for construction sites, so we have an interest in real estate in common. Eventually, I get around to telling him my Aaron story (I had vowed to stop whipping out that baby, but at some point he asked how long I'd been single, and well, it went from there . . .) and hopefully, in my telling, I come across as someone dealing with it in a humorous, sane fashion. I spare him the dirty details, and just mention that my boyfriend had come out. Like most others I'd told, he has a story of some woman he knows to whom the same thing had happened.

As I work my way into my second drink (actually my third as I'd stopped off at The Hog Pit on the way in), I can't figure out if I'm feeling any sexual frisson or not. We get along fine, but I'm not feeling the urge to lean over and kiss him—not that I would've done that anyway in a place like that, in the sober pale light, at that little round table, surrounded by other people at little round tables.

He gets better looking as the sun goes down and the vodka intake goes up, but I'm still not sensing any magnetic vibes. I can't tell on his part. The twinkle seems to deepen and flash into something more palpable occasionally, but that might've just been the effects of his second Mojito.

"Maybe it's a foreign thing, but in Canada you don't really date more than one person at a time," he says. "I'm just getting used to the idea that this is what people do in New York."

It turns out he lives in White Plains and drives back up there every night. Talk about geographically undesirable. He also has a dog at home that he feels guilty leaving alone for too long, so he likes to leave the city by 10 P.M. At least he won't be trying to talk me back to his apartment.

When the bill comes, I almost choke. I'd mentioned earlier that drinks were on me—I'd felt that was fair considering I'd been the one to ask him out—but I immediately regret it when faced with a tab of fifty-eight dollars for four drinks. Seeing my reaction, he pushes forty dollars across the table, but I take only half. I'm in such a state of sticker shock I even leave a twenty percent tip.

He walks me to the subway and we chat like old friends. When I say goodbye, I lean into his face and get a slightly stiff cheek kiss in response. As I turn down the subway steps, he doesn't ask to see me again. I figure if he asks me out, I'll go, what the heck. But if he doesn't, I won't be disappointed.

The question is answered for me the next day when William doesn't email—the first time he hasn't since we'd met. He could've at least thanked me for the grossly overpriced drinks, but I guess that would've been awkward without also asking to get together. I am relieved and peeved at the same time.

James emails and asks if, on Saturday afternoon, I want to go to Plage, a roof-deck bar with a pool where French Tuesdays was going to hold a France vs. Brazil World Cup party.

"I have a sauna in the private club on ——rd Street," he adds. "Would you care to visit it? And would you mind being blindfolded and tied to a water pipe?"

"Friends tie each other to water pipes?" I ask. "I've been missing out on this friend thing."

"The best friendships test each other's limits," he says, a little too accurately.

"You like to test me, that's for sure."

James is beginning to win me over with his single-minded persistence. Especially now that I don't have another man showing any interest.

chapter thirty-four

James keeps up a steady stream of flirtatious emails over the course of the day. I'd once been convinced that his job kept him busy in meetings, hence his lack of email frequency, but I now realize he just hadn't felt like emailing much in the beginning.

About 9:30 P.M., still at work, I step outside and return a call from him.

"Are you going to Plage on Saturday?" I ask.

"Yes. Will you come?"

"Probably. But James, I'm going to be honest with you. I've had a stressful week. I can't have another scene like we had. I just want to have some fun and relax."

"What scene?"

"You weren't very nice to me at China Club." I refrain from bringing up the whole "we don't have chemistry speech." It's clear by now that that had all been bullshit.

"Okay."

"You and I are on some rocky ground here. I don't want to toss it away, but one more scene like that and I will. Let's just have a good time."

"I agree."

After my date with William, I realized how important sexual chemistry was. Now if James and I could only get the mechanics of it down. Though there was a part of me that didn't want that to happen—as long as I left his apartment disappointed, I had some upper hand in the relationship because I'd be willing to walk away from it.

The next night, I sit gulping vodka-soda after vodka-soda at Last Exit where Aaron is doing a stint as guest DJ. I don't get drunk, as I had requested that the drinks be watered down, but I don't want to leave. For as Aaron stands next to me spinning records, he feels like the only friend I have in the world, the only person just as lonely and confused as I am. When he finishes his set, I ask him if he wants to go to Loki to play a little pool.

"And then you can go . . . wherever it is you go," I say.

"I could do that."

But I have an ulterior motive for choosing that particular venue. I hope I might run into Rahil. I don't want to hook up with him, but I'm insanely curious about his retreat, and wonder if seeing him might give me some clue into deciphering it.

At Loki, about three games in, I look over and there he is—a stunned grin on his face. Even though I'd somewhat expected it, I still find myself genuinely flustered.

"How awkward is this for you?" Rahil laughs.

"Not at all. It's your neighborhood."

I introduce him to Aaron and they shake hands.

"I'm going to go get a drink," Rahil says and wades through the crowd. Half an hour later, when Aaron and I leave, he is nowhere to be found. The fact that he's out by himself at Loki, that he hadn't tried to meet up with me, clarifies the situation. There's no misunderstanding going on, no misreading signals. The sign says, "I have no desire to see you."

Aaron and I go to Excelsior, the Park Slope's only gay male bar. It's weird being there with him, but not as intensely mind altering as I'd feared it would be. Maybe I'd consumed just enough vodka to be able to handle it.

"Now we'll run into one of *your* booty calls," I say.

"I don't think so."

No, of course not. Aaron got his men from the online classifieds and was out the door in minutes. No complicated pseudorelationships for him.

I tell him how Rahil, the guy he'd just met, had been in avoidance mode for the past three weeks, giving me stories about being too busy to make contact, and how that very day we'd emailed (again at my initiative), and this time he'd spun some tale about being distracted by a "tragedy" that had happened to a close friend of his.

"You can see how tragic this must have been that he's out trolling bars by himself."

"It's a little suspicious," Aaron agrees.

I ask him what had happened to John.

"It was a bit disappointing," Aaron says, looking wistful. "I'd hoped he'd be my mentor through this thing, but as soon as it got out of the fantasy stage and I was actually available, he disappeared off the face of the Earth."

"Sounds familiar. There's always going to be people who chase you, but only if you're running."

I wondered if this was something in a man's DNA, left over from his days as a Neanderthal hunter. See something run, chase it. It stops, you freeze. It turns and heads in your direction, you book like hell, lest it eat you alive.

Prehistoric biology could also explain why a woman got so anxious when she didn't hear from her man. There must've been plenty of times her hunter never made it back to the cave with a meal.

Aaron and I finish our drinks and catch a car service back to our hood. As we pull up to my building, he asks if he can come inside and visit with the cats.

"Of course. You can stay over if you like. I won't hit on you, I promise."

We go upstairs, play with the cats, smoke, and talk some more. It feels so incredibly good and comfortable to have him there. He sleeps on the couch that night and leaves in the morning.

About noon, I get a wild hair up my ass and call Rahil.

"You didn't have to run out of the bar," I tell him.

"I didn't run out!" he sputters. "I sat there for half an hour having a drink and then I left. I didn't know if that was awkward for you or what."

"It wasn't awkward until you made it so. That was my ex-boyfriend, and he doesn't even know who you are."

"Well, I didn't know if that was the old Aaron or some new suitor."

"Didn't the moustache give it away that he's gay?" I joke. Lately,

Aaron had been sporting a 'stache worthy of entry into the Village People.

"I'm just saying," I continue. "I can't avoid the bars I've been going to for years. I did last month, because I owed that to you, but this new weirdness is all your own. I won't inconvenience myself over it."

"I'm not being weird! Why do you keep saying that! I told you how much stuff I had going on!"

I break into his tirade. "All right, all right . . . forget it."

"Are you okay?" I then ask, referring to the "tragedy" I suspected didn't really exist.

"Yes! I'm okay! I told you! There's nothing going on!"

I break in again.

"Rahil, Rahil. Relax. I'm referring to your friend. Is everything okay?"

"Oh . . . well, uh. . . . it could be a tragedy, it might not be, we don't know yet . . . I don't want to talk about it."

But I won't let him off the hook. I'm getting too much pleasure out of listening to him squirm. "This person is in the hospital?"

"Yes, hospital, all that—"

Uh-huh.

"Well, I'll let you go. You might be busy writing a sympathy card or ordering flowers or something."

"Let's get a drink sometime soon," he says.

"I won't wait by the phone," I say cheerily, and hang up.

I'm relatively certain that's the last time I'll ever hear from Rahil. Well. I'd wanted to taste what it was like to be with a bad boy, and the bad boy elixir was bound to drain out of the cup quickly. I'm not devastated or even surprised, just sad.

"I've been thinking about the Raheel situation," Tyler emails. "He keeps in touch until the moment you let him in, and then he disappears. The timing is too uncanny. This was payback for you breaking it off with him before."

"How sociopathic of him," I reply.

Sociopath or not, I'd always remember our Sunday together. Hell, I'd remember all our time together.

Sitting with Julie and Jake outside on their terrace, I tell them about my Friday night, how Aaron and I had run into Rahil, and how Aaron had ended up sleeping over.

"Is there any sexual attraction?" Julie asks, breathless.

"It's not like that. I still think he's an attractive man—except for that moustache—but I don't want to sleep with him."

I tell her about Rahil's disappearing act and my theory of how a man's DNA causes him to chase, but only if you're running.

"My editor at *Cosmo* used to say don't call a man, don't text, don't email, don't send cute little greeting cards, don't do *anything*."

"Sure," I say, "but if you don't do *anything* and the guy disappears, then how do you know it wasn't your fault?"

"True," Julie murmurs, perplexed.

I didn't remember any of this advance-retreat dance when Aaron and I started dating while in our mid-twenties. Maybe it was because we were both young and barely employed, with small social circles that didn't offer much else in the way of entertainment. But once we'd decided we liked each other, we got together every single night. The way people act in their thirties, with jam-packed work schedules and myriad social obligations combined with a reluctance to commit to anything more time consuming than a last-minute booty call, I couldn't figure how anyone paired up, ever. I wondered if Western civilization might simply cease to exist in a few generations—a victim of commitment phobia.

The next day, bored and anxious to meet someone new, I start emailing guys on Craigslist who sound at least halfway sane. It's a continual
loop of disappointment, but at least it happens over the course of an
hour rather than months.

When one man hints around about a physical encounter, I tell him it
would depend on whether we have sexual chemistry. He calls me "cyni-
cal." In other words, I'm supposed to fuck him no matter what, but he
doesn't want to hire a hooker. After he twice ignores my question as to
whether he'd like to chat on the phone, I figure he's married and this is
his little fantasy. I bid him goodbye.

Another guy stops emailing as soon as I ask for a photo. One guy
does ask me out, but to a movie. A *movie*? As if I wanted to get stuck in
the dark for two hours with a stranger I couldn't even talk to. When this
particular guy finally sends his photo (I had to ask for it three times), it's
a blurry picture of a fifty-something Indian guy with glasses and a big
paunch. I politely decline.

I hadn't gotten an email from anyone on Match.com for a while either. James didn't get in touch all weekend. The well was officially dry.

I have a good little cry about it. It's July Fourth, a day I'd always
remember as the last time I saw my niece healthy and running around,
before her quick, gruesome slide into death.

It was easier to think about men and the general ways in which they
could raise your expectations, get you attached to them, and then let you
down. But that was part and parcel of being out there. I didn't want to
turn into one of those women who never took a risk. At least, I didn't
want to turn into her today.

That night, I attend a Fourth of July rooftop party on Columbia
Street, overlooking the East River. It had a picture-perfect view of the
downtown fireworks. I thought it might be sad being there with Aaron,

and not being together as a couple as we had been every other time. Instead, I find his presence comforting. At 9 P.M., just before the display of unbridled Americanism is to start, I get a text from James: "Hey! U coming tonight?"

"I usually don't with you," I murmur to myself.

I can't believe the nerve. I hadn't heard a peep out of him since our last phone call, and here he was asking if I was going to French Tuesdays' Fourth of July party. It's not as if I hadn't already hammered into him how I hated being asked to do something last minute. I decide the answer that will irk him the most is silence—certainly it gets *my* dander up—so I give him a heavy dose.

I'd wanted to give James one more chance because I'd always been big on second chances. Aaron had acted abominably three months into our courtship, turning cold on me and then taking off for England for a month, but he had come back to become the best boyfriend ever (up until the gay part). Because of that, I'd been the girl who ran around saying to my exasperated friends, "Guys can change." But, thanks to Rahil, I'd since learned that giving a rat a second chance only meant giving him one more opportunity to fuck you over.

Yet in the morning, my hormones are raging so bad I remember why I'd put up with all of Rahil's nonsense. I didn't ever remember getting this horny in my twenties. Was it because I'd had Aaron there to satiate myself before I got clinical? Or was it true what they say, that women don't hit their sexual peak until they turn thirty-five?

My body is thrumming with so much sexual agitation that I draft an email to Rahil: "Hey! Aren't guys wired for sex? Don't I give good blowjobs? I must have turned you gay . . ."

I come to my senses and trash it.

During my lunch break, I walk to Barnes & Noble and browse the

Relationships section—something I'd always scorned and pitied other women for doing. I thumb through the books. The female dating "experts" all say the same things: ignore the man, don't call, don't email, and certainly don't stick around for breakfast. One expert even advocates never, ever kissing on the first date. (Shit, I'd rather be home with my vibrator.) But a tome by a trio of male gurus gives the opposite advice: initiate a call, ring up to say "Thank you" and "I'd like to see you again." Men, they insist, are riddled with insecurities. If you don't show them you care, they'll feel rejected and flee.

Hopelessly confused, I leave empty handed.

chapter thirty-five

I get weak and make contact with James again, though just by phone and email. As usual, he tries over and over again to get me to go to his apartment. I don't know whether to be flattered by his persistence or insulted that he can't even ask for a genuine date as a prelude to getting laid.

It comes as a slight shock to me that men still have such Madonna/whore complexes. If you sleep with them, you are shunted into the "good-time girl" category, and that means a lot of last-minute text messages looking for sex. What it doesn't mean is that men are going to spend a lot of time (or *any* time) courting you with dinners and movies. I guess on some level I couldn't blame them. If they knew you were seeing other men, why should they put themselves out there emotionally and financially? But it's irritating me. So I resist James's entreaties, which, with my tight schedule and slight cold, isn't too hard. Besides,

I'd made plans to go to the Bastille Day ball at the Puck Building. French Tuesdays, along with a few other clubs, is throwing the bash, and I knew James was also going. Sleeping with him before then would only mean he'd forget my name that night.

Still, I didn't want him clinging to me in the man version of a candy store.

"Listen," I tell him on the phone, "don't cock-block me all night. You do your thing and I'll do mine, and maybe we'll meet up at the end of the evening."

With that kind of romantic attitude, perhaps it wasn't too surprising that James wasn't making reservations for two at The Waverly Inn.

A couple of days later, he shoots me an email.

"It looks like I'll be bringing a girl to the ball, so you don't need to worry about me cock-blocking you," he writes. "Happy Hunting!"

First he gives me some story about the girl being a "friend." Then she turns into some girl he had met at a cafe and had "accidentally" told about the ball, and that he'd gotten "cornered" into asking her to it.

Either way, I guess he was off-limits that night, though I email back, "If you want to ditch her, let me know." A girl has to keep her options open.

At the ball, Lily, Anne, and my journalism school friend Pam, who is visiting again from Los Angeles, man hunt around the room in a *Sex and the City* foursome. When we first arrive, I think I catch a quick glimpse of James sitting with a brown-haired girl at one of the tables, looking quite bored. I quickly hightail it in the opposite direction.

A couple of hours in, the girls and I step outside onto the terrace. A short Indian-looking man stands near us. I hear him speaking French, so I turn and ask him how to say, "I want to suck your cock." Leave it to me to be classy and demure with strangers. But he is game.

"*Je veux sucer ton pipe*," he says.

I repeat it. Get it wrong. He says it again. I repeat it. A man walks by us, hears this going on, and laughs so hard he almost falls down.

"Can I buy you a drink?" the Indian-looking man asks. "My friends want to head to the main bar."

"Sure."

I'm not really attracted to him, but frankly, no other guy has shown much interest in me so far, so why not. The Indian-looking man tells me his name is Adi.

The four of us follow Adi and his friends through the packed crowd.

"Why are we going there?" Lily hisses in my ear. "It's too crowded. Let's ditch this guy."

"Lily, he's going to buy us all champagne. Stop complaining and just go with it!"

"But his friends are ugly!" she whines.

We trail Adi and his friends until we finally push through to the main bar. There, the three of them take out their cell phones and stare into the tiny glowing screens. This seems to go on forever. I wasn't that interested to begin with, and now here I was playing second fiddle to a cell phone.

"Forget this," I tell the girls. "I have to go to the bathroom anyway."

While Adi and his friends are distracted, we take off. But half an hour later, he spots me in the crowd.

"Hey, what happened to you?"

"Here's a little advice," I snap. "If you ask to buy a girl a drink, don't make her stand there for an hour while you fiddle with your cell phone. It's rude."

He opens his mouth to say something, but I flip him my palm.

"Buh-bye!"

With that, I spin on my heel and stalk off.

Where the hell is James? It's getting late and he hasn't texted me, so I guess his "non-date" must be going well.

About an hour later, still hookup-less, I head outside for a smoke. I see Adi in the corner of the terrace and sheepishly make my way to him.

"Hey, sorry about before," I say. "I just hate that kind of thing."

"It's all right. You spoke your mind. I respect that and wish more people did the same."

Damn. There was something to this theory that men like a bitch.

"And I wasn't on my cell phone," he continues. "I was trying to figure out if we had enough drink tickets. And for the record, I wanted to buy *you* a drink, not all your friends."

"Okay, fine. Bygones."

I take out my business card and hand it to him. "Maybe we can go for a drink sometime when we don't have to worry about friends and drink tickets."

"I'd like that. But can I buy you a drink now? No cell phone, I promise."

"Sure."

I thrill to the way he grabs my hand and leads me through the crowd. It's take-charge in a way that Aaron had never been.

Adi isn't bad looking, though his longish black hair is thinning quite a bit on top. Truth is, with his lilting British accent and Indian (it turns out to be Pakastani) heritage and alpha-male demeanor, he reminds me of Rahil. This gets my juices flowing.

We head upstairs to the second floor and before long we're dancing and kissing. But then . . .

"There's something I have to tell you," he says.

Uh-oh.

"I'm married—"

My eyes get wide. He finishes his sentence in one fast, long breath.

"—butImseparatedandgettingdivorced!"

I dance about ten feet away from him, getting ready to run.

"I just wanted to be honest with you," he implores. "To tell you before you found out later and said, 'What an asshole.'"

I catch my breath and stare at him for a good thirty seconds.

"Do you two still live together?"

"No."

"Children?"

"No."

Was I going to give up what could be my only flirtation of the evening because he's legally married? He'd been honest (as far as I knew) and had told me early. A married guy hiding his ring and out to cheat on his wife wouldn't have told me, would he? Besides, I wasn't looking for anything serious.

"I should have told you before I kissed you," he says.

"Kisses aren't contracts," I reply.

And the night is on.

Lily and Anne say their goodbyes, and Pam seems to be getting along with Adi's pudgy, balding British friend, Alex. When the lights come up on the ball, the four of us head to SoHo House, a (real) private club where Adi and Alex are members. We have a drink before it's off to the Meatpacking District club Hiro, where the employees greet Alex and Adi as if they're conquering soldiers back from war. Regulars apparently.

Adi and I kiss and dance. He has the same Rahil-like verboseness and overt sensuality. I love the little frown he makes as he's kissing me—as if he is concentrating so hard he has to grimace from the effort.

"Oh my God, you are so sexy," he breathes into my mouth. "I want you so much. I want to make love to you for hours and hours . . ."

An American guy would have said "have sex with you." He would have been afraid to use the word "love" in any context so soon.

Eventually, Pam and I end up at Alex's apartment. Adi and I sit on the terrace, kissing and fondling. It's beginning to get light out. We move to one of the bedrooms, but I won't let him go down on me, nor have sex.

"We have to save something for the future," I say. "It's boring to do it all the first night."

"I agree."

But then he tells me that he is so turned on, if I even so much as put my lips on his cock for a second, he is going to come. I have to test this theory.

He's right.

"That wasn't a blowjob," I tell him. "I was more like a receptacle."

Adi curls up behind me, caressing my hair, and kissing my cheek, but I feel a wave of pensiveness emanating from him.

"Was that your first sexual experience since your separation?" I ask him.

"Yes."

"It will be all right," I soothe.

In the morning, Adi and I lay on one couch in the living room while Pam and Alex are sprawled on the other. Adi and I stare into each other's eyes. His are dark and liquid.

"I want to cook for you," he says.

"I'd like that. What's on the menu? I don't eat meat."

"Do you like corn?"

"That's my favorite!"

"I'll make you a corn curry."

He tells me he's leaving the next day for Miami for the week. "But I don't want you to think I'm blowing you off."

"I don't."

Pam and I finally make our exit about 11 A.M. Still in our evening dresses and high heels, it's the longest walk of shame ever to Pam's friend's apartment where Pam is staying. Later that afternoon, Adi begins seeping into my brain and bones. He replaces Rahil in my sexual fantasies. I call Julie and tell her about him.

"He's like Rahil," I say, "but normal."

That probably means he'll disappear as fast as Rahil too. And I worry about that because, so far as I can tell, this is the first guy I've felt a genuine connection with. He's only thirty. He's only been separated for a month. And while he'd said the separation was his idea, and that he hadn't been happy, I knew how these things went. Once you got out into the big bad world, you could begin longing for the comfort of the familiar.

Adi sends me a cute text the next day, which I think is a good sign. With him, I don't want to get shunted into the booty call category. Yet I don't know how to get myself reclassified without all the hard-to-get game playing that apparently had to be done to get you into the girlfriend category.

Not that I was ready to be anyone's girlfriend—as the next French Tuesdays proved.

chapter
thirty-six

One of my oldest pals, Angelica, whom I'd met as a freshman in college, is in town. I take the day off work so she and I can get ready for French Tuesdays, to be held that night at Tavern on the Green. I'd promised her lots of hot guys.

The night before, we had been walking to dinner in Cobble Hill, my old neighborhood, exchanging sordid sex stories. Angelica lived in the Caribbean and was juggling more booty calls than I could've done in a year. I had just finished lauding Rahil for his sexual stamina when I looked up and there he was, walking directly toward us, blue-green eyes twinkling. I'd almost doubled over in surprise.

"This isn't your neighborhood!" I blurted.

"It used to be. There's a Thai place here that I love."

It was a stifling hot day, and he was wearing his work clothes—

a wrinkled, long-sleeved Polo shirt, tan slacks. I had the urge to roll up his sleeves and caress his arms. I introduced him to Angelica, who recognized the name and grinned. He was sporting a small soul patch. Uh-oh. *Facial hair.*

"We were just talking about . . . sex," I stammered. Not a minute before, I'd been telling Angelica about his Energizer-bunny libido. Could he have possibly heard any of the conversation? "Well," I added. "I'd say 'see you around,' but I guess I won't."

"It's time to do that drink," he said.

I didn't respond. No way I'd keep falling for that.

"Oh my God, I can't stop running into him," I breathed after he had walked away. I was suddenly thankful that I'd decided to glam up before I'd left the apartment—makeup done, miniskirt on.

"He has nice eyes," Angelica noted, approvingly.

That day, James and I kept up a steady stream of dirty emails. He was horny as hell and desperate to get together after French Tuesdays. Maybe his "non-date" from the Bastille Day ball hadn't put out.

Angelica and I decide to have a little fun with him.

"My friend is here from out of town and we share everything. Can you handle it?" I email him.

"Shall we be ravaging you together or shall she be assisting me in ravaging you?" he queries, always the pragmatist.

James gave good email. Julie and I had observed that the more verbose a guy was in real life, the worse email he gave. James, the guy most likely to blush and stumble his way through a come-on, gave the best, most titillating email of all.

We arrive at Tavern on the Green early. Meeting up with James about an hour later, I introduce him to Angelica, who is a tall, attractive brunette. He grins like crazy, no doubt anticipating his ménage à trois. Fool.

James's hand is glued to my ass. Once he realizes a ménage isn't in the cards (Angelica has some dark-haired specimen backed into a corner—not that I would have gone there anyway), we debate the merits of going back to Brooklyn for the evening versus leaving Angelica at the party for a quick romp at his place. Naturally, he doesn't want to inconvenience himself and come to Brooklyn.

"After all, the three a.m. train rides I've taken back from your apartment!" I scold, jumping up and almost leaving, but he grabs me and pulls me back into my chair. He sits watching me intently for a moment, then takes my hand and charges me through the crowd. I love it when he gets all caveman on me.

Outside, there's a downpour. A crowd of people surge toward the taxi stand.

"I don't think this is meant to be tonight," I tell him. "We'll never get a cab."

"They're all idiots. Let's go over to the Trump Hotel and hail one from there."

With that, James lifts me into his arms, and runs out of Central Park through the rain and across the street to the hotel. While still bouncing me around in his arms, he commences chasing various cabs up and down the avenue. We get soaked, but I'm laughing the entire time. It's flat out the sexiest thing a guy has ever done for me, carrying me around in the rain like that. It's almost worth the end of a ten-year relationship.

The second we enter his studio, he slams me up against the wall, digs his hands under my skirt, and begins tearing off my underwear.

I hear the bling of a text message coming in. It's Angelica, asking where I am.

"I'll be back by midnight. Stay there!" I somehow manage to type in the midst of James's ravaging.

Twenty minutes later, I'm getting dressed to leave.

"Are you going to go back to the party?" he asks.

"Hell, yes. The night is young."

Angelica calls, urging me to return. James walks me outside to a cab and soon I'm back at Tavern on the Green.

I find Angelica sitting with a big plate of food.

"You're a thirty-six-year-old woman surrounded by food, wine, dance, and men, and you can't amuse yourself for an hour?" I rail.

She just laughs.

"I'm not leaving here before I get a number," I announce, and stalk outside for a smoke. I was truly on a rampage.

The first guy I see standing alone is short, cute, full lipped, and has a mop of dark hair. I ask him for a light. His name is Drake and he works for the United Nations.

Then Angelica comes outside, trailed by a Serbian hunk named Krav. The four of us head to the Hudson Hotel. First, Drake and I stand outside smoking. I feel the delicious before-the-kiss tension starting to mount. Finally, he leans in. Upstairs, we find a couch and begin fooling around. I put my hand down his shirt and discover he has absolutely no chest hair. His body is as smooth and hairless as a baby's ass.

"It runs in my family," he says. He's part American Indian, his skin a light cocoa color. He starts trying to talk me back to his apartment. The come-back-to-my-pad refrain is becoming so familiar I could have recited it in my sleep.

Angelica comes over to inform me she's is headed to Krav's place.

"He might kill her," Drake stage whispers. Drake has something against Serbs. He thinks they're all murderers. "But he might not, as she's not Muslim."

"Angelica," I chide, "you were such a brat about staying alone. Now that *you* want to hook up, you have no problem taking off on me."

"But you got laid earlier!" she whines.

Drake does a double take. I offer a little apologetic shrug. "It's not like I'd just met the guy," I say, sheepishly. "We've been seeing each other a couple of months."

I write down directions back to Brooklyn and hand them to Angelica; Drake and I hop in a cab. He has his fingers up inside my underwear and isn't doing a bad job at all. He's murmuring a million varieties of reasons why I should accompany him home.

Oh, what the hell. Whom was I kidding anymore? I'd gone back to Alex's apartment with Adi after knowing him for only five or so hours. What was the difference if I'd only known a guy for three? Might as well own my sluttiness. Embrace it, even.

"All right, let's go to your apartment."

There, he manages to do what neither James nor Adi had done—give me an orgasm. I go down on him and he comes in about two minutes; then he lies next to me breathing heavily.

"Oh my God, I haven't come that way in years. And even when I did, it would take forever. I can't believe it."

"Do you want to smoke?" I ask him.

"I just want to lie here for a minute. I'm so happy."

My ego jets through the roof. I am the blowjob queen!

Drake yammers on about the UN, and his upcoming trip to Kenya, then gives me a little history lesson on the origin of the term "third world country." I have nothing against hooking up with bartenders or janitors, provided they're hot enough, but the guys from French Tuesdays (rapidly becoming Fuck Tuesdays) got me sex *and* a minicourse on international relations.

We sit in the living room smoking. Drake tells me he's only been single for about six months, and that he's stunned at how bad most women are in bed.

"Bad how?" I ask, intensely curious.

"They use a lot of teeth, gnashing down on your penis. Or they're down there for two seconds."

"I guess I've been pretty lucky so far," I say.

"Did you really get laid earlier in the evening?" he asks, slightly disbelieving.

"Yes. And, uh, if you see me at FT, it's not like we can't talk, but if I'm with a guy—"

"I won't say anything."

"He knows we're not exclusive. But why set him off?"

The conversation is straightforward and buddy-buddy. There aren't any romantic sparks.

Drake walks me to a cab and, blowjob queen notwithstanding, doesn't ask to see me again. I'm probably too much of a slut for him. Well, let him have the hard-to-get, game-playing girl who doesn't know how to give head. He'd cheat on her with a girl like me.

The next day, James texts to inquire as to whether there had been a "Round 2" after I got back to the party. I ignore the query. Then he asks again by email.

"I didn't have sex," I reply. Granted, I am using the Clintonian definition. "I hooked up with some guy and we messed around. I don't want us to lie to each other. I have no plans on seeing him again. I'm sorry I'm so crazy, you got me at a weird place in my life."

It takes him awhile to email back, and I'm afraid that might be the end of it. But then comes the answer: "A little promiscuous, are we? No need to apologize for being crazy. I kind of like it."

Good old James.

chapter thirty-seven

Day 134 Julie and I go to a restaurant on Flatbush Avenue owned by a very cute guy, Zach, whom we'd met two weeks earlier. Julie and I had hung out with him and his friend all night in Park Slope, and Zach and I had bonded over our recently ended long-term relationships (he was getting out of a twelve-year marriage). When the bar had closed down, he'd walked me to the subway and kissed me. No tongue. Just a soft-lipped kiss like you might get at the end of a date in the 1950s.

Zach is pouring drinks that night, so Julie and I hang at the bar for a few hours. I can't get much vibe off him. He talks to Julie as much as to me.

While Julie and I sit outside, Adi texts me, asking if I'd like to have dinner on Sunday night.

"Sunday," I say to Julie. "Does that mean I'm not worthy of a Saturday night or does that mean he figures since it's already Friday night I must already have plans for Saturday?"

"I don't know," Julie says, helpfully.

We put the question to Zach.

"Sunday means he wants to marry you." I can't tell if he's kidding or not.

At any rate, I text back: "Definitely."

I'm just happy I'd heard from him despite the fact that he'd probably already relegated me to booty call status.

"What is it about men?" I ask Zach. "They try so hard to get sex from you, but it doesn't seem like they really want it. What they really want is some girl who pretends she has no sexual needs and puts them through an obstacle course before she reluctantly 'gives in.'"

"Personally, I'm not one of those guys who would press for sex right away. You have to deal with a human being the next day," he says.

Julie and I sit outside in the garden, and she encourages me to ask Zach out.

"Nah. Doesn't seem like he's into me."

"Just because he's being nice and not all over you? Maybe you should try a guy like that."

"I haven't got to the point yet where I'm going to ask out a guy who doesn't seem interested. Besides, it sounds like he's going through a lot of his own stuff."

Zach seems to be a sweet guy without much game. Or maybe that *was* his game.

Julie and I head to Loki, where I pick up a short (what is with me and short guys?), very handsome guy who, it turns out, can't kiss worth a damn. At first, he doesn't use his tongue at all. It's like sucking on a hole. When he finally finds his tongue, I can hardly feel it through the barrier of his teeth, which keep clashing into mine.

At 4 A.M., the bar closes. He waits outside with me for the car I'd called and keeps trying to talk me back to his apartment. I give him my business card, more to placate him than anything else. I can't deal with a guy who can't kiss.

The next day, I run through imaginary speeches to give Adi. I'm supposed to be having dinner at his apartment the next night, which means he might expect to get laid. Especially since, the last time I'd seen him, I'd entertained him with a laundry list of sexual things I'd like to do to him.

By now I'd heard and read enough to know that putting out early meant guys assumed you did that with everyone, weren't worthy of long-term status, and therefore you were headed for a six-week-Rahil fling or a James email-you-when-I-want-sex type deal. Listen to the language: "putting out" "giving it up." It was the woman who lost, the man who gained.

And what about this marriage of Adi's? Was it a trial separation? Definitely over? Or was it up in the air? As Zach said about his soon-to-be-ex-wife when Julie asked if they'd ever get back together: "Anything's possible." Things were a little different when your ex hadn't turned gay.

I decide that the best course of action is just to see how it goes and to try and keep my emotional baggage from spilling out on to the tarmac.

I hadn't been good at that so far.

At 10:30 P.M., as I sit home nursing last night's hangover, James texts: "What r u up to? A hot date? I'm at a boring birthday party."

"I guess you should learn to ask out people who interest you then," I tap back. No response.

At 5:30 A.M., I wake up and work myself into a mental froth about the

Adi situation. I don't know whom to ask for advice. I really want a guy's opinion, but I had no real guy friends. I thought it was inappropriate to ask Aaron. Besides, what did Aaron know about what men wanted from women? He was trying to figure out what men wanted from men.

Would it be right to ask James? While he'd definitely shunted me into the booty call girl category—and wouldn't ask me out on a proper date no matter how much I cajoled—this also made him the perfect person to instruct me how to avoid it.

That afternoon, I leave a message on James's voice mail telling him I'd like some dating advice. But by the time he calls back, this seems like a spectacularly bad idea.

"Never mind," I say, "it's totally inappropriate for me to be asking you these questions."

"Go ahead."

"Are you sure you want to discuss this stuff?"

"Yes. Why not?"

"Okay, well . . . I know I've been put in the booty call girl category with you, and I'm fine with that, but—"

"No, you haven't."

"Yes, I have. And it's okay, but I—"

"No, you haven't."

"Then why don't you ever ask me out?"

"I asked you out on Friday, but you didn't answer my email."

I had left work early on Friday and not seen the email.

"Okay, but I'm sure you just wanted me to go to your apartment. And why would you wait until Friday afternoon to ask me out for that evening?"

"I never think what I'm going to do until the last minute."

"You were just waiting to see if something better came along."

"No, I wasn't."

The conversation wasn't exactly going as planned.

"This is the problem with having this discussion," I say. "We're going to bring it back to us, and I'm not talking about us."

"Okay."

"Well . . . I guess what I want to know is, how do you not get into that category? Am I supposed to pretend I'm not a sexual being? Am I supposed to make a guy take me out to a bunch of expensive dinners and then reluctantly 'give in' as if it's some painful experiment? I have dinner with a guy at his apartment tonight, and he's going to expect something. And I don't want to play the prude, but I don't want to be put into that category."

"I guess . . . if you talk about sex . . . right away . . . then you figure that's all the girl wants."

"So I'm supposed to talk about work? My hobbies?"

"If you want to see if you have anything in common, if there's something deeper there."

"How boring. Can't people talk about sex *and* see if they have anything deeper?"

"Maybe . . . it's when you start talking about other guys. That's not very romantic. And then you just start thinking of the girl in one way."

"Hmm. I was just being honest."

"I know."

"And I only talk about other men because you ask about them. I don't want to lie to you. I *hate* liars."

"Even if you didn't mention it, I can tell these things."

"Can you? I couldn't. My boyfriend cheated on me for years. I had no idea."

In one of my very first conversations with James, I'd said, "You're free to do what you want, with whomever you want." I'd assumed this sort of freedom would put guys at ease. But maybe that's not what they wanted at all. Maybe Rahil had run, not because I'd stopped playing games with him, but because I'd mentioned James, mentioned Match .com, mentioned joining French Tuesdays for the men. But hadn't that been what he'd wanted? This was the man who'd told me to keep my feelings in check, who'd said he didn't have one ounce of romantic feeling for me. I'd thought letting him know I was seeing other people would make him more comfortable. Shit. This stuff was so complicated.

I'd hardly dated at all in my early twenties, before meeting Aaron. Here I was, in my mid-thirties, a sexual and emotional schizoid, trying to relearn everything. I felt like someone had bound my feet, thrown lye in my face, told me I had a terminal disease, and then asked me to delicately navigate the obstacle course of dating. And I had to do it while I was hornier than I'd ever been in my life.

"I'm very good at being monogamous," I tell James. I thought it was important that he know. "It's my natural state. I did it for ten years. I'd like to see *you* do it for ten years."

"I think you should cancel on this guy. Then he'd really appreciate you."

"I don't think so," I laugh.

"You could come over here for some predate training. We could work on it."

"Thank you for the offer. But I think I've got it. I'll wear my suit and pearls and talk about my bug collection and show him my vacation photos."

"You could come over later and tell me how it went."

Good old James. We'd been messed up since day one, but for some reason we were both still hanging in there.

Later, Adi calls. He's buying wine and ingredients for dinner. Maybe I was on the romance track after all—the dinner taking place at his apartment notwithstanding.

Don't talk about sex. Don't mention other guys.

At 8 P.M., Adi greets me at the door to his sublet. With his big black eyes, long lashes, and perfect teeth, he's more handsome than I remembered. He'd gotten a haircut and it suited him. Within minutes, we're kissing heavily. He finally manages to get himself together enough to make pasta with pesto sauce. I stand behind him at the kitchen counter and molest him while he attempts to cook.

"Do you think the Food Network would be interested in a show like this? Sex plus cooking?"

Apparently I wasn't very good at this not talking about sex thing.

"I think it would," he laughs.

We eat the pasta and kiss some more. Suddenly, he deflates, props his head on my chest and apologizes, blaming it on the heavy meal.

"Don't worry about it," I soothe, caressing his forehead and the palm of his brown hand. It's a much more vulnerable Adi from the one I saw at the French Tuesdays ball. He is a gaping emotional wound. We lay on the bed together, snuggling. Euro dance music wails in the background.

"This is so surreal," he says. "It's my first time being with anyone since my wife. What was it like for you the first time after your breakup?"

"Very intense. Once you've been with another three or four people, you start to come down to Earth and see it for what it is. But that first time . . . very intense."

Sensing hesitancy on his part, I glance at him.

"We don't have to do anything you don't want to do," I say, sounding like a man trying to seduce a woman, sounding like Rahil.

"Would you be upset if we didn't?"

"Of course not. I wasn't going to have sex with you anyway. I'm not ready for that." Naturally, I'm slightly suspicious and insulted. But I hide it well.

"Good. Neither am I."

I didn't know what happened to the guy who, at French Tuesdays, had vowed to tie me up and tease me for hours. He's hiding under the couch, I guess.

"I've been told not to say this sort of thing, but if we do have sex, you know, it doesn't mean you can't continue to do what you want to do. You need your freedom right now."

I figured a guy like Adi might think that sex means instant relationship, and that might prevent him from taking that step. And, of course, I wanted to keep my own options open. Wasn't it smooth how I phrased it?

Yet, maybe this was the wrong thing to say. During our conversation, James had told me how he liked it when a girl showed possessiveness and drew boundaries.

"Oh, please," I'd said. "If I started telling you that you can't do this, can't do that, you'd be out in two weeks."

He hadn't argued.

Adi gives me one of his T-shirts to wear. Then we go to the window and share a cigarette.

"You have a nice ass," I tell him, cupping it.

"My sister always says I have no ass."

"What's your sister doing feeling up your ass?"

He laughs. We finish the cigarette and get back in bed.

"You're doing much better than me," I tell him. "I was so weirded out with the first guy that I could barely have a conversation with him. I'm surprised he put up with as much as he did."

"How many guys?" he asks.

I hold up two fingers, conveniently leaving out the men with whom there'd been no penetration. "That's not bad, is it?" I ask. "For four months? If you keep up this way, one woman every month, you'll have double in the same amount of time."

"Well, I'm not in a hurry." He grins. "Thank you for being so cool." He buries his lips in my hair and whispers, "I'm so attracted to you."

He asks me if I want to stay the night, but I demur. I'm in a miniskirt and high heels. I didn't think the tramp attire would go over well at the office in the morning.

Standing in the hallway, waiting for the excruciatingly slow elevator, I come back to kiss him again as he stands by the door watching me. I wave at him as the elevator finally arrives and the doors part.

Walking down the darkened street, I'm giddy. He'd kept saying things like, "The next time I see you . . ." and "We will have to try that sometime . . ." I felt the future opening up before me.

But my date with Adi teaches me one thing: No matter how great you thought a date went, or how much you laughed at each other's jokes or finished each other's sentences, or how much time you spent kissing and caressing, or how much he complimented you, or told you how attracted he was to you, or how many times he said, "Next time I see you . . ." until you got asked on that second date, there was no guarantee it would happen. The crackling and buzzing of electricity around you may only be the exhilaration you feel in the other person's presence, and not necessarily what that person is feeling in yours.

The long silence that followed my date with Adi was a brutal reminder of the harsh, nonsensical reality of single life.

chapter thirty-eight

I n the morning, I receive an email from James asking how my date
went. Then he goes on:

"Our conversation last night has made me think I need to get a
girlfriend sometime soon. So I went on this East European dating
site . . ."

I can't believe the transparent attempt to make me jealous. It doesn't
really work. At this point, I'm too certain of his interest in me, even if it
is mostly fired by competitiveness. But I decide I'll make him happy and
get a little riled up.

"Figures you'd go to a mail-order bride site to hunt for gold-digging,
hollow-eyed, ill-educated seventeen-year-olds who want nothing but a
visa," I respond.

Toward the end of the day, he asks me out for a drink and then adds
that I can come up to his apartment to see his "vacation photos."

"You mean I get a drink first?" I ask. "I'm honored. How about to-morrow?"

"Okay. Tomorrow then. :)"

"Okay. :)"

Good old James.

Later that night, Sahana calls. "Guess who I just ran into?"

I know it before she even says it.

"Rahil!" she cries.

"Jesus. He's everywhere!"

"He was right outside my apartment," she says, "with Hayden and her *father*. He introduced me."

My heart sinks a little. Actually, I'm surprised how much it sinks.

"Maybe I came across as rude because I was running to my therapy appointment and didn't want to say where I was going." She pauses, then intones: "He must be back with Hayden."

"I guess so. That's probably why I haven't heard from him."

"I felt like saying to her father, 'Congratulations, you've raised a wonderful trapeze artist,'" she laughs.

"You should have asked Rahil when was the last time he fucked Kiri."

"I couldn't do that," she gasps. "Her father was there!"

"I'm just kidding."

Then Adi, James, everyone recede into inconsequentiality. My heart keeps up an irregular, heavy thumping.

I guess you never forget your first relationship after your first relationship.

chapter
thirty-nine

Day 138 When the protective bubble you've been living in for ten years explodes; when the pain you've spent years inoculating yourself against rushes into your bloodstream; when your road map for life gets torn to shreds and scattered to the wind, something happens.

I sensed the descent starting.

I felt the dangerously alluring tug, heard the demons rattling the bars, thrilled to the chemicals in my brain churning.

It was the desire to see people as they were, to know what they were capable of, to stare cruelty and heartlessness in the eyes, to take the hurt I'd been avoiding, to take it straight on the chin, in fact, to invite it in. And I found a willing partner. Damaged people can sniff each other out like trained dogs.

Over the past couple of weeks, I'd stumbled upon a whole new James by email. We'd spend most days exchanging erotic messages. At some point, we began trading sexual conquest stories. Hearing about me with other men, he said, not only inflamed his jealousy, but excited him. So I tell him about meeting Adi at the Bastille Day ball, and how that had progressed.

"Now you," I say. "And don't lie or embellish."

Far from moping around the ball with some boring girl, as I'd fancied, James's date had been a twenty-two-year-old hot babe whom he'd had little trouble enticing up to his apartment, where he'd had sex with her "three times, in every position imaginable."

"Jealous yet?" he asks.

Heart thumping, hands a little shaky, I confess that I am.

"This is a strange game," I say. "But fun."

I'd wanted to try this kind of relationship—one based on ruthless honesty—since Aaron had broken my world with his dishonesty. Why not know everything in a man's heart, including all the ugly shit you didn't want to know? You'd find out about it eventually.

I'd toe-tested this type of thing with Rahil, but hadn't counted on the visceral jealousy that eventually overtook me. James was a better candidate. Perhaps he would inspire jealousy, but only to an extent that would be more spice than poison.

From then on, James would tell me about his dates, his flirtations, the girls he led on, but had no real interest in. Then there was the time he'd shown up so tired two months ago for our date in Brooklyn. Turns out it was because he'd been fucking two different South American girls almost nonstop the entire weekend.

He also gives me some telling insight into my date with Adi and the reason he didn't want to sleep with me: "The only time I might find myself unsure about whether to have sex with a girl is if she seems more into me than I am into her," he says. "Then I don't want to hurt her and involve myself in an emotional mess."

Great—just what I wanted to hear. That was probably exactly what Adi had been thinking.

At his apartment, James throws me down on the bed and growls: "Tell me exactly what you like."

The very words I'd been waiting to hear from some man, any man, coming out of the man I'd least expected to hear them from! I tell him how to rub my clit and suck my nipples at the same time. He does. I could've told him exactly how to go down on me, but for some reason I'm still nervous about this. I'm not sure he likes it. Or maybe I don't want to orgasm and give up any power to him. Or maybe it's that his big cock is so tempting. Whatever the reason, I tell him just to fuck me. It's semiviolent, sweaty, and sexy as hell. Afterward, we lay there in a heap, breathing heavily, neither one of us able to speak for a few minutes.

We move to the couch and have a conversation about our lives. For the first time, James opens up about his family—his parents are divorced, his siblings sound like screwups. Maybe not screwups, but they definitely did not share the intellect gene that James had inherited. He plays a bad French pop tune and translates the lyrics for me. Then he lays his head on my shoulder while I caress his cropped hair (always kept short otherwise it frizzes, he says) and I kiss his forehead. Then we wrestle around and slap and beat each other up playfully.

"Why did you tell me we didn't have chemistry?" I finally ask.

"To piss you off," he says.

It's probably the most truthful statement I'd ever heard out of him.

Somehow James had unexpectedly morphed into the man I felt most comfortable around. With him, I wasn't constantly reining myself in, being careful not to seem too interested, too crazy, too talkative, too opinionated, too whatever. He got quite a bit of amusement out of whatever mood I showed him. And nothing could dampen his sexual desire of me. I knew that either he or I would meet someone else who would take our attention off each other, but for now it was nice to have his company.

chapter forty

A man I had met for about thirty seconds at the Bastille Day ball, a doctor named Caleb, asked me out through a friend. I didn't have high hopes. First, Julie knew him and didn't like him, calling him an egotistical mama's boy and high maintenance.

Second, no sooner did I agree to have a drink with him than he began emailing me about where we could meet—long missives detailing a variety of different bars and restaurants, weighing all their respective attributes, from the food to the décor to what angle the sunlight slanted through the windowpanes.

I was so certain nothing would come of it that during one long day of erotically charged cyberbanter with James, I suggested that he go to the restaurant where Caleb and I would meet, watch us on our date, and then follow me on a trip to the bathroom where he'd "ravage" me.

"Yes!" James responded. "Let's do it."

I was just in the heated frame of mind to do something like that too. But then I came down with a raging case of strep throat. I had to cancel the date and stay home from work (Aaron fetches me the only thing I was able to swallow, watermelon, then stays over all night watching me drool white goop into a cup). Caleb bombards me concerned emails and, being a doctor, threatens to come over and culture my tonsils. After realizing what a nice guy he is, I tell James we can't go through with our plan.

Caleb continues to email or text me every day throughout my illness. I'm amazed how solicitous guys are in the beginning—when they know virtually nothing about you. In the thirty seconds it had taken Caleb to meet me, what, other than a fleeting glimpse of some kind of personal beauty ideal, would indicate I was worth so much attention?

But it was all part of the courtship game wired into the male brain. I was learning not to read much into it. The early eager-beaver mating dance was for the girl he thought you might be, some girl stored in his imagination, not the girl you *were*. You had to be careful not to confuse the two. "This is not for me," I began telling myself. "This is for some girl he is hoping to find, and he temporarily thinks I might be her."

The next day, a combination of cabin fever and achy heart overtakes me and I text Adi a little goodbye: "Hey Adi- Have not heard from u, so I guess that's it. That was a short one! I have been sick with strep throat all week. Hope u don't have it too. Good luck to u. It is tough out there, as I am learning."

I didn't expect to hear back. But it was immensely gratifying to get the last word in with a guy who tried to drift away on a blanket of silence.

About five hours later, Adi texts back that he's been swamped at work and traveling, but he wants to see me again, and that he deserves a "spanking" for not being in touch.

Who was at fault here? Me, for expecting regular contact from a guy

I was barely involved with, or the guy, who didn't have the brains to know that he should get in touch with a girl a few days after a date, just to say hi, that is, if he wanted to see her again.

Since Adi is doing the "I'm busy/I want to see you" hybrid blowoff, my guess was he *did* like me—just not that much.

Adi got put in the doghouse.

I return to my computer and harangue James via email again for never asking me out properly: "I'm tired of those other sluts getting restaurant meals and asked to balls when I'm putting out and get squat!"

His reply shocks the hell out of me: "In that case, want to come up to Canada with me on Thursday and spend the weekend on a lake at my parents' home?"

I stare at the screen, disbelieving. Here's a man who won't ask me to dinner, but he'll invite me up to Canada to meet the folks?

Part of me is tempted. But another, much bigger part of me, is terrified. James and I had a very odd relationship. It wasn't exactly emotional. It wasn't exactly a relationship. And yet canoeing on his parents' lake (the next email, hoping to persuade me, described just this) was exactly that, something a nice, normal, emotionally involved couple would do.

If I went, we'd be together round the clock for four days (Thursday through Sunday). Thus far, James had only ever seen me under the most controlled circumstances: dressed to kill, meticulous makeup and hair, slightly drunk. Yeah, there'd been a morning or two where I'd woken up in his bed, hair a bird's nest, makeup smeared, eyes puffed into slits, but I'd quickly managed to restore myself in the bathroom before he saw too much. What if I got acne, diarrhea, or some other not-so-romantic thing that would move us from the realm of wild sex partners to something more intimate and, yes, more disgusting?

Also, what do you do way out in the country like that? *Talk.* Talk on the lake. Talk at night. Talk during drives. We'd know our respective life stories within days, and then we were supposed to come back to the city and pick up with our kinky sex and open dating situation? Yeah, I'm sure I'd be just fine with him trolling dating sites and banging random twenty-two-year-old girls he met in cafes after I'd spent days canoeing on a lake with him, exchanging hopes, dreams, and childhood traumas.

But I don't tell him any of this. I merely tell him the truth: that there's no way I could get more time off work, after I'd been out sick so much the past week. But I offer to come over the night before his departure to help him "pack."

M y first day back at work, and I'm still feeling weak. The antibiotics I'd been prescribed for my strep (as well as perhaps my increased sexual activities) had given me a mild yeast infection. James continues to try to cajole me into going to Canada with him. Yet I also know he's meeting a young (of course) big-titted (his words) Serbian girl at French Tuesdays that evening.

I tease him about what his "plan of attack" will be and tell him that my date with Caleb, the doctor, is that weekend. James says he's jealous and tries to get me to cancel.

What a twisted relationship. But there's something exhilarating about it.

"He's in love," pronounces Helen Fisher, the famous biological anthropologist and author.

She's referring to James. I'm interviewing her for a story about "men who love the chase," which I'm freelancing, and I'd just finished recounting for her how James had carried me several blocks through the pouring rain, all so he could find a cab and get me back to his bed.

"Oh no," I protest, "far from it. He's sleeping with other people. *Lots* of other people."

"You can sleep with other people and still be in love with one person," she says, as if that's the most obvious thing in the world.

I guess the past year should have taught me nothing if not that very lesson.

Fisher explains how the reward centers of the brain light up when a male is in courtship mode and trying to win over a female and how dopamine continues to flood those centers as long as he isn't getting what he wants. As soon as he gets it, the chemical recedes. So a woman who takes longer to acquire feels more valuable to a man than one he bags in short order.

"*That's* why women play hard to get!" I exclaim, mental lightbulb flicking on.

"Oh, women have known this for eons," she drawls.

But some men, Fisher continues, actually enjoy the dopamine flooding their nerve centers so much that they get stuck in the courtship phase and never graduate to the all-important "romantic attachment" phase, which involves another chemical, oxytocin, and feelings of pair bonding.

Hmm. I suspected Rahil, James, and Adi were all dopamine fiends.

Fisher then describes the "serotonin type" man. He hates the chase, is uncomfortable in the courtship phase, and is quite relieved when it's over and he can start bonding.

"That sounds like the guy I was engaged to," I say. "I don't think he ever chased anyone in his life."

"You're not still together?"

"No, he decided he's gay."

"How old was he?"

"Thirty-six."

"Fascinating!"

Fisher is careful to point out that the ebb and flow of chemicals doesn't guarantee much of anything—that there are plenty of men who don't respond to hard-to-get women, and that, in fact, there are men who stay madly in love for decades past the initial dopamine rush. Human beings are not glass beakers into which compounds can be mixed and matched to create certain reactions.

Unfortunately.

After I get off the phone, I notice that Adi had texted to ask if I wanted to do dinner or drinks the next night. Previously, an invite like this would have sent me floating around the apartment on an ecstasy cloud. But now I barely take notice of his message. I don't even reply to it—let dopamine flood his nerve centers for a while.

chapter forty-one

At an uptown salon, my eyebrow shaper, Lena, has me in the same position a few people have me these days—flat on my back.

"How are things?" she asks in her thick Russian accent, threading some floss between the tips of her fingers and ripping the hair out from my arches.

"Good. Busy. It's busy being single."

She peers down at me through a triangle of floss, her lips puckered with concern. I'd already spilled the details of my breakup with Aaron. I had that kind of big mouth.

"Someday . . ." she sighs.

"Someday what?"

"Someday you'll find the one."

Irritation seizes my body like an electric shock. I'm the pitiable single girl.

"I'm having a lot of fun," I insist. "I was part of a couple for ten years. I'm not looking for that now."

"I'm sorry," she says, either not believing or not understanding.

Back outside, I check my phone and see a text from James that he'd sent me last night: "Just felt up her big boobs and ass." He means the big-titted Serb he'd taken to French Tuesdays. I'm flattered that he'd taken a moment out of his "courtship" to text me on his progress.

"When does she go back where she came from?" I reply. "I'll have to tell my friend at the INS about her."

Back at work, we start emailing. "I have two dates this weekend," I tell him. He'll be in Canada at that time. "Jealous yet?"

"You are *not* going on any dates unless you want to get slapped and punished when I get back!" he replies.

I laugh. That sounded fine to me.

That evening, I meet Caleb at an upscale sushi place in Greenwich Village. I sit at the bar until he arrives. When he does, I'm slightly taken aback. He's only my height, five feet five inches tall, and he doesn't look a day under his age: forty. However, he's in good shape and has nice sensual facial features.

The only problem is that, from the second he arrives, he's completely infatuated. I hadn't had to deal with a guy like this since I was single in my early twenties, and it can be a bit disconcerting.

"You're dangerous," he oozes at me over dinner.

"Why?"

"Because I like you."

"Why is that dangerous?"

"Because you might not feel the same."

Too much information.

We share the sushi taste menu (I catch a glimpse of the only-a-doctor-wouldn't-blink-an-eye $200 tab) and then we move to a joint that plays live salsa. He's a good dancer and patient with me. I kiss him just to figure out if there's any sexual chemistry and the kissing is all right—not perfect, but then neither was James's kissing at first, I keep reminding myself. Speaking of James, I find myself thinking about him an inordinate amount while Caleb and I dance.

"What are you doing this Sunday?" Caleb hollers over the rollicking salsa beat.

"I have a date."

"You would go out with other guys after me?" he asks, not quite kidding.

It turns out he himself has two more dates planned for that weekend, but he volunteers that he'll cancel them for me.

"I like you more than I like them, more than anyone I've dated so far," he says, twirling me into him. "Is that overwhelming?"

"A little," I admit.

I don't want to run from the guy who wants me and isn't playing games about it—isn't that what I'd been complaining that men were doing to me? But somehow the strong come-ons of Rahil and Adi didn't bore me the way Caleb's do, probably because theirs were sexual while his seemed emotional. He was just too damn easy.

"What is it about me that you like so quickly?" I ask. I'm genuinely curious, considering he knows almost nothing about me.

"Your frailty," he purrs.

My frailty?!

"Most people think I'm pretty tough," I counter.

"That's just your cover."

No, it isn't, I feel like saying. Plenty of people would have curled up into a rocking-back-and-forth ball of submission after the couple of years I'd had. Caleb not only didn't know me, he also liked some quality he imagined he saw in me that would've allowed him to play protective father figure.

Nevertheless, I agree to (or am pressured into) a second date. I keep thinking about how many times I'd almost dumped James for being boring and sexually selfish, but after scratching the surface, I'd found someone a little more exciting and sexually adventurous than maybe I was ready for. So, my reasoning went, if I scratched Caleb a little deeper, maybe I'd find someone more relaxed and challenging.

Ten minutes after I arrive home, Caleb texts me, thanking me for the date and saying he looks forward to the next.

I'd have to scratch this surface very hard.

The next night, I meet Adi at a French bistro on the Lower East Side. He's looking quite cute, but I'm determined to play it cool until I see how he's feeling.

"Come here," he growls, pulling my stool closer to his. I guess he's feeling okay.

"So you'd written me off," he says.

"Not really. I just wanted to say a little goodbye. I like to wrap everything up in a little bow. I'm not used to a guy taking so long getting in touch—at least, not if he wants to see me again."

"I don't have an excuse," he admits.

"I guess most people just go silent, but I'm still learning all the rules and regulations."

"Me too."

"Adi, whatever happens between you and other women is irrespective of whatever happens between us."

"I appreciate that."

Now that everything is out in the open, I hoped he'd be more at ease, like James was.

After dinner, we go to Stanton Social and make out on the couch. He's fingering my panties under my miniskirt when I dare him to take them off. We are in full view of the bar. He finally manages it.

He tells me he'll be going to Greece on vacation for a week, then to England for another week on business. The week of his return, I was to leave for Los Angeles. That means, after tonight, we won't see each other again for three weeks.

If it's anything my conversations with James and my own experience had taught me, it was that in the New York dating game, at least among a certain sector of busy, professional, socially adept people in their thirties, you never quite knew where in a prospect's romantic journey you jumped on the caboose. He might be in the middle of a divorce, and wary about dating, or even have moved toward a reconciliation in the time it took you to set up your first date. He might be in an on-and-off relationship, and you happened to catch him in an off moment, but three weeks later, it's back on and you're out. He could've had his third date with another girl right before you, and he and that girl click on the fourth, so you're out by the second.

It was all about timing; you couldn't take any of it too personally. You just had to keep juggling, as everyone else was doing, and at some point, the balls would, hopefully, land in the right hands—so to speak.

That weekend, James emails me from Canada telling me he's bored. I respond with a barrage of sexual fantasies.

"Sorry," he replies. "There isn't an opportunity for me to get alone and write something substantive to you on that subject. Anyway, it feels kind of weird discussing sexual fantasies in the living room of my dad's house with my nephew running around."

Christ! He'd invited me up for a family gathering. He was trying to get to know me as a *human being.* And yet all I could do was write, think, and talk about sex. What the hell was wrong with me?

Yet, I couldn't stop. I inform him how vigorously Caleb is pursuing me, and how this is beginning to freak me out a little. I'm trying to make him jealous—so far, jealousy had attracted, not repelled, him.

"I wrote you a long reply," he says. "But it just got erased by mistake. I'll write more tomorrow."

In the early morning, I wake up fantasizing about Adi. Whether he would develop the kind of affection for me that I had for him, I didn't know. As James had put it in one of his emails: affection couldn't be gotten by strategy.

How true. Sometimes it came to you out of the rockiest beginnings. Sometimes it came later than you'd hoped and only after various interruptions and near endings. Sometimes it packed up and left the building unexpectedly. Sometimes it turned gay.

And sometimes it stayed a millimeter just out of reach, no matter how much you beckoned it.

chapter forty-two

Would you like to kiss her?" the tall handsome man with a shirt unbuttoned to his navel asks me. He juts his chin toward the pretty red-haired woman behind him.

"I don't know," I say. "I haven't kissed a girl before."

"She hasn't kissed a girl before," he informs the redhead.

The redhead grins. Then she and I are kissing, and it's just like kissing a guy, if you ask me.

And now I have more pressing problems.

James has disappeared, off in a funk somewhere in the bowels of Plumm, a club on 14th Street, where Cake is having an event. Cake is a group dedicated to "female empowerment," which is basically a euphemism for couples looking to experiment with other couples. James, Julie, Jake, and I had all gone out of mere curiosity. James and I had been emailing about it for weeks—and he'd told me over and over again, in pinpoint detail, how he wanted to see me kiss another man.

Everything went fine until I gave James what he claimed he wanted. I'd found some tall, dark-haired specimen of hunk, dragged him downstairs to where James sat, plopped him between us so James had a good view, and began smooching the gentleman in question.

James took off like a rocket. After my make out partner went to find some friends, James returned and stood next to me, rigid as a monolith. "I'm going to go home," he announced, barely moving his lips.

"Why?" I exclaimed. "I thought that's what you wanted to see me do!"

"It was by *email*. I thought you'd know I was *joking*."

"Would you feel better if you kissed a girl?"

He shrugged.

So we went back upstairs, and soon I was playing wingwoman for James. I introduced him to a well-fed German blonde as "my cousin." I was sure she knews what we were doing—Cake was that kind of place. I also knew James would get her in a lip lock within minutes, so I sidled away, and sure enough, the next time I looked back, he had the heifer's tongue in his mouth.

This is when I get approached about kissing the redhead. Thinking James might find this titillating enough to forgive my dalliance, I turn to him, but he's disappeared again. When I finally track him to his lair in the corner, the blonde is gone.

"Where's your piglet?"

"She left."

"Do you want to go?"

"Yes."

He still refuses to so much as even glance at me.

"Are you going to give me the 'let's be friends' speech again?"

He manages to laugh a little. "No."

"Because if you are, give it to me now."

"No."

So much for James being sexually adventurous.

In the next day's email exchange, he sends me a portion of an email that a girl had sent him at 2 A.M., wherein she laments that she doesn't know *why* she's emailing him at 2 A.M. *How about because you're desperate?* James tells me he finds her stalkerish communiques "endearing."

Jealousy unexpectedly rips through me, forcing me outside, where I sit smoking with slightly shaky hands.

I knew this was exactly the kind of reaction he'd tried to provoke, but that didn't do anything to lessen it. The sight of him making out with a hard-bitten German blonde at Cake didn't cause me one ounce of the vexation that a 2 A.M. email from some infatuated girl did. Infatuated stalkers, as pathetic as they may appear, could still end up as girlfriends.

The night before, I'd sent Caleb an email telling him that I didn't quite feel the kind of romantic connection with him that would justify another date, but that I'd be happy to have drinks with him "as friends." To my astonishment, he'd answered that he was fine with that. So we meet up at Coffee Shop in Union Square.

On my way there, the sky opens up, soaking me from the waist down. Caleb gets his karate pants from the car and I change into them. Because he's so small, they almost fit me. With the pressure of a date off us, I find myself being brutally honest about the fact that his heavy-handed pursual had turned me off. He apologizes, tells me he's like that with everyone, and promises to tone it way down. I'm glad I'd decided to meet up with him. He's fun, smart, and even cute in a way that normally would've attracted me. But for some reason there just isn't much sexual chemistry. Maybe I'm worried about leading him on. Maybe it just isn't there.

Meanwhile, I know James is out having drinks somewhere with 2 A.M. Email Girl, but he texts me four times during the evening. When I get home, I call him. He tells me that he'd also been caught in the downpour, and had used his wet socks as an excuse to cut his date short.

"I'm glad you had a boring evening," I tell him.

I wasn't sure how much longer we'd be able to keep this kind of relationship up without it imploding. I knew that I couldn't enter into a "real" relationship with James—we didn't have enough in common to sustain it. But I also knew that I had the capacity to throw myself fully into it anyway and be monogamous for the long term, as I had done with Aaron. I really didn't think James had that in him. By the time he'd cheated on me and we went through all the spasms of a dying relationship, I'd be another six months or a year older. With the clock ticking away on my face, I didn't feel as if I had that luxury. On the other hand, I had now bonded with James to the point that the mention of other women began to drive me a little bonkers.

Implode it would, I just didn't know when, or which one of us would end up getting most hurt.

The next day, James tells me he has another date, this time with some girl he'd found on Match.com. Again the news sends me into paroxysms of jealousy. When I confess this to him, he apologizes and says he will stop telling me about other women.

"Oh no!" I respond. "I appreciate the honesty. This is the kind of relationship I need right now. I'm still adjusting to it, that's all. If I get jealous, it's a natural human reaction. I can handle it."

I think.

A couple of hours into his Match.com date, James sends me a text that the girl isn't as pretty as she appeared in her photos. Soon he is on his way to meet me in the West Village, where I'm at a party. When he gets there, we sequester ourselves by the makeshift bar and kiss. Before long, we're in a cab on the way to his place. He fondles me under my skirt and lays his head on my lap. Aaron used to do the same thing—lay his head on my lap in a cab, that is. He was never much for fondling under the skirt.

At his apartment, James's attitude toward me is noticeably warmer. He cuddles with me during the night, wrapping his legs and arms around me and burrows his head into the crook of my neck. In the morning when I try to get up to go home, he prostrates himself flat on top of me and refuses to budge.

"Are you going to let me leave?" I finally whisper.

He vigorously shakes his head no and I fall back asleep. There's nothing like a man who wants to seriously cuddle with you. But I make sure to let him make most of the moves. I don't went to come across as needy. James had the same ability Aaron had—to shut down. He could be cold as marble when he wanted to. But he was also beginning to show me this other side, one that was incredibly soft, vulnerable and affectionate. I devour it, but I also know how dangerous it is. It's this side that can suck me in, if it hasn't already.

chapter forty-three

Day 156 So much for the softer, more affectionate James. We made plans to see a movie on Sunday evening, but in the afternoon he calls and says, "Let's see the ten p.m. showing. I'm supposed to meet an Argentinian slut for coffee at five."

"Are you kidding me?" I blast back. "You made a date on a night when we have plans?"

He says that it "isn't a date," and he'll cancel it if I feel that way. But nothing can douse my rage. I'm being scheduled around his sluts!

I take my revenge by flouncing off to the restaurant Zach owns. But after sitting at the bar watching him pour drinks for about an hour, I remember why I hadn't bothered to pursue him any further. I can't get any vibe off him whatsoever. Maybe he's shy. Maybe he isn't interested.

James texts me that he is sorry, stupid, and not used to this kind of relationship, so I go outside and call him. But he's on his way to meet the Argentinian.

"I'll call you later," he says. But I know if he and the Argentinian hit it off, he'll be too busy working to get her back to the private club on ——rd Street.

I give up on Zach and text Aaron. We agree to meet at Last Exit.

There were two fights that convinced me Aaron was in it for good. Sometimes it's the fights, not the lovemaking, that let you know. In one, I was raging about something, Lord knows what. I did quite a bit of spontaneous raging in my twenties.

I'd stormed out of the living room of the West Village loft Aaron and I had shared with two, sometimes three or more, other transient souls, and into our small back bedroom, more like an extra large closet. It just barely fit a bed, a table, and some clothes. I was still raging when Aaron followed me, carrying a chair. *Is he going to hit me with it?* I briefly wondered. Then he put the chair on the floor and decisively sat in it, blocking me from going anywhere.

"What can I do to make this better?" he'd asked. Woah. No one had ever responded to my hostile irrationality with quite this brand of loving but firm rationality before. I immediately calmed down, and we talked through the matter.

The second fight occurred some months later, at the same loft. I'd opened our mailbox and found a letter stamped "RETURN TO SENDER." I recognized Aaron's handwriting on the envelope. My heart kicked up a wild beat as it dawned on me what had happened. Aaron had sent a letter to his ex-girlfriend, the single mother he'd dated right before me, who lived in Florida, and since she was no longer at that address, it had been returned. This was in the days before either of us had access to email.

With shaky hands, I tore open the letter and stood breathlessly devouring it right by the mailbox. It didn't say much of any import, but one line, where he wrote that he'd fallen in love with a beautiful woman, caught my attention. I assumed he meant me, but for some reason, this declaration did little to comfort me. I actually became convinced he'd written that to make her jealous. Inside the loft, I tossed the letter at Aaron and broke up with him. What followed was like something out of a Greek tragedy—Aaron gnashed his teeth, he wailed, he threatened to throw himself into the Hudson River (which, since we were on the West Side Highway, was conveniently right outside the door).

At some point during the fireworks, I looked down at his wrists and realized they were bleeding. Aaron had taken a butter knife—not a very effective tool if you want to kill yourself, but definitely effective if you want to make a point—and tried to slice his wrists open. It crystallized then that this man loved me, truly loved me.

That was the last time we would ever have such a dramatic scene. I slowly came to trust not only that his feelings were genuine but that they were permanent. Deep into the relationship, I looked back on those early days of doubt and insecurity with headshaking bemusement.

And yet, after these two bruisers of arguments, there'd been no ravenous make up sex—just a lot of hugging and reassuring. Should I have known then?

At Last Exit, Aaron is exhausted. He says he'd been holed up in the studio with his band all day.

I tell him about my issues with Zach and James. We get on the topic of sex (ironically, something we could never really discuss while we were having it), and I mention how James had made a small tear in my vagina, which my gynecologist discovered—because of his large penis.

"Yet he's been wanting to stick his dick up my ass!" I exclaim.

"It's an acquired taste," says Aaron.

My eyes go wide.

"Does that mean you've tried it?" I practically shriek.

Aaron looks sheepish.

Aaron. On all fours. With a dick up his ass.

It's a vision I really don't need or want residing in my brain—like if you walked in on your parents fucking. Too late. It's seared there. Forever.

James does call that night (the Argentinian either not to his liking, or maybe she wouldn't put out) and tries talking me up to his place, but I refuse. Double booking indeed!

chapter forty-four

Day 160 With Adi in Europe, Zach unreadable, and James busy with his various sluts, I had to find someone to distract myself, since that's still what it was all about: distracting myself from myself.

My friend Lily and I attend a party at Marquee nightclub. The place is packed with young gorgeous models. Now I not only felt old but short. The only men there are young (probably gay) male models or old model-hounds. We give up on meeting anyone and dance the night away by ourselves. The highlight of the evening occurs when Adi texts me from Greece, telling me he's watching the sunrise and that he looks forward to his "spanking" upon his return. The text leaves me floating.

Yet soon I'm sucked back into the highly antagonizing but weirdly irresistible vortex that is James. He'd once again stopped bothering about my needs in bed, and as we lay together on the couch one night, he launches into one of his repressed speeches about how it's "mechanical" and "unromantic" for me to talk about sex in a practical way, to compare likes and dislikes. He says I might as well draw up a map and ask him to read it.

"Women are made differently from men," I calmly explain. "A guy can give himself an orgasm just by having sex, the woman is reliant on the man to do what she likes."

"A lot of women don't care about that," he sneers.

"Maybe that's why none of your relationships have lasted very long," I counter.

"No. It's because I got bored."

"Maybe *they* got bored."

He turns his back on me dramatically. As much as I hated the women who came before me who'd allowed James to get to this point where he imagined his cock alone made him a fabulous lover, I hated myself more for being another party to it. Why did I continually schlepp to his neighborhood so I could be with a man who only cared whether he was satisfied?

I could only conclude it was because right now I felt that a good hard fuck with a man who would push me up against the kitchen counter was better than staying home and watching bad television—and much better than staying home and wrestling with my emotions.

The intense affection James had shown me a week before—wrapping himself around me like a boa constrictor—also went by the wayside. He was back to sleeping on the opposite side of the bed.

I can't wait to see Adi again. But then I know Adi is a slippery slope. He's a guy I could get attached to, and a rejection by him would hurt like hell. James is a plaything. Yet, despite his aloofness, when I get into work, he is again emailing me like crazy. He's my dream man in terms of witty, rapid-fire banter.

And the next day, he astonishes me by doing something suitorlike. He invites me to see the Metropolitan Opera's performance of *La Traviata* in Central Park.

After the opera, James holds my fingers as we stroll through the park. He throws me down on a bench to kiss me. I'm acutely aware that something about the situation is temporary—that whenever I walk through the dark winding pathways of Central Park in the future, I'd think about the time I'd done that with James and wonder what had happened to him.

The next night I have a dream that Aaron wants to introduce me to his significant other (male). I'm as reluctant and squeamish about meeting his new man as I used to feel as a child forced on visits with my absentee father. I don't want to acknowledge this imposter, this personification of betrayal. And yet he is there, and I must.

The boyfriend is a good-looking, tall, brown-haired man. I'm sitting with a bunch of people at a table in the backyard of my childhood neighbor's home in Connecticut, where I'd spent much time playing as a youth. These people, whoever they are, also seem reluctant to meet the stranger. Aaron flutters around us, nervous and hopeful.

His companion approaches me—even more nervous, knowing he might be rejected—and I shake his hand. I introduce him to the people at the table. I'm dispassionate but not hostile. I allow him to sit next to me. Somehow, I know the man is barely holding back tears—one or two even slip out. He sits, relieved and grateful for the little bit of acceptance I show him. But I keep my body as far away from him as possible, and I can't bring myself to look at him.

chapter forty-five

Day 174 That night, I meet up with Julie and some of her friends at a restaurant in Brooklyn. James comes out to join us. Julie starts off the evening telling us about a foursome she and Jake had attempted with another couple over the weekend. It'd been excruciatingly awkward and culminated with the girl throwing up in the bathroom.

"Jake swears it wasn't me, that it was because the girl was so drunk," says Julie, not looking convinced.

From beginning to end, the tale is one of a sexual fantasy gone—as they have a tendency to do when transferred to real life—horribly awry.

"I mean," Julie continues, "there's four people, and no one knows who does what, or what goes where. There needs to be a director!"

None of us can stop laughing—except James, who never starts. He remains as stiff and motionless as a wax figurehead.

But without any men around with whom he can imagine I'm flirting, he at least reverts back to the "affectionate" James at my apartment, snuggling with me all night, and even dealing gallantly with the cats, though he claimed he was allergic.

In the morning, as we walk to the subway, he begins stammering out some story about having to go to Canada in two months to deal with a visa issue. He pauses and then says, haltingly, "Maybe you'd like to come."

I'm touched that he's optimistic enough to think we'll still be seeing each other in two months. But I manage to refrain from voicing this, take his arm, and say, "Sure."

That night, as I'm sprawled on the couch relaxing, he calls. He says he's home watching a French movie and this reminds me of a girl he'd recently mentioned who would come over to watch French movies with him (and no doubt indulge in other activities). "Faux Frenchy isn't there to keep you company?" I ask.

"No," he says, "haven't seen her in a few weeks."

"Aw, that's a shame. What happened?"

"The first time we were together, she told me we were made for each other."

"Really?"

"Then she just vanished."

"Do you like it when girls say something like that right away, or does it weird you out?"

"It would weird me out if I didn't feel the same," he says.

My heart unexpectedly kicks against my chest. Did I misunderstand what he'd just said? Had he actually just said that in the time we'd been seeing each other he'd also been involved with a girl he'd felt he was "made for"? Not that I felt James and I were made for each other—far from it. But it bugged the crap out of me when he told me this stuff.

"Don't you have your date with Muhammad tomorrow?" he asks.

"His name is Adi, thank you, and that's Sunday."

I decide I will go up to James's apartment to watch a movie with him, but then he calls five minutes later and says his friend is in town from Paris and leaving the next day, so could we postpone until tomorrow? Knowing James's brilliance for inventing excuses to cover his dalliances (he'd once told a date that a water pipe had burst in his apartment so he could slip away and fuck a different girl), I have my suspicions that another prospect had opened up.

But I can't get too worked up about it. James and I are what we are. Two people who enjoy each other's company, enjoy having sex, and are biding our time until someone better comes along.

chapter forty-six

I get ready for my date with Adi. Because he'd been out of the city visiting his brother all day, he suggests we keep it low-key, and order in food at his place. His apartment is a haul for me—the far Upper West Side—and I'm not certain I want to go straight to his pad without any preamble, but I can't bring myself to argue. One thing was certain: I had to start dating Brooklyn men.

That night, James has not one, but two Match.com dates, both of which he makes sure to tell me about—one with a Polish girl and one with, finally, an American. Perhaps he ran out of foreigners.

I hadn't had one date via Match. I got plenty of emails from barely literate men in their forties who all looked in their fifties, but the few promising thirty-somethings I'd emailed either hadn't gotten back to me or their misspelled emails had turned me off. The dating age discrimination between men and women was irritating. To find nice-looking thirty-somethings, I had to pick them up in bars so they could see for themselves that a woman my age wasn't falling apart. I figured James could email any woman of any age and quickly get a date. That made me resentful.

As I'm walking to the subway, Adi calls and suggests we meet somewhere more convenient for me (a nice change from James). We rendezvous in the East Village, and he leads me to a nearby French restaurant. It's a beautiful clear evening, finally, after several rainy, windy days.

Adi and I have easy conversation. We have a lot in common (incredibly, he too loves the Rita Hayworth movie *Gilda*, which I had unsuccessfully been haranguing James to watch), and we relate in a way that James and I never did.

Still, something is off. I'm feeling too friendly toward him, not sexual enough. Occasionally, he grabs my hand from across the table. It isn't helping.

We decide to go to another bar and begin kissing in the cab. He suggests we go straight to his place.

"Sure," I say. What's the point in playing hard to get?

But damn, the kissing is slightly "mechanical" as James would say. What's happening?

At his apartment, we have oral sex. His technique is masterful. He tells me that's because when he was twenty, he'd had an eight-month affair with a much older woman, and she had "forcefully" taught him what to do.

"Kudos to her," I say.

But I'm not experiencing that rush of feeling toward him that I had the last few times we'd been together.

I know what the problem is. James had wormed his way under my skin. I surreptitiously check my phone a couple of times to see if he's texted me, but he hasn't. That means his date(s) is going well.

Adi gives me one of his shirts and we slip into bed.

In the morning, we begin kissing, and it looks like it might lead to sex, but I'm not gung-ho about it. I had texted James while I was in the bathroom, asking what he was doing. I wanted to head to his place after I left Adi's.

"Should we be bad or good?" Adi asks, as we lay feeling each other up on the bed. He has to leave soon to be at the U.S. Open.

"We can be quick."

"I don't like being quick," he grins.

I thought that was kind of ironic, considering that the longest he'd ever lasted had been about twenty seconds.

My phone rings and it's someone from the animal shelter telling me that no volunteers had shown up that morning, that the cats are hungry and lying in their own excrement. I'm almost relieved to have the interruption—well, not relieved. But I don't mind. I tell Adi there's an emergency and I have to go.

"See you in a month?" I tease.

He laughs. "I'll be in touch soon."

Right.

The second my feet hit the pavement I call James.

"Slut, slut, slut," I tsk into his voice mail. "One of them put out because you haven't answered my text message. Must have been the Pollack—they're stupid."

I don't hear back from him until later that afternoon as I'm leaving the shelter. Turns out the Polish girl had cancelled their date, so he'd stayed with the American. He didn't leave her place until about 6 A.M.

that morning. He claims they hadn't had sex, just kissed. Supposedly, she'd had her period and didn't want to go any further. But for him to spend that much time with her . . . What did they talk about? Did they laugh as much as we did? Did they snuggle in bed? She was probably young and very pretty, otherwise he wouldn't have bothered that much with a girl who only wanted to kiss.

"Do you like her?" I ask.

"She's very . . . wholesome."

"Until she got a couple of drinks in her," I smirk.

"I threw her up against a wall and began kissing her."

Remembering all the times he'd done that with me, nausea rises in my throat.

"That usually works," I say, tightly. "Well, I guess I'll head back to Brooklyn." I hope he'll suggest we get together that night.

"I'm going to take a shower," he answers.

Disappointment pools like molten lead in my chest.

Suddenly I remembered my date with Caleb and how we'd been dancing and I'd been thinking about James. Why hadn't I seen this train barreling down the tracks?

By 4 P.M., the situation had resolved itself. I'd broken with James.

chapter forty-seven

I t starts as I lay on the couch, minding my own business, trying to recuperate from the night before. James texts and asks me if I'm outside enjoying the beautiful day.

For the first time ever, my heart leaps when I see his name appear on the cell screen.

I ask if he's up for doing something "low key" that evening or if he's too hung over from the night before? I figure if he doesn't want to get together, then I've just handed him a diplomatic "out"—he could just say, yes, he's too hung over.

But like an idiot, he doesn't take the "out." He texts back that he's rescheduled his date with the "Polish slut" for that evening, and then he has to do the laundry.

HAS TO DO THE LAUNDRY!!!

I fume and ignore the text for a bit. Then I decide to let him have it.

"So I'm below the laundry now?" I rail into the phone.

"What?" he giggles, nervously.

"That is the *lamest* excuse I've ever heard! Don't pursue me so much and let me meet other people—"

He tries to interrupt but I cut him off.

"*Don't* pursue me so much and let me meet other people! Goodbye!" Then I hang up. I wished I had an old-fashioned landline so I could have slammed the receiver in his ear.

About an hour passes before it begins to sink in that what had galled me so much wasn't being lower than the laundry, but the shift in power. There were plenty of times when James had asked me to come to his place and, for various reasons, I hadn't. Either I was too tired or I was too lazy to leave Brooklyn or I was busy at work or I just didn't feel like it. That was because James was running second—to Rahil or Adi or even my own general disinterest, which was heightened by my confidence in his interest.

Now he was in first place. Adi didn't quite sock me in the gut the way I'd expected. And after hearing how James had spent all night kissing some other girl, I wasn't feeling too confident in his interest these days either. So while the laundry comment was uncouth, it wasn't any more insensitive than other things James had said or done. But my reaction was different.

When you start to have real feelings for someone and he tells you the laundry takes priority, the results won't be pretty.

Then I do what I usually do when I'm feeling low, when the world seems so brutal and cold that I don't know how I'll survive it—I call Aaron. The very person who'd flung me out there to begin with.

I invite him over. We order in Thai food and I tell him what had happened with James. Aaron suggests that, considering how complex our relationship had been from day one and how I myself was dating other men, I might owe James an apology. Laundry did, indeed, have to get done occasionally.

Also, maybe it was time to tell James how my feelings had morphed. Then at least I'd know if laundry was just laundry, or laundry was a big "screw you."

So I draft three email apologies. The first one lays it on the line: That I had thought about him far too much while I was with Adi, and that I had allowed myself to get attached to him even though I knew this to be the dumbest idea ever, therefore my reaction was blown all out of proportion. A couple hours later, I draft a second email. This time I say I hadn't felt the spark with Adi that I had in the past and I attribute that to spending so much time with him, and it's a dangerous situation and maybe we should cut back on seeing so much of each other.

The third merely apologizes, says I'm going through some "stuff" and I took it out on him, and if he doesn't want to speak to me for a while, I would understand. That's the one I send.

The solution is the same: I needed fresh meat. James had moved to the front burner, not only because of his relentless forward momentum in that direction, but because no one else was really in the picture. He'd gone on at least ten dates in the past few weeks—hell, he'd gone on two over the weekend alone—and I'd gone on only two since I'd met him. He could afford to treat me cavalierly.

His response comes quickly: "That's okay. By the way, it wasn't just the laundry. I actually just felt like being alone tonight (besides meeting with the Polish slut), and getting ready for the week ahead. The date with the Polish slut was a bad joke. She basically embodied every negative aspect of Eastern European girls that I grew to despise when I lived in Europe. You would've laughed. Wish you a good night. If you feel lonely and need to scream at somebody, feel free to give me a call."

Good old James. We kept looking for other people and, for some reason, kept finding each other.

chapter forty-eight

After getting rejected by James for his laundry, I'd emailed about a dozen guys on Match.com. A couple of the better-looking ones viewed my profile and didn't get back to me—a real ego bruiser. But to my surprise, I got three responses, one from a calendar-worthy fireman; another from a cute Indian guy; and the third from a decent looking forty-three-year-old whose profile was sharp, who said he was looking for someone "witty," and who told me I was "adorable."

I, of course, keep James informed of all of this.

The next night, I meet the third responder from Match.com, a man named Carl, at the Olives bar in the W Hotel. As soon as he makes his way to my table, I practically sigh audibly with relief. He's deadly cute, with pouty lips, a full head of hair, and zero percent body fat—all at forty-three.

Conversation is easy, but as he rattles on about cooking, I again have the unsettling feeling that this is more of a friendly connection than a romantic one. So I'm relieved that when we exit the restaurant and stand awkwardly on the sidewalk, mentally debating whether the evening is over, he dives in for a kiss. I'm doubly relieved that his technique is passable.

When he begins wending me through Washington Square Park, I know exactly what he's doing. Working me in the direction of his apartment, which he'd told me earlier was in Greenwich Village. I call him on it and we sit down on a bench. As he delineates the various techniques men use to get women in the sack, my interest piques a bit. It's better than listening to his ideas for cooking shows.

I agree to go to his apartment. I'm curious to see what will happen and, frankly, I have to use the bathroom.

We sit on his couch and begin kissing. Clothes come off—and he begins going down on me. But I'm either too drunk or too disinterested to get any pleasure out of it. I ask him if we can move to his bed, but for some reason he wants to stay on the couch. Maybe he reserves the bed for special occasions or something. I go down on him with the same technique that had quickly gotten results with other men, but with him it just goes on and on and on. Perhaps this was the downside of dating a guy in his forties—sore jaw muscles. I finally give up and ask if I can smoke. He leads me into his "smoking room"—a small den—and launches into a story about wanting to start a winery on Long Island. I figure I'd better leave before I fall asleep.

Outside, I proceed to drunk-dial James.

"I need to get laid tomorrow," I slur into the phone. "Either you're going to do it or someone else will."

Classy.

I felt completely empty. I was no longer even luxuriating in the happy shame that came with being a slut for the first time in my life. When I emerged from the relationship with Aaron, I'd been sexless for so long that I was like a virgin. Everything was shiny and new. Now it was old and beat-up.

Nor is there any challenge involved trying to get a guy in the sack. Men, at least, had that—they never knew if a girl would go there, and if she did, at what point she might suddenly put a halt to the proceedings. With men, you just kind of waited until they put the moves on you. If they didn't, you waited a little longer. If your patience wore thin, you made the moves yourself and there was no argument. No wonder women focused on the emotional aspects of a relationship. Trying to get a guy to say "I love you" is a heck of a lot more of a challenge than trying to get one to fuck you.

But a part of me knew I was just fooling myself. The problem was plain and simple: I'd fallen for James.

chapter forty-nine

The next day, I make sure to tell James about my date with Carl. He retaliates by telling me about the "wholesome" girl he'd spent the night kissing, who had since emailed him that she was hesitant to see him again because things had happened so fast between them and she'd never experienced that before.

"Oh please!" I shoot back. "That's the old 'I'm really a good girl and I've never done anything like that before' ploy. It's all designed to keep you from getting turned off in case you thought she was loose. And she's trying to flatter you. 'Gee, I've never met someone who makes me throw all my morals to the wind like that!' What *bullshit*. Write back and say, 'Fine, we don't have to see each other.' She'll change her tune."

"I think she's quite serious," he responds. "If I was a betting man I'd say I'd never hear from her again."

One could only hope. But I had to hand it to her, she was playing her cards well. What man didn't salivate at the idea of a "good girl" losing self-control because the overwhelming virility of her date caused her to engage in "uncharacteristically" slutty behavior?

But I also figured she was the type who, if anything of a physical nature did happen again, was going to start pricing diamonds. I couldn't wait until she started pressuring James for a commitment. His frantic feet would accelerate so fast he'd leave a smoking trail behind. *Meep meep!*

Carl writes asking me out again and I accept his offer.

Adi never gets in touch. I'm glad whatever it was I'd felt for him had seemingly evaporated or I would've been crushed.

My birthday was in two days. I'd be thirty-seven. Thirty-seven years old and crazy about a cold, snobbish, bitterly sarcastic thirty-one-year-old banker who was sleeping with every foreign chick within ten zip codes. Oh, and who thought I was thirty-five.

Fabulous.

chapter fifty

Julie, Jake, Aaron and I gather at a local restaurant to celebrate my birthday. Over seared tuna, I launch into a story about how that afternoon, a clipboard-wielding fund-raiser had waylaid me as I was walking to my office and implored, "Can you spare a moment for gay rights?" I had turned on him and barked, "My boyfriend turned gay, so I think I've done my part!"

The table, Aaron included, cracks up.

Later, we head to Loki (no Rahil this time). Once Julie and Jake leave, I suggest to Aaron that we go to his gay bar.

"Are you sure?" he asks.

"Yes, why not?"

I don't know why I'm perversely drawn to accompanying Aaron to gay bars. Maybe I want to take away their power—their dark secrets.

By the time midnight rolls around and it's officially my thirty-seventh birthday, the man next to me—an old queen with a stereotypical high lisping voice—is insisting on buying me a birthday shot.

"I can't believe I'm sitting in a gay bar with my fiancé on my birthday," I sigh.

"Can we go on record saying this was your idea? Can we please go on record?" Aaron pleads.

Aaron sleeps over, and in the morning I apologize for the repeated ribbing about his homosexuality that I had given him over the course of the evening. He tells me how he'd asked the gang at Last Exit to stop making gay jokes. Being so confused, he is sensitive about it.

"It's just that we don't know what to say," I explain. "It's like there's this big elephant in the room, and we joke about it in order to deal with it." I refrain from calling it a "pink elephant."

I promise him I will stop making jokes, even though I think I have every right to do so, as his sexual switcheroo affected my life as much as his own.

Then James begins texting me. I tell Aaron, who is sitting on the couch drinking coffee, how James is the opposite of most men: he was all action, no talk. He'd email, he'd text, and he'd always want to see me. But he simply wouldn't give me any clue into his thoughts or feelings.

A few hours later James writes: "Women in this city are even more manipulative than the men!"

"Maybe it's the women you are choosing to spend your time with," I respond.

"Well, I need a new strategy, because I am getting morally exhausted."

I have no idea what he's referring to. He'd told me earlier he was sitting in a plaza outside, reading. He must have just had some kind of encounter with a female, one he'd tried to pick up or vice versa.

"Maybe you need to stop strategizing and allow yourself to feel something real once in a while," I suggest.

Affection couldn't be gotten by strategy. And conversely, and most horribly, it could take root when and where you least wanted it to.

Overcome with the urge to suffer, I dial James.

"So why are women manipulative?"

"I ran into that faux Frenchy the other night and we decided to go to a concert."

Going to a concert on a Saturday night was, of course, something he had never invited me to do.

"She acts all interested but then I never hear from her," he says.

"Some people are just flaky," I reply, my heart doing a little flop of sadness.

"I've just had to adjust my expectations."

"Yeah, I've had to adjust mine too," I retort, pointedly.

Damn this. James had been perfect for so long precisely because I hadn't been able to dredge up much emotion for him. But, as had happened with Rahil, I began to get attached. This must be some biological thing, designed to keep women from trading in the fathers of their children every few months.

After a long pause, James ventures, "Maybe you want to come over and watch a movie."

"I would, but I might go out with Carl tonight for a drink. I'm waiting to hear from him once he gets back from Long Island."

Maybe I should have hopped on James's offer, but I'd been doing too much hopping for James.

We hang up and I stew over the faux French girl. Goddamn. It hurts when someone you really like likes someone else more—someone who doesn't even seem to be around very much.

The lyrics to a Fiona Apple song drift into my mind:

It's dangerous work
trying to get to you too
And I think if I didn't
have to kill, kill, kill, kill,
myself doing it
Maybe I wouldn't
think so much of you

chapter fifty-one

If you'd told me six months ago that I'd be lying in bed with Aaron, the love of my life for ten years, and yet couldn't stop thinking of another man, one who never gave a damn about me, I would've told you that would make a very ridiculous book.

Aaron and I had spent Friday and Saturday nights together, and then went to Last Exit for the usual Sunday evening get-together of the regulars. After that, we'd moved on to Loki, where I had to pick up my birthday present from Julie (a travel book for India) that I'd left there by mistake.

I'm not sure at what point in the evening I glanced over at Aaron and, through an alcohol-induced haze, began directing my sexual restlessness toward him. It had been two weeks since I'd been with James. I did remember that Aaron had a nice big dick, and he was looking pretty good these days—he'd lost some weight and his facial hair was finally

237

shaped into something less resembling the 'stache of a Studio 54 bartender, circa 1977.

In the cab on the way home, Aaron turns and uses his pet name for me, "Mrs. P——." Hearing him call me that inflates such a tumultuous balloon of emotions in my chest that I burst into tears, which makes Aaron feel terrible. We head to our local dive bar for a last beer to calm down. Then it's back to my place.

"I don't know if I should say this—" Aaron begins.

"I know what you're going to say," I interrupt.

You weren't with someone for ten years without knowing a little bit about what is going through his mind—even if you didn't know everything you should.

"Tell me," he says.

"You're thinking about sleeping together."

"I was going to say it always bugged me when you clipped your toenails on the dinner table"—for this, in fact, is what I was currently doing—"but yes, I'm thinking about that, too."

"I don't think we should," I sigh, putting aside the clippers. "I wouldn't want to ruin what we have going on."

But I begin thinking how I will see James at French Tuesdays in a couple of days and will probably drunkenly throw myself at him unless I get laid, and laid soon.

So I get on top of Aaron and begin kissing him. Our kissing technique had always gelled perfectly, but I wasn't feeling anything extraordinary. It's rather what I'd felt recently with Carl, a painless way to spend some time, but not much else. Aaron, on the other hand, is doing a lot of sighing, and seems really into it.

"Was that a test?" he asks, when I pull away from him.

I feel his cock and it's hard. Guess he passed.

"If we can't fuck each other when we're drunk and horny, who can we fuck?" I ask.

We relocate to the bedroom. I begin going down on him, but he says, "I want your pussy," with more enthusiasm than I ever remembered. But within moments, he loses erection and blames it on the alcohol.

"Are you sure it's the alcohol? Does this happen with men?"

"Yes."

"You don't have to lie."

"It definitely does."

But we fool around anyway, and then head out to the living room to smoke a cigarette. He tells me how he has a "cigarette fetish," and that there are even videos dedicated to this fetish, which involves sexual activity combined with smoking. Not the usual smoking after sex—but *during.*

"Sounds kind of dangerous," I say. "Don't burn the house down."

We go to bed and I don't feel any distance or discomfort emanating from him. On the contrary, he seems quite content to be in our old bed with the cats poured around us.

But my mind only reels with thoughts of James and how, perhaps, all this time, through all these months of constant emails and text messages and get-togethers, all at his insistent initiation, that perhaps he'd been consumed with an on-off affair with faux Frenchy.

It was so disheartening when you finally moved someone to the top burner just as you got shunted to the back. Only in movies did it seem that everyone's hearts aligned perfectly just before the credits rolled.

I knew, too, the potential danger of the situation with Aaron. Unlike James and Rahil, Aaron is a man whom I could, and did for a very long time, respect and love. And since Aaron was still attracted to men, this could end up being a big pain in the ass, no pun intended.

I also knew I couldn't tell any of my friends what had happened with Aaron. They would never understand it was born out of loneliness, affection, deep love, sexual frustration, and, of course, booze.

After Aaron leaves for work, I email him: "Thank you for the pleasant head last night. And yes, this is a girl writing you."

After another day of torturous emails with James—we exchange flirty messages that other people had sent us—I begin to think he's doing me a favor. I barely notice the few emails I get from Aaron and Carl, nor do I really care that Adi had nosedived off the face of the planet again. James was keeping me from getting too worked up over the other men in my life.

But I vowed not see James until I was more certain of his feelings, or less certain of my own.

chapter
fifty-two

James's emails suddenly pick up their flirtatious banter, and after yet another one of his dates that apparently had gone nowhere, he begins texting demands for sex.

My vow not to see him crumbles in the face of extreme horniness, and I agree to meet him late Saturday night, after a friend's wedding reception. The time I spend with him is clarifying—he's the same old James, highly sexed and desirous of me—but no Rahil. He gets his pleasure and assumes that's enough for me, or maybe he doesn't care enough to assume one way or the other. In the morning, he is consumed with his French music, his French movie, and reading aloud to me passages from a Marcel Proust novel, none of which occurs to him might be boring me to tears.

I also feel self-consciously old with him. He isn't that much younger than I am, but I know he is accustomed to being with women who hadn't yet developed crow's feet. I catch myself looking away from him in the harsh morning light, and being reluctant to smile, so that he won't see the lines around my eyes, which seem to be deepening by the day. The irony is, the stress of my time with James was probably a main contributor to my wrinkles.

I go on my second date with Carl and am relieved to be with someone older than I am—though he certainly doesn't look it. "Where's your portrait, Dorian Gray?" I tease.

We have dinner at a sushi place conveniently located near his apartment. Conversation flows, we laugh a lot. He's full of stories about his female friends and the many ways in which they'd "screwed up their chances" of getting married by picking the wrong guys.

"Don't chase younger men!" he warns me. "All the women I know who went for older men are married; and all the ones who went for younger men aren't."

"I guess it depends what you are looking for," I mumble. All the men I'd dated so far (barring Carl) were younger than I was, and of course none of them went anywhere.

After dinner and a couple of drinks at a nearby bar, Carl talks me up to his place with a casual, "Want to go to my apartment?" No begging and cajoling for him.

We sit on his couch, drink wine, and listen to music. He likes the same kind of music I do (he even puts Kate Bush on the iPod) and we have similar taste in movies. We discuss the merits of Woody Allen's films—something I couldn't have done with James, who considered anything executed in the English language to be barbaric. The only thing that troubled me was that, while we were at the bar, he'd referred to himself as the "man with no feelings," something his friends apparently call him.

"What does that mean?" I'd demanded.

I'd pretty much had it with men with no feelings.

"Just that I don't have any baggage. I'm not in mourning about some past relationship."

I wasn't sure I bought the explanation, but I'd let it go for now.

We kiss and caress on his couch but I won't let his hands inside my underwear, as I'd pledged not to be such a slut this time. For what purpose, I didn't know.

Around one in the morning, I leave Carl's apartment feeling fairly buoyant. I'm relieved when in the morning he, rather than James, takes up most of my thought space.

But as James and I start our usual all-day email exchange, I once again get a heavy feeling settling in my chest. I tell him I'm confused and irritated that he doesn't want to see me anymore except for the occasional booty call, and he, of course, makes no effort to clarify anything. That makes me cry, which I hate doing, because a crying jag at thirty-seven never quite leaves your face.

Don't chase younger men.

When I get home, I text Adi, the youngest of them all, inviting him to a party that Friday night. "I would like to keep this friends idea alive," I write.

I'd ignored Adi for two weeks. Therefore, I'm convinced that he'll get back to me right away. So convinced that I put the cell phone next to me on the couch and one eye it. Sure enough, within two minutes, he texts back that he would love to go to a party Friday night.

Men are psychotic.

I email James about Adi. At this point, I didn't think he got jealous over me and other men anymore; I just needed to commiserate with someone about the vagaries of singlehood.

He emails back that he'd been out the night before with a Ukrainian chick. I think he must be dating every immigrant in Manhattan.

Don't chase younger men. The caveat goes double for younger men with a penchant for young foreign girls.

chapter
fifty-three

Day 195 I go on my first date with a gay man—if you don't count all those years I'd lived with one.

Vijay, a twenty-five-year-old Indian man I'd briefly met while at the *TV Guide* Emmy party in Los Angeles, had called me to say that he was coming to New York over the weekend and asked if I would like to meet up. I'd suggested we get drinks at Olives, the W Hotel bar in Union Square. I couldn't remember much about him, other than while at the Emmy party, he'd grabbed my hand, led me over to the bar, and continued holding my hand the entire time he spoke to me. I'd liked his aggressive approach, but by then I'd been pretty drunk, so the memory of his looks and demeanor were a bit fuzzy.

So when he shows up at the bar wearing a red knit sweater and tells me, in a rather dainty voice, how he wants to become a fashion stylist and how he loves Paris Hilton and, how he, in fact, is wearing Paris for

Men cologne, I can do nothing but picture his imminent coming out party.

I'm getting a little weary of all the gay men stuck in heterosexual bodies. There's James with his opera and nail polish, Carl with his Kate Bush, Aaron with his cock sucking.

But Vijay is fun to talk to and shows me pictures on his digital camera that he'd snapped of himself with various celebrities around Hollywood. And I'm somewhat flattered that he seems so enamored of me, considering that he tells me he can't find a girl who lives up to his "high" standards, that is, one who looks like Paris Hilton or Eva Longoria (he volunteers that he owns a shirt emblazoned with "Mr. Longoria"). But the sexual attraction on my end is zilch—even after he lunges at me for a tongue-probing kiss, which I oblige. The whole time, I fixate on his overbite, which makes kissing him somewhat like tonguing an elderly man with a jutting set of false teeth.

I manage to escape and head downtown to The Delancey for the birthday party of someone I don't know. Julie had invited me, and it's the party I'd invited Adi to, who had emailed me the day before that he was definitely coming and looked forward to seeing me.

By the time midnight rolls around and Adi still hasn't shown, I send him a text message: "Hmm. . . . is Adi coming?"

He responds that he's at another party but will leave there shortly. Then, over an hour later, he texts back asking me if the party I'm at is *good*.

Maybe it's the booze. Maybe it was the date with the gay Indian. Maybe it was my earlier email exchange with James, where I'd once again admitted that I'd developed feelings for him, only to get a message back divulging his plan to meet up with not one, but two girls that evening. Maybe it was the fact that I was in the midst of another one of Adi's disappearing acts. Whatever the reason, his question bugged the fuck out of me. If my presence didn't make the party good enough to warrant attendance, then screw him.

"Don't bother coming," I text back.

He responds that he didn't mean to upset me, but that he thought it was an open, casual invitation.

This from the man who, the day before, had said he was definitely coming. I just wanted him to be a man and say, "Hey, I don't think I can make it. Sorry." Fuck the whole "friendship" thing. I didn't want a friend who didn't want to see me. I already had one in James.

"Lateness I don't mind, but you're just being your usual flaky self," I shoot back. "Please lose my number."

Don't chase younger men.

I engage in a little contest with another woman, where we compare sexual text messages we'd received. I flash her at least half-a-dozen texts from James along the lines of "Will Madame be sampling the great northern nine-incher this evening?"

"You win, hands down," she laughs.

Good old James.

Upstairs, I start flirting with a couple of guys. I think the bald one is cute, but Julie cock-blocks me and starts up an intense conversation with him, ignoring Jake, who sits near her silently fuming.

"Are you single?" I ask the bald guy's friend.

"Yes. Just broke up with my girlfriend on Tuesday."

"How long had you been dating?"

"Six months."

"What happened?"

"I didn't feel there was a sexual spark any longer."

"You broke up with her for *that*? Did she feel the same?"

"No. I broke her heart."

Is he smirking?

"You sound like a total asshole," I scold. "You should call her right now and apologize. I bet you pursued and pursued her until she finally felt something for your sorry ass, and then you dumped her, right?"

Not completely surprisingly, Dylan (this is his name) seems to find my bitchiness attractive.

"You are so hot," he breathes. "Give me your phone number."

Julie, Jake, and their friends take off, leaving me alone with the jerk.

"You're going to come to my apartment," he commands.

"No, I'm not. I've got enough booty calls. If I want to get laid, there are five men I could call." Not necessarily true, but whatever.

He begins kissing me. "I like this game we're playing."

Sick bastard. Naturally, I find this a turn-on.

"Give me your number," he says, whipping out his BlackBerry.

"No. I'm not attracted to you."

"I'm not attracted to you either. You're too skinny."

"Why, you like fat girls? I bet your girlfriend was a heifer, that's why you dumped her."

"I like girls with a little meat on their bones."

"Yeah. Fat."

"You're such a bitch."

We kiss some more. He isn't bad. At least he doesn't have an overbite, nor does he seem gay in the slightest.

I give him my number. Then we go downstairs and dance. Soon he drags me out of the bar and pushes me into a cab.

"Where are we going?"

"To the subway."

But he gives the driver an address uptown. Before the cab can start moving, I open the door, leap out, and dart into another cab.

"Hope you got home safely, sweet thing," he texts at 4 A.M.

"Who is this?" I reply, knowing exactly who it is.

"One of the population of men who would like to fuck you."

"Oh, you. The bastard."

"You are so hot." A minute goes by, then another text: "Bitch."

Ah, yes, just what I needed. Another man who likes bitches and can't commit.

That's when my rage at the male of the species prompts me to do something I'm not proud of. I'd always regretted that I hadn't gotten in a good parting shot at Rahil. That I'd allowed him to fuck me dozens of times and then disappear without so much as a "Thanks for the type of blowjobs my girlfriend could never give me." That I'd never let him know what an asshole he was.

I'd let Adi know.

I send him a text: "Oral skills good; cock ridiculously small. Might not want to play hard to get in the future."

What the hell. I'd already burned the bridge. Might as well burn down the neighborhood.

There were a million nasty things he could've chosen to text back, but he doesn't. He'd probably just dismissed me as psychotic.

I suspect he is right.

In the morning, I don't feel good about what I'd done. But a part of me is a little giddy. I hadn't let this one slink away unnoticed. I'd given Adi the textual equivalent of a drink in the face, with a penis insult thrown in.

James leaves me a message that he's working on burning a CD of classical music to give to me.

A few weeks earlier, I would've read too much into this. In all likelihood, he'd fucked two different women last night, but he's working on a CD for me? He doesn't want them! He woke up thinking of me!

But by now I knew better. When I ignore him, he texts a few hours later, "Don't even respond, ungrateful bitch ;)"

He noticed I didn't respond! It bothered him! He must like me!

Nope. Didn't do any of that either. James did like me—and half the female population of Manhattan. Mentally, he was where I was in the weeks immediately following the breakup: horny, out for sex, excited at the prospect of meaningless encounters. Only he was there permanently.

I call Aaron.

"I never used to go for the bad boys," I tell him. "I never understood girls who did. I'd grown up with enough emotional pain, why court more? But I went for the good guy—the one who should have worked out—and look what happened. This is all your fault."

"I know," he says.

I think of my sister, who had brought up my niece "naturally:" breast-fed her until she could walk, served her only organic food, treated her colds with homeopathic remedies. Still my niece got cancer and died.

Sometimes you can do everything right and it still ends up all wrong.

chapter fifty-four

Thank God, I was free at last!

That's what I felt like shouting to the rooftops as I left Carl's apartment at midnight. It took three dates with him, but I finally felt *something*, some kind of passion.

And I might have had James to thank for it.

I'd planned to meet Carl at 8 P.M. at The Delancey, where I'd forgotten my credit card and driver's license during my drunken Friday night haze.

Around 5 P.M., James had texted: "What are you doing?"

I couldn't imagine why he was asking. I knew he had a date with a Brazilian slut that evening. And he hadn't asked me to do anything in ages.

"Why?"

"Somebody is still pissy," he'd replied.

"Why is that pissy? I am meeting up with Carl tonight."

When I got no answer, I called him just to tell him I wasn't pissy. After hanging up, we have an almost two hour exchange of mocking text messages. After he tells me the Mexican girl he'd had two dates with had masturbated in front of him, I reply: "Of course she masturbated. That's the only way she's going to get off, poor girl."

"At least finish your drink before you give him head," James returns, referring to Carl.

"It's smart of you to date a Mexican laborer," I shoot back. "This way, she'll do all the work in bed and won't ask for a little reciprocation like we pesky Americans!"

Something about the textual sparring got my juices flowing. Then Carl showed up at The Delancey looking gorgeous.

After a couple of drinks, we headed back to his place. I was so happy just to be feeling the type of passion that came close to what I'd felt with Rahil and James, and this time with a guy who didn't appear to be a complete man whore. (Though, Lord knows, I'd been wrong on that count before.)

After sex, we lay on the couch talking.

"My last two girlfriends were Asian," he says, apropos of nothing.

"What is it with the Asian girls? Every guy I've dated either is dating or was dating one. Funny, this guy I was seeing was getting stalked by an Asian girl. She would send him emails at two a.m. and—"

"*Was* seeing?"

"Oh, we're not seeing each other anymore. Maybe we never were, who knows."

"When did you stop seeing him?"

"Last week? Week before? I really don't know. But Carl, please, get it out of your mind, because I'll never sleep with him again."

"Why not?"

"He's one of those guys who has to nail everything that moves. You know the type. He's grossed me out, really. Besides, he's a bore."

The bore and I email all the next day. I tell him he's a "sad Benny Hill figure, forever running around, lifting up girls' skirts, hoping it will somehow make you younger, stronger, more of a man." He snipes that he doesn't feel like there's any spark between us unless we're riling each other up or talking about sex.

"I tried to show some interest in the things you like," I email. "But if a girl doesn't come 'pre-packaged' with every single quality you want, then she's not good enough for you. You are going to have a long search ahead of you, good luck with it."

"How I love to feel the warm glow of Kiri's directed rage," he responds.

But I'm sure he doesn't like this attraction any more than I do. I wasn't the twenty-two-year-old European polyglot and classical music aficionado he'd always imagined himself ending up with and no doubt it baffled him why he couldn't go even one day without contacting me.

The next night, James and I attend French Tuesdays together, and then I end up back at his place for the first time in weeks. He starts off kissing me in a way that can only be described as tender, and dare I say it, loving. But as we loll on the bed, I hear the bling of a text message come into his phone, and curious as to which slut would be getting in touch at 1 A.M., I run and grab the cell, which he manages to wrestle out of my death grip.

He throws me back on the bed, then pins me down, peppering my face with tiny, soft kisses.

"You don't mean it," I say, weakly trying to slap him away. "You're a whore."

I was becoming intensely ashamed of letting a person who would mind-fuck with me in this manner continue to have some kind of strange hold over me. I normally wasn't susceptible to assholes, just closet cases. Had I allowed this to happen so that when James betrayed me I could shrug and say, well, what did you expect? Whereas when someone like Aaron did it, the foundation of my soul was rocked? Perhaps James, with his myriad little pedestrian and predictable hurts, was nothing more than an unorthodox way of insulating myself from real heartbreak.

Only it wasn't quite working.

chapter fifty-five

C arl and I plan a date for that Saturday evening, and I clean my apartment in preparation. The date will be in Brooklyn (unlike James, Carl was more than willing to commute to see me), and I expected it might end up back in my bed.

At that moment, I felt like I could care for two different men, in two different ways.

Carl and I head to Joya, a Thai place, for dinner. There's something strange about a fourth date, when you've had three previous good ones. The expectation for fireworks and emotional intimacy are pretty high—maybe too high. But Carl had that worst of James/Aaron qualities: he kept his emotions under armed guard. I couldn't figure anything about him. At the restaurant, his tone is so sarcastic, his expression so stone-like, I begin to get it into my head that he doesn't like me after all. I look off into the distance and start to tear up a little because I'm just so tired of trying to painstakingly pull, bit by bit, wrist over wrist, a thought or feeling out of an emotionally stopped-up man.

But when I tell him what's bothering me, that I think maybe he doesn't like me, he appears genuinely flabbergasted.

"I need to work on this then, because that's 180 degrees away from how I'm feeling," he says. He admits that his former girlfriends had accused him of the same thing. They never knew what was going on in his head or heart. What did this society do to our men that they had such a hard time expressing anything, even making it impossible to say, "I'm very attracted to you," when clearly they were? Then again, Rahil and Adi had been full of effusions, and what had it really mattered? Neither one had stuck around very long.

We do end up back at my place. But after sex and sitting around talking and listening to music for a couple of hours, he casually says, "So how about that car service?"

Again, I'm simultaneously relieved and peeved. Peeved that he has no intention or desire to stay over, relieved he's leaving so I can be alone with my thoughts. The sensation was so frequent now I'd have to come up with a new word for it: Pelieved?

After he says goodbye, I feel like crying a little, because he hadn't shown me that tender side that James had occasionally deigned to bestow upon me. And I wonder what slut James is out with that night, and if he's thinking of me, and if he misses me like I miss him.

The next day, James texts me around 4 P.M. and says he'd "like another foot massage again soon." I take that to be some kind of veiled request to get together that evening. I'm game, and bring my overnight stuff with me to Last Exit, where the gang is gathering for one of the bartender's last shifts.

A couple hour later, I'm having phone trouble, and unsure if James can reach me by text. I leave him a voice message saying, "My text messages aren't working, so if you need to beg for sex, you'll have to call me."

It isn't until 11 P.M., as I'm exiting the subway and heading back home, after having given up on hearing back from James, that I receive a voice mail from him saying, "Looking for my foot massage."

I'm liquored up and the message whips me into a frothing wrath. I call and get his voice mail. "James, I called you at six, and you don't call me back until eleven, probably after you've tried every girl in the Manhattan phone book," I say. "I'm not your last minute booty call. Just when I think you respect me as a friend, you pull something like this. Listen to me carefully—do not email me anymore, and do not call me."

Perhaps that would be the last of James. Lord knows I'd said that before, but I certainly hoped this time it would stick. For how long could I be his bed warmer while he went about his search for someone he deemed worthy of serious status? To be fair, I had been using him for the same thing. But at least I didn't call him at 11 P.M. and expect him to haul ass to Brooklyn.

That was the thing about being single. You could get wined, dined, and fucked every which way on Friday and Saturday, but by Sunday, they had all fallen away, and you were again alone.

The next day, it begins to dawn on me that James's voice mail was probably a joke. He loved to press my buttons, and there's no way he could've seriously thought I was going to make the trek to his place that late.

For the first time in months, we'd gone all day without emailing. Then that evening, I write:

"I suppose it's possible that you were just joking last night. I got your message when I was exiting the subway, exhausted, inebriated, and couldn't hear your voice very well. Listening to it again today, it sounded so presumptuous and over the top, that I'm beginning to think it was just another 'button pressing' technique of yours—asking me to do something you know I wasn't going to do. If it was a joke, then I am sorry for my nasty overreaction. But perhaps it is just another indication that you and I will never really 'get' each other, and also that I'm just a little too emotionally fragile to have someone with your particular nature in my life on a regular basis."

He emails back that he's glad I figured out that he was joking. He doesn't apologize.

"This whole rela. is exhausting to me," I type, not even having the energy to write the words out fully. "I def. need a break from it. Maybe we can catch up later, when I'm not so crazy, and you're not so insane."

I'm beaten down from the emotional wear and tear of liking someone, knowing I shouldn't like him, not knowing if he liked me, feeling that he did, but not knowing if he would tomorrow.

James had ceased being the man who was taking my mind off my problems, and had become them.

chapter fifty-six

I finally had what I had supposedly wanted all along—a man who would ask me out on Tuesday for a Friday night. It was Carl. I presumed this meant the man liked me, inscrutable as he was. I didn't really feel it progressing anywhere; I didn't feel that flush of emotion with him like I had with Adi, but then again I'd gotten over that feeling by date number four. I hoped I had the brains to refrain from ruining it with Carl because he wasn't filling my head with a bunch of empty romantic talk. I knew his emotional stonewalling could be a big problem down the line. If he couldn't even tell me I looked pretty, how was he going to communicate if we ever hit more complex relationship topics? But I thought I should at least keep giving it a try. He was the only man who'd entered my life so far who seemed reliable and didn't have me on the booty call track.

Around midnight, I begin tossing and turning with that now-familiar missing-a-guy ache in the gut. I do a Google search on James and cry over some banking memo he'd authored. I'm aware that while I'd been seeing James, I'd mourned the loss of that idiot "Raheel," so I know I can get over this. It's just going to take longer. James had been around for five months, and we'd been in contact every single day for at least three of those. He'd wormed his way in much deeper than Rahil ever had.

I'd always half-wondered what might have happened if I hadn't dumped Rahil that Sunday afternoon, the day after he'd run out to see Hayden. Perhaps if I'd just stuck with the momentum—and outwaited his Hayden fixation—something might've come of it. And now I'd dumped James. Should I have kept the momentum going and outwaited his desire to see other women, none of whom had taken up much of his time or attention?

Or was I wisely preemptive dumping?

Since I couldn't see Carl on Friday (it was Sahana's bachelorette party), he and I make plans for Sunday evening. But I'm not excited about it. Carl's actions were of a man who genuinely liked me: he'd ask me out early in the week, he'd ask me to go on things like wine tours with him. But I got no electricity off him. When James looked at me, his eyes sparkled and he grinned from ear to ear. But he wouldn't ask me on a date. Which was better?

I find a perverse pleasure in my light-grade post-James breakup suffering. I enjoy going home, being alone, smoking a cigarette, thinking about how he never really wanted me, and getting a little misty eyed. I don't know what about it pleases me. Maybe it's because this type of adolescent mooning isn't the death-rattle of shock and aloneness that confronted me in Aaron's absence. It's more like the feeling you might have gotten in high school if you saw your crush kissing another girl. Maybe it reminds me of youth, of possibilities. I practically luxuriate in my sadness and the crisp self-awareness of knowing my heart is aching for someone who never really thought that much about me, other than that he liked having sex with me and found me amusing.

The reality of life with James would be a nightmare. He wasn't communicative, he could go cold without warning, and I'd suspect every moment he wasn't with me that he was hitting on some foreign exchange student. But the ideal of it was enticing enough that I had a hard time letting go of it. James fulfilled one of my deepest, darkest, longest-running fantasies—he bantered with me in a viciously sarcastic manner, kind of like those couples in the screwball comedies from the 1940s.

Despite my demand that James stop contacting me, we email all that afternoon. By the time I'm out with Sahana and her girlfriends for her bachelorette party, he's texting his usual, "Get ur ass over here." I don't go. I'm still so messed up about where I stand. My brain and body were saying *yes, why not, continue.* My heart was bleating, *give me a break, please.*

After the bachelorette party, Julie and I stumble our way into Loki (no Rahil). She begins giving me shit about the "cock ridiculously small" text I'd sent Adi.

"You probably destroyed him!"

"He must know it."

Julie tells me how she has "zippo" sex drive these days. But Jake had generously offered not to have sex with her for a year, which made her sex drive spike slightly.

How well I remembered the latter years of Aaron's and my sex life. We'd be lying on the couch, watching TV, and I'd know that we'd planned to have sex that night, but just couldn't bring myself to make a move. Neither could he. Sexual identity confusion or not, after a certain amount of years, sex somehow became a chore. It made me think about James and how, what the hell, I should just continue with him. It wouldn't be too long before I was a certain age and perhaps men wouldn't be so intent on having sex with me. I should take advantage of it while I still had it. But I knew the complicated emotions that would ensue, and I was just so tired of them.

By the time Sunday rolls around, I'm keen to cancel my date with Carl. He hadn't called me or texted me or done anything during the week (other than to firm up our plans by email) to let me know that he was thinking of me in any way, shape, or form. I dreaded that once we got together, his lack of emotiveness would tempt me to drunk-dial James again.

So I send Carl a text asking if we can postpone until next Friday. I hoped a fun Friday night out with some friends, rather than a sedate Sunday evening, might put to rest some of my reservations about him.

But I'm still not at the point where I can spend a Sunday evening alone—and apparently Aaron isn't either. He comes over and we make our old "couple meal," tuna pasta, and watch some ridiculous movie. I knew I couldn't live with a man who preferred men, but damn, I was beginning to think Aaron was the best man I was going to find in this lifetime.

chapter fifty-seven

Rahil married Hayden.

In one of my occasional exercises in self-torture, I'd visited Hayden's social networking page. Sometimes it had new photos or information, and I was able to glean little bits of what Rahil was doing with his life.

Getting married, apparently.

It was an Indian-style wedding, Lord knows where. There were only three photos. I might've thought it was just some fancy party, but one photo of Rahil looking at Hayden in red dupatta was labeled "Wedding."

My hands shook so violently I could barely type, but I somehow managed to tap out a congratulatory text message: "U r the last one I expected, but I'm happy for u!"

He never responds.

This from the man whose life goal it was to oversee a five-woman harem.

The pictures had been posted in late September, which meant they must have gotten married at least a week or so before that, and the ceremony looked fairly large, so there were probably weeks of prior planning involved. It had been mid-June that we'd last been together.

He must have left my bed and run straight to the nearest diamond retailer.

"Maybe she got preggers," one of my coworkers offers when I tell her the story.

It certainly cleared up why he'd vamoosed out of my life so suddenly. A part of me is relieved that the mystery was solved. I hadn't been dumped for some random chick he'd picked up in Loki, but for Hayden, his future wife, his true love.

The other part of me felt like crawling into a hole. I'd not only made a straight man gay but a nonmarrying man into a husband.

I email James about the situation and, uncharacteristically, he writes back that he's too busy to respond.

Aaron and I meet up for a drink at Boat, and he tells me he's considering going to a leather bar with his regular booty call, John Doe.

For ten years, I wasn't able to get Aaron to try anything even slightly risqué, yet here he is talking about going to a leather bar with his fifty (yes, *fifty*)-year-old bear. (Not to mention that he never even wore leather.)

"Sometimes he acts all romantic towards me, other times he tells me he's a confirmed bachelor," Aaron laments into his beer.

All romantic. A man. A big hairy leather man. Towards my fiancé.

I get home and call James. I really felt like he'd let me down, not responding to my email about Rahil. James was another story—I'd finally caved in and met him at his apartment the night before, giving everything and receiving nothing in return but his smile, the sparkle in his hazel eyes, and the exquisite uncertainty of trying to read his body language. For some reason, I'd decided to give myself over to the apparent pleasure I was getting out of this unbalanced arrangement.

With James, I'd have no expectations and just go along for the ride. At some point, there'd be a crash, and I'd end up bruised, possibly bloodied, but it would be nothing fatal, I was certain. I wouldn't try to alter its course. I'd tried too many times before and failed. Officially, however, we were still just "friends."

But my "friend" hadn't given me any feedback on the Rahil thing, nor tried to comfort me. So I called him.

"Why are you so upset about it?" he asks, somewhat peevishly.

"I'm not upset," I lie. "I'm shocked. Imagine if I stopped seeing you out of the blue, and a month later you found out I was married to an ex."

"Then I would say I didn't know you very well."

"That's the question, James. At what point do you ever know anyone?"

"Think of all the good you're doing," he drawls, "making guys want to get married."

guess I'd known deep down Rahil would end up going back to Hayden, just as I knew James would ditch me as soon as he found some young European girl who met all his intellectual and artistic criteria. The one thing I hadn't known deep down was that Aaron was gay.

James sounded like he wasn't seeing anyone these days—or at least, all the girls he'd recently dated had fallen by the wayside, including the masturbating Mexican, whom he said he was "trying to bump into the friendship category."

"James has this idea of what he wants on paper," I'd told Aaron at Boat. "I'm sure an American girl in her late thirties who writes about celebrities and likes to talk openly about the mechanics of sex was never in his game plan."

Just to make the day rabbit hole upside down from start to finish, Aaron told me he was jealous of James. I didn't really know what to do with this futile bit of information or even how it could possibly be true. I very quickly filed it away in the drawer of my brain that stores interesting but useless snippets of trivia about celebrities, old movies, and gay boyfriends.

Rahil. Married.

At the time I'd known him, the relationship between him and Hayden had seemed anything but solid. She'd just moved out of his place, and he was not only fucking me but hitting on everything that moved. He was also vehemently declaring his stance against matrimony, monogamy, children, a regular job, anything, really, that smacked of commitment.

If a guy like that, within the space of a few months, decided to switch gears and become a committed adult, maybe there was hope for us all.

chapter
fifty-eight

O n Friday night, I meet up with Carl, and I was glad I hadn't cancelled again. He looked so gorgeous, his lips so lushly pouty, that I couldn't help spontaneously kissing him a few times on the street. We go to his apartment after dinner and finally have some real fun—just the two of us.

We get really drunk, and Carl, it turns out, has some wonderful fingers when he puts his mind to using them, all with "blaxploitation" music in the background (Sly and the Family Stone, Rick James, Isaac Hayes), which made me feel like I was in a porno flick. Unfortunately, he had to interrupt the proceedings when he got light-headed and ran to the kitchen to drink juice. No, it wasn't our passion that overcame him. Carl, I learned, was diabetic.

During the date, James texted to ask if I was doing anything "interesting."

"I'm out," I tapped back.

"Slut," he responded.

I shut off my phone.

In the morning, Carl officiously goes about making cappuccino and omelets. He doesn't have that gleam in his eye and bounce in his step that James would've had the morning after, but I was getting accustomed to his insularity. The fact that he revealed a vulnerability—his diabetes, and how he had to insert a needle into his stomach three times a day— endeared him to me.

The next night, as I'm getting ready to leave the shelter, James texts and, to my surprise, wants to go out (it's a Saturday night, after all, usually reserved for one of his sluts). I'm wearing my shelter clothes—ratty jeans and sneakers—and my insecurity with James is such that I can't risk walking around looking like a frump when pretty girls in cute outfits might be catching his eye, so I find myself in the humiliating position of scrambling around trying to buy fashionable boots and a miniskirt at 8 P.M., just as all the stores are closing.

We go to an opera bar. Typical James, but it's fine with me. I always got to experience the type of thing with him that I never would with my friends, who stick to the local pub scene. In the cab on the way home, he receives a couple of text messages from girls, and allows me to read them. They ask what he's doing, which apparently is the universal booty call signal. James ignores them and tells me the Mexican chick (one of the texters) wants a relationship with him.

"And how do you know this?" I ask.

"I can tell."

I'm sure she has no idea what she's dealing with.

He also described a sentimental email he'd received from a French girl he'd dumped two years ago, and with whom he'd had an open arrangement. However, from what he'd told me about her stormy crying scenes, the arrangement sounded more to his liking than hers.

"What's the magical ingredient all these girls are lacking that makes you not want to have any of them as your girlfriend?" I ask.

"They're not very interesting."

He's sweet and attentive to me all night, except for at one point when I ask him, "But you care about me, right?"

"What do you mean 'care'?" His lip curls.

"As a friend," I clarify.

"Yes."

It's a sudden cutting reminder that, with James, the "caring" only goes so far.

Luckily, right now I was in a good position. I was fairly passionate about both James and Carl, and they seemed to offset each other so that I didn't get overly eager about either one.

On Monday night, James asks me to come over. Of course, he'd waited until I was back in Brooklyn.

"Why don't you ask me these things before I leave Manhattan?"

"Because that would be a commitment."

"It's not a commitment, James, it's common courtesy."

The thing about Aaron was that he'd always been trainable. I'd get mad at him about something, and if I got mad enough, he'd stop doing it. James, so far, had proven as trainable as a retarded puppy.

The next day, James doesn't return a couple of my emails, nor a phone call to his office, which sends me running to the nearest bar to gulp a glass of wine like a true obsessive. But soon we touch base, and I end up at his apartment.

There, after five minutes of half-drunken blubbering on my part about my cherishing our so-called "friendship," he attempts to shove his cock into my mouth.

"No!" I holler, trying to push him away. "Why can't we just be friends like you and the Mexican? Why do we always have to have sex?"

"We can have both," he says.

In what world were you friends and lovers and not one iota more than what we were? In James's world.

We watch a bad French movie and get into bed. He then proceeds to bury his nose in a volume of Proust. I force myself to view this as him allowing me to see his "true" self, other than what my paranoid mind is edging me to believe, which is that he's ignoring me.

Sometime in the very early morning, I feel him tightly curling his hand around mine. When I attempt to pry my fingers from his so I can go to the kitchen to get water, he grunts his disapproval and clings tighter.

It's moments like these that kept me coming back, I suppose.

Alone in the apartment after James leaves for work, I take a good whiff of his pile of shirts in the closet. I remember having done the same thing early in my relationship with Aaron.

That night I have a dinner date with a guy from Match.com. At first, I think it will be a verrrry long evening. He is decent-looking, with deep-set eyes that remind me of Rahil's, but not much of a sense of humor. After a glass of wine, he perks up and his dark eyes start glowing. But he has a high-pitched girly giggle that I could gladly live my entire life without ever hearing again.

"Would you go on a second date with me?" he asks, before the check has even arrived.

"Email me. I have to 'digest' the evening."

Is that a gentle enough no?

chapter fifty-nine

Day 223 October 20. My niece's birthday. She would have been eight years old.

Tomorrow is Aaron's birthday. He'll be thirty-seven.

After James leaves the office that night without offering a goodbye or, God forbid, asking me to do anything with him that weekend, I seethe with anger, despite the fact that my weekend is already booked. Maybe I just needed the satisfaction of saying no.

This was typical James, behavior that continually frustrated me: a build-up of intimacy over a course of days or even weeks, which would then lead to him shutting down, or disappearing, or booking a series of dates with other women. I didn't think I could ever fully understand how someone could curl his fingers around yours in the middle of the night, and want to spend four nights in a row with you, and then, a few days later, not care about seeing you at all.

Yet, somehow, I was as acutely aware that James's reservations about emotional intimacy had as little to do with me as did Aaron's sexual preference for men. The two were protagonists in their own emotional dramas, and I was merely a supporting player who alternately helped and hindered their progress, just as they did with mine.

That didn't mean that James's convoluted signals didn't make me bat-shit.

I take Aaron out to Joya for a birthday dinner. My turbulent relationship with James and my not very deeply buried grief about my niece, Ana, have put me on edge. So when Aaron remarks that he knows his friends don't want to see him with a man, I snap, "I don't either, Aaron. Neither does anyone else. Even in New York, you risk getting your head bashed in if you hold a man's hand on the street. And it's disgusting. Because I wish everyone who wanted to be gay could just be gay and leave people like me the hell out of it."

The tirade culminates with me in tears and Aaron too begins welling up. Just the speech he wanted to hear on his birthday, no doubt. I hold his hand tightly and beg his forgiveness with my eyes. I love him, and I resent him, and sometimes everything erupts at the most inconvenient moments.

The next day, Aaron is leaving for San Francisco. Purportedly, he's going to visit some close friends of ours. But I also suspect that the gay capital of the world holds additional charms for him.

After dinner, we head to Boat for a drink so we can end the evening on a better note. I didn't want to risk that his plane might crash, and the last words I'd said to him were those volatile ones in the restaurant.

I had a right to cry about Aaron and Ana. But I had no right to be waterworky about James, as that particular torture I had chosen for myself and continued to choose for myself. And yet knowing we deliberately choose something bad for ourselves and can't stop choosing it, is somehow sad as well.

Saturday night I go to Carl's. He'd spent two hours cooking me a vegetarian meal, bought white wine, and rented *Last Tango in Paris* at my request. Let's just take a moment to compare this to James, who not only had never cooked me anything, but never taken me out to dinner; who continued to stock nothing but red wine even though he knew I preferred white; and who, when I suggested we rent *Last Tango* one night, responded by suggesting three alternative movies he'd prefer to see.

And yet James had wormed his way under my skin so successfully that when Carl falls asleep on the couch halfway through the movie, I sneak into another room and begin texting him. When the exchange goes on a little too long, I tell him I'm at Carl's and shut off my phone.

"Are you done text messaging?" Carl mumbles when I return to the couch. The man has good ears.

"My friend Lily on some bad date," I say.

To his credit, or maybe his detriment, he plays it cool.

The next night I spend at James's apartment. As he's pulling out his Halloween costume from a shelf in the closet, a slew of bras, panties, and negligees comes tumbling down. Since the pieces are all marked XS for extra small, I at least feel relatively confident the lingerie doesn't belong to him.

Later, with James at work, I go into his closet and dig around on the shelf until I locate a packet of pictures that had fallen down with the lingerie, but which he had refused to show me. I slide out the photos. There is the girl in the lingerie. She's cute, but no great beauty, and appears to be about twenty, her face still moon shaped with baby fat, the look in her eyes vacant, slightly gooey, the puzzled stare of an adolescent who hasn't yet seen one ounce of real-world strife. His attraction to little girls really brings him low in my eyes.

The next night, James is off to Lincoln Center for a Shostakovich concert, courtesy of the masturbating Mexican, who got a couple of free tickets through her employer. I knew I had no right to be restrictive with him, but that didn't mean I had to be gracious about it.

"I think it's wonderful that Maids R Us has such a cultural program for its employees," I snipe on the phone.

James had said earlier he only felt platonically toward the Mexican and didn't want anything physical with her anymore. But I tell him I find it hard to believe that a woman who likes a man enough to masturbate in front of him and take him to a Shostakovich concert wouldn't want something physical in return.

"Poor Kiri," James retorts, "she's never had a male friend, so she doesn't understand how a man and a woman might want to just go to a few concerts together and not have it be a prelude to fucking."

Well, he's right about that. But if I'd never had a platonic male friend who wasn't gay, it wasn't my fault. Lord knows I'd tried. Even a gay one had sex with me for a decade.

"She must be dead ugly," I pronounce.

In the morning, I call Aaron to see if he can feed the cats that evening. Since the breakup, we'd shared custody of them like children.

"Are you sick?" I ask him. "You sound tired."

"I was out with Amber last night. That woman is going to kill me."

Amber. Always Amber.

"I don't know why you and Amber don't just get together, you spend enough time with her."

"Well, there's that little issue of sexual orientation."

"That didn't stop you for ten years!" I snap.

Aaron is getting it from me these days.

I take James to a friend's pre-Halloween Halloween party. O.J. Simpson and his glove were a better fit than James and my crowd. They all do their best to be nice to him, but James just isn't a social character. At least, he's not a social character if he isn't in a room full of Francophiles or young girls he's free to hit on.

Predictably, we get into a fight. I'd been pawing him a little during the evening, trying to make him feel welcome and comfortable in the unfamiliar crowd, when he sneers, "Why are you being so clingy?"

"Clingy!" I screech. I couldn't imagine being called a more horrific word.

At that moment in my life, I hadn't yet disabused myself of the notion that I was the opposite of "clingy." I imagined I was free floating, mercifully cut asunder from human attachments, and therefore invulnerable to their wicked instabilities. So I berate James some more for calling me "clingy," and then we decide to leave.

Once we make it back to his apartment and are alone, we get along perfectly. James and I just didn't do well in social situations, it seemed. Which, being a social gal, is difficult for me. In the morning, I weave my fingers through his and we hold them like that for at least an hour.

I spend most of the day at his apartment so I can leave straight for the animal shelter in the late afternoon. He knows I'm meeting up with Carl the next day and makes a couple of sneering asides about it.

"Does it bother you that I'm seeing someone?" I ask, genuinely curious. I couldn't imagine that it would.

"No. I always knew you were a slut."

But about a week ago, I'd noticed that he hadn't kissed me in a while, and when I'd asked him about it, he'd responded, "I don't know where your mouth has been."

"Well, you know the alternative," I say. "Monogamy. And I'm good at it, but I think you'd last about two weeks. If you want to take opportunities, I'd rather you do it without it being 'cheating.' I'd rather be jealous than be betrayed."

"Yeah."

I couldn't tell if he agreed, disagreed, cared, didn't care, or even if he'd heard me. One could never get a straight answer, or any answer really, from James.

chapter sixty

arl and I drive in his Mini Cooper to the Hamptons. At first, I'm not sure how the day will go. He gets frustrated at some traffic, slams his fist on the steering wheel, and begins yelling. Having grown up with a stepfather who routinely beat the daylights out of my mother, the sound of a man yelling is anathema to me. My heart goes cold and begins thumping against my ribcage.

"Are you going to be like this all day?"

He doesn't answer but calms down when the traffic lightens.

We tour a couple of wineries and then ensconce ourselves in a rustic little Italian restaurant. I confront him over the fact that he doesn't want to date a woman over forty (so says his Match.com profile) because her ovaries might not be good enough for him—he wants children. Being three years away from forty, I'm a little sensitive to the topic. He gets beet red with embarrassment as I state my case as to why men should be willing to date women their own age, but surprisingly, after my lecture, he asks if I'd like to accompany him on a trip to the Dominican Republic, where he has family. I tell him that India is on the schedule for that month, so another trip wouldn't be feasible, but that I can do it in the future.

What I don't mention is that idea scares me silly, and not just because he's a yeller. My guts still turned to jelly at the thought of a "real" boyfriend.

chapter sixty-one

On Halloween night, James and I are arguing before we even reach our first party. I'd noticed he was being a little distant, and when I would try to take his arm as we walked, he would pull away from me.

"Are you going to be like this all night?" I say, keeping my tone light, as if I was asking him about his favorite vegetable.

"Uh-oh. Are you starting already?"

"Well, James, every time I try to take your arm, you pull away. What's up?"

"I don't like pretending we're a couple. We're not a couple."

"Umm. Okay, but we're together now. Can't we be a couple while we're together?"

"You're always saying we should just be friends. So let's do that," he says.

"You just decided this tonight? I wish you had told me earlier so I could have brought a date." I grin, but James's face remains immobile.

I suspected this was all about my spending Sunday in the Hamptons with Carl. I try to lighten his mood by forcefully grabbing his hand, swinging our arms together, and announcing, "This is my boyfriend!" to various passersby. He cracks a smile.

By the time we get to the second party, a costumed French Tuesdays event, James is acting normally. Well, normally for James. He even betrays a bit of chivalry, buying a drink for my friend Lily after I accidentally knock her over. Back at his place, we cuddle and fall asleep without sex. But in the morning, while I have him in a good mood, I decide to get to the bottom of things.

"Why did you say that stuff to me last night?"

"To be cruel," he says.

"Why would you want to be cruel?"

"Sl-ut," he whispers, drawing the word out.

So I ask the question I'd been thinking about putting to him for months.

"Do you want me to stop seeing other men?"

"No."

"No you don't want me to see other men, or no you don't want me to stop?"

I get no answer. "I'm only going to ask this once, James."

"No."

"Um. No you don't want—never mind. So I'll continue seeing other men. But you can't act this way if that's what you want."

Not surprisingly, it soon comes out James has made a date for Friday. There isn't much I can say about it. If he'd wanted monogamy, and if

I'd agreed to it, it would have been a mistake. It's so easy to fall into a relationship, then you blink, and ten years have gone by.

I wasn't one to put my life into the hands of fate, but this time I had to. James and I were not only inviting temptation, we were actively courting it, so fate had its work cut out for it. Still, I felt that if we were supposed to be together, it would happen when we were both ready. Of course, leaving things up to fate is a great way not to have to make a decision.

Meanwhile, Carl had slipped into what I termed his "comatose" courting technique. By Thursday, he hadn't asked me out for the weekend, a first in five weeks. I was beginning to realize why this guy hadn't found the wife he supposedly wanted so badly—just as the momentum picked up, he'd curl into himself like a snail.

The day James leaves for Montreal for a business dinner, he shocks me by calling me from work "just to chat" before he heads for the airport. Then he scours the Internet looking for a ticket to fly me up there that night. But last-minute tickets are exorbitant.

Since his mother and stepfather are coming into town the next weekend, I say, "I guess I won't see you on a weekend before I leave for India."

"You can hang with us."

Hang with him and his family? Well, that was James for you. Want to fly a girl to Montreal, invite her to meet the folks, not like it that she sleeps with other men, but not want a relationship.

Friday night, James returns from Montreal and calls me at 9 P.M., just as I'm getting back into Brooklyn.

"Aren't you supposed to be on a date?" I ask.

"I cancelled. Too tired."

He pushes to get together after he's had a nap. Typical James. Call me at 9 P.M. and expect me to haul my ass back to Manhattan. *And* wait until he's had a nap.

Somewhere along the line "Good old James" had become "Typical James." I decline the offer.

The next night, I'm out with some friends, and Carl, whom I'd hardly heard anything from all week, texts me at midnight, asking if I'm in the city and whether or not I'm wearing a miniskirt?

I become flushed with annoyance. How, in the course of one week, did I go from being the girl he drives to the Hamptons to the girl he drunkenly texts for last-minute sex? The switch is so whiplash fast that I feel nauseous.

I should have just ignored the text, but I'm liquored up and, frankly, looking for an excuse to extract myself. So I text back that indeed I'm in Manhattan and yes, I'm wearing a mini. When he falls into the trap and replies that he'd like to examine the outfit up close, I call him. He's clearly out at a bar, which he hadn't bothered to invite me to.

"I don't respond to booty calls," I say.

"Then goodbye," he snaps.

"Then goodbye," I snap back.

In the morning, I send him an email saying, "If a guy wants sex, he takes me out and spends the evening with me. I'm not a call girl." I ask him not to contact me again.

I'm torn between letting James think I'm still seeing Carl so that I'd have some upper hand, and letting him know I'd broken off with him to see if this puts the brakes on his own dating.

I decide to go with the latter.

"So Carl is gone," I say, after telling him the story at his apartment.

"Oh, that's too bad," he drawls. Five minutes later, he's on top of me. So perhaps he approves.

But nothing changes. The next night, I call him and his phone is turned off. After a few hours of not hearing back, I leave him a message. "Slut, slut, slut," I cluck, rather amiably. "You must be on a date. I can't wait to go to India; I'm going to blow every Indian I see. Indian cock, mmm, good. And don't call back because I have to get up early tomorrow and the phone will wake me."

But at quarter to midnight, the phone shatters my sleep. I let voice mail take it. James leaves a message saying he is walking home. I don't call back.

At 4 A.M., I wake up convinced I can't keep courting heartbreak in this manner. I want to punish him, drop out of sight, fuck dozens of other men.

Waiting to see which girl he would replace me with was like waiting for the guillotine to drop.

The next day, as I stand in line at the Indian consulate so I can get my visa, James calls. It turns out he hadn't been on a date after all—but at a movie with the masturbating Mexican (whom I was now relatively convinced he was merely friends with). He asks me if I will go to French Tuesdays that night, that he thought he'd stop by after work.

I decide to stay home, but around 10 P.M., I sent him a text: "This is a test of the emergency slutcast system. If you do not respond to this test, I will know you are chatting up a slut."

At midnight, he calls. I answer the phone in a nebulous wake-dream state. "I'm not sure how long I can be in this type of relationship," I slur, barely coherent to myself. "It bothers me when you go out to pick up other women."

"You do it all the time."

I didn't think he meant I picked up other women all the time.

"Doesn't it bother you when I'm out with other guys?"

"No."

I had to stop asking that question. I was never going to get the answer I wanted.

"I was just out with my coworkers anyway," he claims.

The next day, I'm not sure I'll hear from him. Hadn't I just confessed a little too much? Wasn't I getting a little too possessive? But to my surprise, he actually emails an apology for waking me up.

I might never hear what I'd like out of James, but he was smart in that respect. One couldn't be held to something one never said.

chapter sixty-two

Day 245 When James's mother and stepfather arrive in town from Canada, he and I slip into a sort of pseudo boyfriend-girlfriend arrangement. I go with the three of them to dinner, and for that night and the night after, James hides out at my apartment, as they had taken over his bed.

"We haven't had a talk about anything," I tell Jocelyn on the phone. Jocelyn had met James the night before when he'd joined us at Marie's, a piano bar where the patrons sing along to Broadway show tunes.

"Maybe you don't need to," she says.

"I don't want to. But if we keep seeing this much of each other, there's a perceived monogamy. And one of us could be in for a rude awakening at some point."

I begin to wonder if I'd had James wrong all along. Was he not the slut he appeared—or maybe he was, but only when he didn't have a girlfriend? Because the James who stayed over my apartment was incredibly sweet, affectionate, and attentive. Seemingly the perfect boyfriend.

But it wouldn't be the first time I'd been dead wrong on that count.

Since I'm leaving for India later that week, James invites me to his place after his parents fly home. To my astonishment, he has bought wine—not the red he prefers, but the white he knows I do—and stocked his cabinet with vegetarian meals.

"Why did you buy all these?" I ask, fingering cans of lentil and vegetable soup, when previously I'd only seen steak stew.

"For you," he says.

Hmm. White wine, meals I can eat? Maybe he had a brain tumor.

We have a glass of wine, and he tells me stories about his former girlfriends—most of whom seemed possessive to the point of mania. One girl, whom he'd dated briefly but hadn't seen for a few years, met up with him on vacation in Argentina. He'd thought it was going to be a casual get-together until the girl expressed her sudden expectation that they would be getting married. As for his college girlfriend, she was even threatened by two-dimensional women. If a pretty girl came on TV, she'd grab his crotch to feel if he had an erection. If he did, there'd be hell to pay. Another time, she flew into hysterics because she'd found a Victoria's Secret catalog in his apartment, which had been sent to the former resident, and she imagined he must be doing dirty things to the lingerie-clad images. Yet he'd loved her and stayed with her for two years.

"I find it ironic that you go for the possessive type when some of the first words I ever said to you were, 'You can sleep with whomever you like,'" I say.

"I saw beneath that."

"So I let you sleep with whomever you want but am a crazed jealous lunatic underneath?"

"The perfect combination." He grins.

"Give a man his freedom, and he won't want it."

"It's part of your strategy."

"Affection can't be gotten by strategy, remember?"

While I'm far too old to be indulging in the antics of a love-crazed teenager, the idea that my giving vent to obsessive and lovesick behavior might cement his feelings for me takes up potentially dangerous root in my mind. Women are so accustomed to being instructed to act aloof and indifferent that when a man seems drawn to the opposite behavior, it's bewitching.

In the morning, before I leave, he kisses me quite a lot, and quite tenderly. He also suggests we fly to Paris over the Christmas holidays. I admit to him that I'm scared of making a big plan like that so far in advance.

"The only reason we've been getting along lately is because we've both been good," I say.

"Or there's perception of being good," he replies, attributing the quote to Machiavelli.

The perception of being good. Relationships shouldn't be based on perceptions. And how much they were. Whether it was the perception of monogamy or heterosexuality, how much was real and how much perception, I didn't think I would ever know again.

While I'm in India for Sahana's November wedding, James and I keep in frequent touch through my BlackBerry and the hotel computer. He even writes a long email that sounds suspiciously like he wants to spend New Year's Eve together. But there's one night when he texts me, and it's 3 A.M. his time. *Whom is he out with that late?* And then I text him three times while Julie and I sit in the Delhi airport—it's about 11 A.M. his time. He doesn't get back to me. Is his phone off? Is he still sleeping? Or is some bimbo in his bed, preventing him from responding? I wouldn't ask him. I didn't want to know what he did while I wasn't around.

But I did know one thing: When I got back, I'd have to diversify my man portfolio. James and I had gotten far too exclusive before my departure without any of the guarantees of actual exclusivity.

Upon my return, I get a text from James telling me to make sure my "pussy is moist before deplaning and heading to ——rd Street," and by that evening, I am over there. He greets me at the door with a big hug and many kisses.

chapter sixty-three

James and I spend most of the next weekend together, but by the dawn of Sunday morning, the little romantic cocoon I'd spun around myself bursts in a big way.

I'd so far resisted the temptation of snooping into his cell phone—knowing in all likelihood what I would find. But as our intimacy deepened over the weekend, and I found myself less and less inclined to answer any Match.com invites, and my fantasies ripened about James really being some sort of good monogamous type under the bad boy persona, I decided I should know what I was dealing with. Asking him flat out had never gotten me anywhere.

One of the things that had kept me in the dark for so long about Aaron was my lack of snooping. Had I once, in the past couple of years, checked his browser history or personal folders, I would have caught on to his secret gay life. Some part of me was thankful I hadn't discovered it as I was fairly certain that, as the first leather-clad scrotum came into view, I would've instantly dropped dead of shock.

I didn't want to be the girl illuminated by the blue light of the laptop screen in the wee hours of the morning as she busts into her man's email. And yet that girl was taking charge, telling me to stand back, dumb ass, while she went about her cracking work—because she was disgusted by the stupidly oblivious girl I'd allowed myself to be.

So about 6 A.M., as James lay sound asleep, I grabbed his cell, tiptoed into the bathroom, and locked the door.

"Drinks and tapas sound good. Meet you at the theater at 8:30 P.M.?" someone named Mindy had texted. This was last Friday night—it was the next morning that I couldn't reach him from Delhi. There was also a text in his outbox asking another girl to a concert. My hands shook and my heart beat fast and light. James had invited me to a concert on the same previous Saturday night, but we didn't end up going for some reason. Had he invited this girl before me and I was his backup plan?

I crept from the bathroom, perched next to him on the bed, and then batted his face lightly until he grunted out of sleep.

"Why'd you invite another girl to the same concert you invited me to?" I ask.

"What are you talking about?" he mumbles.

"I checked your text messages."

He sighs heavily.

"How did you think you were going to juggle that?"

"It must have been an old message."

"No, it was the same date."

"I didn't invite anyone else."

"And you took someone named Mindy to tapas and the movies?"

He says nothing.

"Did you fuck her?"

Nothing.

"Okay, you fucked her. Do you like her?"

"Not really."

"Why not?"

"She's kind of boring. We have nothing in common."

"You and I have nothing in common. Are you bored with me?"

"No."

I hold his head in my hands and cry a little. He edges up next to me.

"It's just that . . . I can't get interested in anyone else," I say, almost choking. The feeling was, believe me, completely involuntary.

"I can't either."

I think about telling him I love him, but I don't know if that's true, or if I just want to see his reaction.

I settle for: "I feel like we have a real connection."

"I do too."

We hold each other tightly. The morning stretches on indefinitely. We cuddle, we fight, we cuddle some more, we fight some more. At one point he leaves to fetch coffee and I furiously get dressed, hoping to clear out of the apartment before his return, but just as I'm about to leave, he comes back in.

"Where are you going?"

"Don't call me. I don't want to see you anymore," I say, sweeping dramatically by him. But when I reach the elevator, I realize there's no milk in the coffee I'd taken with me, so I sheepishly return. He opens the door.

"Can I get some milk?" I tearfully request.

"Do you want to come in?"

"It hurts when you sleep with other people," I say, sliding past him.

"It was just one. I don't have the desire to do it when you're here."

"I can't be here all the time, James."

I knew that, technically at least, he hadn't cheated. I was just disappointed to learn that he hadn't gotten to the same point I was at—where he simply had no desire to be with anyone else. For James, and men like him, fucking a girl was like watching a movie—something to do to pass the time.

I had done the same. I remembered the night at French Tuesdays when I'd left James's place only to end up at Drake's. I'd put no more import into being with two men in one night than I would have if I'd treated myself to two restaurant meals in one day. But now sex, something almost purely acrobatic in that past encapsulation, was vibrating with momentous implications. Sex was a funny thing that way. It wasn't unheard of for people to kill over it, after all.

By the time I left, I was exhausted with the whole James thing, and knew I couldn't do it anymore. I couldn't open myself up to other men when I was this attached to him. Goddamn the female DNA.

After I get home, he texts: "I can't remember if you left on good terms or bad."

I call him.

"I just feel we've known each other long enough that we should give this relationship a try. If not, I need to move on."

He hems and haws. "You're just going to change your mind."

"No, I've felt this way for a while . . . and I would think about saying it . . . and then I would change my mind," I say, somewhat proving his point. "What's your opinion?"

"I'd like to keep things the way they are."

"Well, I can't. Is there something you're ambivalent about?"

"We don't always get along."

"James, we don't get along because you're either fucking someone else or I am."

"Let me think about it. I can't keep talking about this all day. I want to take a walk." His voice is friendly and intimate, even if his words aren't.

"Okay, you think about it and I'll think about it and we'll talk later."

I hang up and lay on the couch in a catatonic state for a couple of hours. I can't watch TV, read, sleep, or even smoke. I stare numbly out the window.

Then he texts: "I did enjoy the way your head banged up against the wall the other day when I took you from behind."

"I'd like to bang your head up against the wall," I reply. But I smile for the first time all day.

When he calls later, my desire to hash out the situation has completely evaporated. I don't pick up. I'm so emotionally drained and physically weak from not eating all day and smoking a hundred cigarettes that I collapse into bed around 9:30 P.M. and sleep the whole night through.

chapter sixty-four

Aaron and I go out for a few drinks and it gets teary. Since James and I are so ambivalent right now and my romantic life so tumultuous in general, I can't be in much of a friendly mood toward him. I still blamed him for casting me out into the soul-killing dating scene.

"I loved you," I tell him. "I still love you." Which is true, but I think I tell him this just to make him feel guilty.

Then James calls, leaving a message that he's walking home, and wants to say hi, and asks me to call him back. But I don't—because I'm in a mood to say "fuck you" to someone who only wants me part-time.

The next day, James emails, asking me why I hadn't returned his call. I tell him a lie: that I'd been on a date with Dylan, the jerk from The

Delancey. James had seen him flirting with me at my friend's Halloween party, so he already had his dander up about him. When he presses me for details, I make up a story about kissing Dylan, fondling him.

James immediately writes back, saying: "I'm disgusted with this whole situation. Especially after our talk the other night."

"Talk?" I shoot back. "Far as I recall, you didn't want to talk about it at all!"

Then he goes silent.

After work, I venture up to his apartment, but he doesn't answer his doorman's call. I text him. I sit in a nearby bar fretting, and call and text some more. The calls range from the accusatory—*You set me up! You could have just told me you didn't want to see me anymore instead of going through all this!*—to the blubbery—*Just call me. For one minute. As a friend. Please!*—to the angry—*Every person I have run this by has said you're psychotic!* I get no response.

The next morning he finally calls. I confess that I had been out with Aaron that night, not Dylan, and he sputters "Yeah, right!"

"It's true. I wanted to see if you were as fine with me seeing other guys as you claim to be. Is this the behavior of someone who is fine with me seeing other men?"

"I didn't say we couldn't be friends."

"Is this the behavior of someone who is fine with me seeing other men?"

"I just didn't want to talk last night."

"Is this the behavior of someone who is fine with me seeing other men?"

"Is this an automated phone call?"

"All I'm saying, James, is that we might want to consider each other's feelings when we do something—at least through the holidays. Is that something you want to do?"

Silence.

"Is that something you want to do?"

"Yes."

And so it was that James and I came to some kind of vague, tentative arrangement to be exclusive.

chapter
sixty-five

O n Christmas Eve Day, I feel I might be having a slight nervous breakdown. Despite being out with Julie and some friends until 2 A.M. the night before, I jolt awake at 7 A.M., jittery and unable to fall back asleep.

I think I know what the problem is: It's going to be my first Christmas alone. Ever. For ten years, I'd had Aaron, and for the years before that, my family.

But I'd decided to spend Christmas Day in the city and go home to Connecticut later in the week. Part of my decision was that I hated traveling over the holiday—it was too chaotic. Part of it was that I had promised James I'd spend the day with him (he didn't feel like returning to Canada to see his family). So I guessed I wasn't entirely alone. But being with James could be similar.

To ensure a pleasant holiday, I decide not to bring up anything controversial with him. And sure enough, we go to Christmas Eve dinner like a normal couple. (Well, like a normal New York couple. We sit in a Thai restaurant and listen to the staff mangle various Christmas carols.)

On Christmas Day, we exchange gifts. Somewhat surprisingly, his are small but personalized and sweet: room spray (for when my cats take a stinky dump); body lotion; a CD of French songs I had told him earlier I liked; and *The Stranger* by Albert Camus, which I'd told him—in a sop to his obsession with French literature—I'd be interested in reading. But the most meaningful gift was the inscription he wrote inside the book flap. It read, in part, "Here's to our continued long-lasting friendship/relationship/whatever-the-hell-it-is! You're a very special person in my life."

Despite our agreement to be exclusive—at least through the holidays—both of us were still on Match.com. I could even see that James was checking his account fairly frequently, though whether out of curiosity or because he was actively seeking out other women, I didn't know. I myself had agreed to meet two different Match.com men for drinks, mostly because I didn't trust James's shaky acquiescence to monogamy. Or was it mine that was shaky? I didn't know if I could ever trust anyone's profession of monogamy again. If Aaron—my precious, steadfast Aaron—could cheat, certainly a guy like James would. And I didn't want to be caught in the dupe's trap again.

As for Aaron, I was entering a new phase of intense anger toward him. We had polite but short conversations when I needed him to care for the cats, but that was all. The thought of him completely out of my life was unbearable, but I no longer felt the need to lean on him as I'd been doing. I was too tempted to tell him—again—how much he'd hurt and betrayed me. Yet there wasn't much point in continuing to lash out at him.

On New Year's Eve, I stand on the subway platform, waiting for a train that will take me to James's apartment, when I suddenly hear "Kiri!"

I knew the voice as well as my own. Aaron. He lived near me, so it wasn't unreasonable that we'd run into each other. But this was the first time it had happened and on New Year's Eve, no less.

In the train, we sit together. I'm silent for a few moments.

"Sorry if I'm being distant," I finally say.

"Do you want me to sit over there?" he asks, nervously.

"Of course not."

Aaron tells me he is on his way to dinner. He doesn't say with whom, so I assume it must be with John, the fifty-year-old mistress. I grow even more distant.

We chit-chat about the cat feeder he had ordered for me as a Christmas gift, which still hadn't arrived. We chat a little about James.

"Jake gave me a good lecture a couple of weekends ago," I say. "He said, 'James is a player, he doesn't deserve you. Aaron was nice.' I had to remind him that 'nice' Aaron was sucking dick behind my back."

I probably said that a little too loud for being in a subway car.

"It's just that I've been thinking about a lot of stuff," I continue, beginning to shift uncomfortably, chafing under the awkward weight of my new personality. "I don't trust anyone anymore. I don't believe in anyone anymore. I'm not the person I used to be."

I don't like the person I am now, I feel like saying. *And it's because of you that I'm her.*

Aaron insists on kissing me before he gets off at his stop.

At James's apartment, we have a bit of wine before heading to Lily's, as I'd promised to stop by her party. The "party" turns out to be just Lily and her cousin. We have a few drinks and play a word game until it's almost midnight. Then James and I say our goodbyes and walk south along Ninth Avenue with the revelers on the outskirts of Time Square.

From a building-sized JumboTron visible from where we stand, we watch the ball drop. We kiss and kiss as the New Year dawns.

chapter
sixty-six

Day 300 James tells me he loves me. Well, he tells someone he loves her, and he directs it towards me, and he's asleep at the time. I'd been dreaming but woke up just in time to hear him growl, clear as a bell, "I love you" before he began sucking on my armpit. Then he fell over and went back to sleep.

I don't mention any of it the next morning. James had already had two instances of murmuring something unintelligible in his sleep and then sticking his tongue down my throat for a make out session. Both times I'd told him about it next morning, and he claimed not to remember anything.

Whether he was conscious of saying it, it didn't matter. I'd have it in my ears. I knew what it sounded like. In case he never said it while he was awake, I still had it.

And I felt the same.

* * *

A couple of weeks later, James leaves for work and I scramble to find his old cell phone. He'd recently bought a new one, and had taken that one with him. It didn't take me long to find the old; it was stored away in the top drawer of his desk. I'd once again become consumed with getting clarification on a cloudy and increasingly more intense situation.

On New Year's Eve, as he and I had sat eating dinner before we went to Lily's, he'd said, "Ask me anything. Nothing is off limits."

"Okay," I'd said, "what is going on with us?"

He looked as if I'd asked him to explain advanced trigonometry.

"I mean," I'd clarified, "are you seeing anyone else?"

"Not right now," he'd said. James was a genius at the indefinite answer. Did "not right now" mean not this second? Did it mean not today, but possibly next week?

Also, there was the little question of his jealousy. The weekend after New Year's, one of his Paris buddies had come to town. They had gone out on Friday night, and I imagined they'd be out trolling for chicks. I'd hunkered down to bed as early as possible, hoping that sleep would leave me blissfully ignorant of whatever they were up to.

But after midnight, he'd called my landline—again and again and again. I knew it was James. No one but James and my mother called my landline, and I could see his name coming up on my cell almost simultaneously. He was checking to see if I was home. I decided to let him wonder. But at 4 A.M., unable to take it anymore, I finally answered.

"Are you alone?" he'd asked.

"No. I have a little furry black guy here with me," I'd said, glancing at my cat, who was sprawled next to me.

And a few days before that, James had checked my text messages. I'd left my phone in his bathroom (on purpose, I admit, as I was curious to see if he cared enough to snoop). When he came back to bed, he'd grumbled, "So who's Bill?"

Bill was an old friend of Aaron's and mine who'd texted me a friendly, but slightly flirty, message. Nothing going on there, I'd reassured him.

All this jealousy. And yet all this ambivalence. I had to know.

It was with shaky hands that I turned on his old phone and went into the inbox. There were a bunch of messages from girls. Most were inconclusive: "Happy New Year's, James!" and the like.

But one text stood out. Not only for the message, which thanked him for a wonderful evening, but because it came from someone with a first and last name. I wrote them down and Googled her when I got to work. Someone with her name went to Columbia University. Was it her?

First, I decide to give James a chance to fess up. Our relationship's status was still murky. If he had slept with this girl, I would feel hurt and disappointed, but not terribly betrayed.

I email him and confess that I'd checked his messages in retaliation for him checking mine. Then I ask him point blank if he'd slept with this girl, whose first name was Elizabeth.

"Of course I didn't sleep with her," he writes back.

Now I felt entitled to know if he was lying. I set up a Yahoo account under James's name and email Elizabeth, whose Columbia address I'd found online.

"How was our date?" I ask her.

I half expected a "Who the hell is this?" reply. Or a "James, I'm married, you know that. What are you talking about?" reply. But a few hours later comes the answer.

She asks which date he's referring to, since they've been on "several."

My throat closes in a vice grip. I run outside to call James from my cell phone.

"Are you dating this person?" I ask, calmly. I theorize that if I don't sound upset, he'll be more likely to give me the truth.

"Who?"

"Elizabeth. She emailed saying that you'd been on several dates. I thought you said you weren't seeing anyone."

"Ohh . . ." he says. "I didn't think you meant *coffee dates*."

"Well, I would classify that as dating!"

We have a quick, short, intense argument and then agree to call each other later in the evening. That night, he reiterates his story that he'd had a couple of coffee dates with this Elizabeth, nothing more.

Again. Information I felt justified in verifying. Elizabeth's signature had been on her email to me. I call the number.

Elizabeth picks up and we spend an hour on the phone comparing notes. "All those dinners, all those walks in the park, he was going to come to my sister's wedding in Florida!" she wails. And, of course, they'd slept together. The night after James and I spent New Year's Eve together, no less.

I'm almost as shocked as the night Aaron told me he might be gay. James apparently had some sort of serious girlfriend on the side. What the *hell* was he doing with me? And how had he seen so much of her when we'd been together four nights out of the week and spoken every night on the phone?

After our call, Elizabeth immediately emails James a raging breakup letter and cc's me on it. I try to call him, but he texts, "Fuck off."

He must have loved her. I had ruined it for him. I send him a couple of long emails and then retire to a night of shaking and crying.

"It's ironic," James emails the morning. "Because I cared little to nothing about seeing this Liz chick again."

Through a series of calls and emails, James explains his side of it: He'd met her a month ago. They'd had two coffee dates, then she pursued him "relentlessly," offering herself up "easily," and he took her up on it once. But he hadn't seen her since and had no desire to see her again.

"You weren't going to attend her sister's wedding in Florida?"

"That's the most fucking ridiculous thing I've ever heard!"

He writes a series of heartfelt (or what sounded heartfelt) emails about us: how he had put up so many defenses; how many times I had hurt him with my escapades with other men; how he wished he could just let go of the past and believe in us.

James, if it isn't clear by now, is not an overtly emotional man. I'd never heard any of this before. That's what made it genuine to me. Not to mention that, in a subsequent phone conversation with Elizabeth, it turned out that James's side of the story stacked up. "Oh, I just mentioned my sister's wedding," she admits. "He said he couldn't go." The "dinners" turned out to be the one dinner she cooked for him at his apartment.

Still, even though they'd only had three dates, Elizabeth was crushed to learn James was also seeing me. I send him a bunch of emails berating him about what a shit he is for not only hurting me, but her.

A few nights later, I agree to have a drink with him to discuss the situation. I didn't expect much would come of it. But when he enters the hotel bar where we'd agreed to meet, he comes hurriedly to my side, tucks me into him, and begins murmuring furious apologies.

I burst into tears. And end up in his bed.

chapter sixty-seven

A few nights later, I'm on James's bed, giving him a massage. Playing one of our little games, I quickly dive my hand into his back pocket to "jokingly" see what is there. But the joke is on me, because I pull out a business card, with a girl's name and cell phone number scribbled on the back.

"That's months old!" he protests.

Once again, I'm on high alert. In the morning, as he takes a shower, I go where I think more business-slash-pleasure cards might be residing: his coat pocket. No cards, but there's a letter from his telephone company, informing him of his new online account's password.

Would the company send a real password in the mail? And the password sounded odd, like some kind of gibberish word. Nothing like what I assumed James would choose: Proust or Camus or Voltaire. Was this a temporary password the company had given him that wouldn't fit any other account?

I take the train back home to Brooklyn so I can feed the cats before heading into work.

First, I turn on my computer. Something inside is thrumming *Don't do it, don't do it, don't do it.* But I'm no longer in control.

Of course, I knew James was still on Match.com. I'd given up confronting him about it. He'd always tell me he was merely making friends, writing to people about opera or art.

I'm not going to excuse my own naïveté here. Some part of me chose to believe this so I could keep up my own Match profile, though I had long ago stopped communicating with anyone. Some part of me was still so new to the single world, that I honestly didn't quite understand *that a man on a dating site was, in all likelihood, dating,* no matter if he told you he was merely collecting recipes or researching his screenplay or whatever else he came up with.

Some part of me was just in flat-out denial.

I go to Match.com, enter James's handle, and type in the nonsense password.

My heart beats in my throat as I watch the blue line in the address bar on my iBook slowly grow longer and longer as the page begins to load.

And then I see it all: email after email after email to girl after girl after girl. There's at least five or six a day. He'd email them right before I came over, and right after I left. He must have had a date set up for every hour I wasn't around. Many of the emails were, as he'd claimed, talking about art or books. But it was clear that these niceties were either preliminaries to a date or follow-ups after one. Certainly, he was acting as if he were completely unencumbered by any kind of commitment anywhere else. In one of his emails, to a twenty-one-year-old girl in Boston, he says that when he's in a relationship, it's the most important thing in his life.

I was far from the most important thing in James's life.

The admittedly shaky and self-delusional bubble I'd been living in bursts so completely and dramatically, I don't know if I'll ever be the same.

It gets worse when I call James at work and confront him.

"You've been emailing girls every day," I say.

"No, I haven't."

"You've been dating girls every night," I say.

"No, I haven't."

James, I was discovering, is the type who would lie, lie, lie, until confronted with irrefutable evidence, and then lie some more.

"I can't talk right now," he says. "Someone is in my office."

"I just checked my Match.com account," he emails soon after we hang up. "I don't know what you're basing this information on."

It's only after I cut and paste several emails from him to various women that he finally, reluctantly, parses that okay, maybe, yes, perhaps he'd been on a few coffee dates, but so what, we never said we couldn't do that, and he was certain I was dating too and—and—and—

After this, I refuse to see him. He sends me text messages saying he is sorry, and that he is going to change. "I'm going to straighten myself out," one promises.

"I'll be curious to see it," I reply.

One day, he sends me three emails in a row. Apologizing. Explaining. Rationalizing. He has depression issues. Match.com had become a replacement for Zoloft—an addiction. He didn't like it. He was tired of feeling so empty. He wanted to fall in love. He wanted something real.

Was he playing some kind of sick, perverted game with me? Was he some kind of sociopath-slut who felt nothing, but said whatever he thought would get him what he wanted?

I pulled up his private email provider and typed in his name. Then. His password.

Loading, loading, *Oh God, it's working,* loading, *oh shit, stop, look away,* loading . . .

And I'm in.

James is emailing me and another girl at the same time. To me, he is sending messages of contriteness. To her, he is sending his address so she can come to his place. He tells her not to *exhaust* herself when she goes to the gym before their date.

chapter
sixty-eight

Day 320 If you can believe it, this wasn't the end of James and me. I could give you various complicated reasons why not. For one, I wasn't even sure why I was fighting for monogamy when most of me didn't even believe in it anymore. For another, I monitored his Match and private email accounts for a week and saw no suspicious activity. But mostly, it was because of his emails: How his body ached constantly for me; how I looked so beautiful when he was kissing me, as if I was opening my soul to him. He even wrote, during one blistering fight, that he wanted to cry and jump out the window.

These declarations are, of course, the type of last-ditch, manipulative emotional appeals that any practiced womanizer would wield to get out of trouble. But I had read through enough of James's emails to other women to know that he didn't approach this level of emotion with everyone—in fact, he did it only with me.

But the thing that got to me the most was the idea that all of this was my fault anyway.

James would enumerate past slights or dalliances of mine in such exquisite detail—he remembered how I'd said my hands were shaking when I found out about Rahil's marriage, how I'd once said I was going to French Tuesdays to find some "French cock," and how I used to call him "staid and boring"—that I became convinced if only I could be a better person, someone more worthy of him, then he would change. Who could blame a man for not wanting to put his heart on the line for someone like me, who had acted the way I had for so many months of our relationship?

Then there was that 1 A.M. phone call.

It was a Saturday, well, early Sunday morning. I'd just returned home from dinner with Sahana and had done nothing but gripe about James.

The phone rang. My heart skipped a beat. Only James would call this late.

"I . . . miss . . . you," he'd mumbled, as if pulling the words deep out of the recesses of his tortured soul.

"I miss you too," I'd said, and began to cry.

"You sound pretty when you cry."

"I don't feel pretty."

"I wish you were here right now."

"So . . . what are you saying?" I'd stammered.

"Mmm. . . . mmm . . ."

"James," I'd whispered, "are you saying you only want to see me?"

"Yes."

Was this really happening?

"Take down your Match.com profile," I'd commanded.

We went to our respective computers. He hid his profile; I hid mine.

"I'm done with all that," he'd pronounced. It was as if the digital mistress who had constantly stood between us was finally banished.

The next day, at his insistence, I cancel a date I'd previously set up. He calls me a couple of times on my landline to make sure I hadn't secretly kept it. I go to his place in the evening.

I'm not even a foot through the door when his mouth swoops down on mine. My overnight bag slides from my hand to the floor. We make our way to the bed without ever once separating our lips.

One of the ironies was that James, just when I was most desperate to end our entanglement, had morphed into a caring, sensitive, and attentive lover. It had never even occurred to me before now that perhaps my own behavior had had something to do with his reluctance to be otherwise.

Then we lay on the couch. He read his book, his arm wrapped possessively around my shoulders. I was so happy I couldn't read, couldn't watch TV, couldn't do anything but kiss his fingers.

In the morning, we stand in his small kitchen, playing around as we'd done in the past. He buries his nose in my neck and whispers, "I missed you."

But it's only the next night that things suddenly change. I call him around 9 P.M., in a panic. I hadn't been able to reach him earlier, and I became convinced he was out with a girl.

"What's the crisis?" he asks, somewhat coldly, "I'm here, aren't I?"

"But James," I stress, "you do realize that being exclusive doesn't mean just taking down your Match profile. It means not getting girls' numbers in cafes, on the street, in elevators . . ."

I knew I was prematurely pushing him. I wanted us to immediately leap from the type of relationship we'd had for the past year to the type

I'd had with Aaron, minus his extracurricular activities with men. I just wanted a partner, dammit, and I wanted it on my own schedule.

James wasn't going to play along.

All the emotion and certainty I'd heard the night before evaporates. He hems and haws. "Maybe this is a bad idea," he finally says.

Devastated once again, I put my Match profile back up. He sees it and follows suit. We argue about it, and he eventually takes his back down, but not before he'd winked at a couple of girls and not before one had the chance to email him, which, as I was still monitoring his account, I saw. She asks him if she'd done something "wrong" last night.

"Last night" would have been Sunday. It was a night I couldn't reach him until 10 P.M. The next day, I'd emailed him saying, "You are obviously still seeing people. I should too." But he'd denied he was seeing anyone. He'd insisted he was home reading and relaxing.

I go to his place. I need to find out what had happened directly from him. The girl's email is too ambiguous, and since he thought I couldn't get into his Match account anymore (he'd changed the password, but I quickly found out the new one when it was sent to his personal account), I couldn't confront him with what I'd seen.

I sit down and make up a story about getting an email from this girl, which asked if I was still seeing him. This was the same girl he'd been making a date with a couple of weeks ago while he simultaneously emailed me about wanting to change, the girl he'd told not to *exhaust* herself. That day, I'd called her, emailed her, and warned her about him. She'd actually thanked me and called him a cheater and a liar.

"Why would she email me?" I ask him. "You must be still seeing her."

James confesses.

Cheaters and liars apparently to her taste, the girl, according to him, had pursued him after my warning, and he'd bedded her. The timeline was iffy. Had he done it before he'd called me and we'd agreed (again) to monogamy? Had he done it after? Or had he done it simultaneously— perhaps she'd been lying under him as he proclaimed his devotion to me on the phone. One never knew with James. One never knew with us.

If, with Aaron, I'd lived in a black-and-white world where the rules had been printed in clear bold type and were broken so flagrantly that there was no doubt where the fault lie, with James the rulebook was cobbled together so loosely, the squiggly lines so fuzzy and gray and mutating, that it was almost unreadable.

Yet I still felt sucker punched to the core. The truth was, I'd been playing a game I wasn't cut out to play. I'd been betraying my nature as much as Aaron had been betraying his.

"I just have one question," I stammer, my lips trembling. "Why did you call at one A.M. and say you wanted to see only me?"

"I don't remember that," he says, his hazel eyes blinking blankly.

I tell him I'm going to use the bathroom and then I'll go home. When I come out, he attacks, pushing me over to the bed, and hiking up my skirt and yanking down my underwear. It was consensual, but if I had wanted to get away from him, I'm not sure I could have. The whole situation disgusted me, but somehow, inconceivably, turned me on. There must be some rationalization for this—anger pumped up the adrenaline so much that maybe the body mistook it for imminent danger and went into some kind of regeneration mode—conceive immediately even though you might die! Quick, one last chance to pass along those genes!

Afterward I get dressed.

"Why are you leaving?" he asks, incredibly.

There had been so much miscommunication in the past, I didn't want any this time.

"James," I say, patiently, clearly. "I care about you more than you care about me. I won't lie here all night in your arms while you pretend to care about me, when you do not."

He doesn't argue. I leave, and stand crying like a baby as I wait for the elevator.

I couldn't feel too sorry for myself. I'd certainly known all along what James was. I had even taken a certain pleasure out of his cruelty to women—because I thought I was exempt from it. I was like one of those grizzled adventurers who lives among bears for years and years and whose last thought, right before the bear devours him, is "I thought I was different!"

Bears are bears.

I email James his password. All this time, he thought I'd been getting into his accounts through some mysterious software I'd acquired. But now I wanted him to know I wouldn't be checking on him anymore. Because what he did or didn't do didn't matter anymore.

"Come on, write something," he pleads by email a few days later. "At least tell me what an ass I am."

"It's boring," I reply.

Nothing would get to him more than the thought of being boring.

chapter
sixty-nine

Two months later The sun warms my face as I
lounge on the patio at the Palm Beach Hotel. It was the first time in
months, maybe even in an entire year, that I'd felt somewhat relaxed,
something less than psychotic.

Of course, my heart was gutted, stomped into mulch. But with the
southern rays pinking my cheeks and the squeals of oblivious souls
splashing in the nearby pool, I was momentarily at peace. I, along with
my father and uncle, had come down to visit my grandfather. He'd had a
couple of bad falls recently, in one case lying sprawled on the bathroom
floor until he was found forty-eight hours later by his housekeeper. By
that time, he was completely dehydrated and had to be rushed to the
hospital. He was back home now, but still would rest on his bed every
once in a while, sucking feebly through the mask of an oxygen tank. Yet
he retained his irascible, cunningly charming personality.

A couple of times I'd abruptly burst into tears. Over James. Over Ana. Over Aaron. Over everything.

"That man. . . ." he'd grumble under his breath. "Disaster."

Perhaps, on some level, witnessing the intense suffering James was causing me gave my grandfather some insight into whatever psychic damage he himself had inflicted on others over the years. Maybe he could really feel it now, understand it, when he saw the toll it took on someone he truly cared about.

"Do people change?" I'd asked him. Being 90 years old, he must have some idea of people by now.

"No," he'd said. "Not men!"

And yet I knew this wasn't entirely true. Certainly, Aaron had changed. Even my grandfather, as essentially selfish and myopic as he was, had changed. For most of his life, he'd looked with contempt upon his birth country, Portugal, and his relatives there. Nor did he seem to have much use for his three sons, my father and uncles. But toward the end of his life (for, unknown to me at the time, my grandfather was nearing the end), his family had become the only thing he cared about—the only thing, really, that he could stand.

Also, there was another change. One incident he'd told me about— small, yet it stood out in my mind like a drop of blood on a blanket of snow.

A few years earlier, my grandfather had recounted a story about running into a young man who lived in the same apartment complex as he did. This man, apparently somewhat in awe of my grandfather's history with the ladies, bragged to him that he was thinking about hooking up with a female colleague at work. The problem was, this young man had just gotten married. And my grandfather liked the lady in question. He didn't know her well, but she always gave him a polite greeting in the hallways.

"If you do it," my grandfather told him, "I'll tell her myself."

Certainly, that was a change from my grandfather's old attitude. It came a little late in life, but it came.

My time in Palm Beach also gave me a chance to step back from the chaos and reflect. I thought a lot about Aaron. For so long I'd felt duped, as if the relationship had been a hoax. But I was realizing that for ten years I'd had a man who loved me without reserve and who saw me through many trials and traumas. I knew now I wouldn't have traded in those years for anything. Once, I'd demanded to know why he hadn't told me, why he'd waited so long. He'd said, simply, "I didn't want to lose you."

I'm sure there had been other factors involved (*The shame of it. . . . I thought it was a sickness that would go away. . . .*), but I did believe him now. It must have been gut wrenching for him to know that to be true to something inside of him, something he didn't even want, yet something he couldn't control or banish or ignore, he would have to lose the most important thing to him—me.

In Aaron, I thought I'd found the perfection I'd been denied until I met him. In reality, I'd found something much more interesting, much more wonderful, and much more confusing and painful—another human being.

As for James, I'd become more aware of the loaded cannon I was when he'd found me. I'd given him as many mixed signals as he'd given me. The truth was, I'd been horribly conflicted. As long as I pushed him away just enough so that he didn't want to commit to me, then I didn't have to commit myself, and I didn't have to risk anything.

Despite this, I stubbornly imagined our relationship should be infallible, solid as an oak, with an unbendable future able to withstand conflict, boredom, illness, and all manner of unforeseen difficulties—

not to mention wrinkles. I already knew there were no guarantees on that front, yet I'd clung to the vision like a fanatic clings to the promise of heaven without any proof of it. I'd welcomed the volatility that led to sexual excitement, and yet I wanted emotional assurance.

It had all added up to one hell of a mess.

It'd been almost two months since I'd stood crying at James's elevator and we hadn't seen each other since. The emails flew fast and furious, of course. We acknowledged that we'd been playing a game in which neither of us quite knew the rules, or we were playing with a different set of rules anyway, and that neither one of us knew quite when to stop, or maybe we'd each stopped playing at different times, only to pick up again when the other person didn't. At any rate, we agreed that both of us (*him* mostly, I'd remind him) had screwed up.

There was plenty of the usual banter—relentless, addictive, ego-stripping, button-pushing banter that went for the jugular and sent me alternately into paroxysms of rage or fits of involuntary laughter. We'd even gotten to some kind of "Hell, we seem to be stuck with each other, so at least let's try to get along" state of friendship.

Yet I still refused to see him.

Driving back to the Miami airport, my father repeatedly asks me if I'm done with James.

"Of course," I say, "I have no desire to see him whatsoever. Believe me on that one."

chapter
seventy

Back in Brooklyn, I'm at home, cooking dinner. The Aaron-less apartment had become my refuge. Miraculously, and with much relief, I'd reached that point where being alone was not only tolerable, not only comfortable, but preferable—and not in some misanthrope kind of way, but in a way that swelled my soul with brightness and optimism.

Perhaps this was the only state of mind to be in if you were going to enter a relationship, to fuse your life with someone else's. To know that if it melted down, you could pick your way out of the smoking wreckage, go back to where you started, and that *you* would be waiting on the scrap heap, and that you and you could build anew.

Suddenly, about 9 P.M., my cell phone peals.

Then my landline.

Then my cell phone.

Then my landline.

It's like a duel of bells rather than swords.

I'm not picking up. I can see from the cell screen that it's James, and only James sends up a cacophony of double calling.

And now I watch my cell phone screen light up as he leaves a message, hangs up, calls again, and leaves another message. Almost simultaneously, his voice, sounding strangely desperate, comes through my home answering machine: "Call me, please. It's important."

At some point it dawns on me that he might be in real trouble. Maybe he was in the hospital or in jail.

Let him rot in jail.

But I knew, despite everything, I was probably the closest friend James had in the city. If something were terribly wrong, I was most likely the only one who could help.

I finally pick up.

"Yes, James," I say, my voice tight. "What can I do for you?"

"It's my Dad," he blurts. "He's collapsed and is unconscious."

I instantly drop my resentful tone. "What happened? Is he okay?"

James's voice is low and ragged. "I don't know. His wife called me on the way to the hospital, but now I can't reach her." His breath catches in his throat. "I think he might be dead."

I'd experienced enough death, of people, of relationships, in the past couple of years to have some idea of what he was going through. Assuming he would say no, I automatically offer, "Do you want me to come up there?"

"Yes."

Of course, this would be the answer. Throughout everything, James had never stopped pursuing me. And now he had more emotional leverage than ever.

"James," I say, unable to help myself, "I don't know if you would be there for me if the situation were reversed."

"I would," he says, adamantly. "I would be there."

Numerous thoughts race around each other and collide. How many other women had James called begging for support? If I went up there, what kind of future turmoil was I setting myself up for, just when I'd gotten to the point where my lungs didn't constantly burn and my sleep wasn't wracked with nightmares?

"Please," James says, breaking the long pause. "I know I don't deserve it. I know this has been all my fault . . ."

"It was both of our faults."

"If you give me a chance, I know I can make you happy."

"James," I say, "let's just deal with the situation at hand."

"It's unbearable being without you," he continues. "I'd rather have you yelling at me than not be with you."

"I don't want to be yelling at anyone."

"I don't want that either. I know you don't want to be with the type of person I've been with you. I don't want to be that type of person anymore."

Maybe it wasn't that people didn't change—it was that they did nothing *but* change. *Life* did nothing but change.

"Let me come down to see you," he insists.

"No," I say. "I'll come up. But just as a friend. Nothing more."

"Okay," he says. "As a friend."

If love couldn't be gotten by strategy or be held onto by strategy, then, for better or worse, sometimes no amount of strategy would send it packing. Perhaps we had to forgive ourselves for that—not just forgive but also take joy in the flawed humanness of it. Maybe love, which didn't listen to what we wanted, or take into account our plans, dreams or preferences, knew better what we needed than we ourselves did. I wasn't sure if it was better to be peacefully alone or to be in a relationship and know that, at any minute, the seemingly secure foundation could give way, sending you careening into weightless air. But I did know this: somehow, I would land upright.

The last time I'd seen James had been so traumatic that I'd gotten off the subway and gone straight to Aaron's apartment. I couldn't bear the idea of being alone in the twitchy twilight of half sleep I'd been suffering lately, constantly jolted awake by flashes of the intense affection James had shown me and the acute belief of how little this had actually meant to him.

I knew also that Aaron's relationship with John Doe had ended. Perhaps he was feeling as lonely and achy as I was. Even now I couldn't stand the thought of Aaron suffering.

Aaron and I had slept in his bed, cuddling like we used to. Not James-type cuddling, but something sexless and soothing. I'd lain all night with my body pressed inside the warm and familiar crook of his arm, my hand draped lightly across his chest.

It helped.

Acknowledgments

This book would dwell nowhere but the dark, lonely womb of my hard drive if it weren't for the laborious birthing efforts of my agent and literary midwife, Jamie Brenner of Artists and Artisans. Thank you also to master negotiator Adam Chromy.

To everyone at Kensington Publishing, who curiously concluded that they wanted to publish these ravings, my sincere gratitude. A special shout out to my champion and editor, Amy Pyle, who was Thinking Straight when I wasn't.

To Fiona Apple, appreciation for your genius, and for allowing me to include it.

Thank you to all the muses and inspirations in this book, especially Bernardo, Anabelle Mae, Marie, and Nan; and to those who loved me during a time in my life when I was most unlovable.